JESUS CHRIST, OUR SAVIOR AND REDEEMER

JESUS CHRIST, OUR SAVIOR AND REDEEMER

Francis M. Gibbons

Sixteen Stones Press

HOLLADAY, UTAH

Copyright © 2015 by Francis M. Gibbons

All rights reserved. No part of this publication may be reproduced, distributed, or transmitted in any form or by any means, including photocopying, recording, or other electronic or mechanical methods, without the prior written permission of the publisher, except in the case of brief quotations embodied in critical reviews and certain other noncommercial uses permitted by copyright law.

Sixteen Stones Press
Publisher website: www.sixteenstonespress.com

Hardback ISBN 978-1-942640-06-6
eBook ISBN 978-1-942640-07-3

PREFACE

The title of this manuscript suggests the two principal consequences of the atoning sacrifice of the Lord Jesus Christ.

First, it guarantees salvation to all mankind, regardless of office, gender, race, national origin, or the quality of their lives. From resurrection they will be assigned to that degree of afterlife that their earthly life has merited. So in his first letter to the saints in Corinth, the Apostle Paul wrote this: "For since by man came death, by man came also the resurrection of the dead. For as in Adam all die, even so in Christ shall all be made alive" (1 Corinthians 15:21-22). So the Savior's atoning sacrifice is a free gift to all, which comes to each regardless of worthiness.

The second main consequence of the Savior's atoning sacrifice is that it provides redemption for the sins of the individual, conditioned upon faith and repentance, followed by baptism by immersion for the remission of sins, receipt of the gift of the Holy Ghost, and by persistence and obedience in keeping the commandments of God throughout life.

It is hoped that this narrative will be helpful to the youth and to others who may be studying the life of the Savior for the first time in depth, because of its narrative style and because of its strict adherence to the scriptural account contained in the four gospels of the New Testament of the Holy Bible and in Third Nephi in the Book of Mormon. It is also hoped that the reader will be benefitted by the practice of reading the scriptures on which the narrative relies verbatim in the body of the manuscript, together with the scriptural citations. It is believed this will enhance readability and encourage scriptural study.

TABLE OF CONTENTS

CHAPTER ONE 1
    The Awakening

CHAPTER TWO 23
    From Infancy to the Temptation

CHAPTER THREE 37
    The Ministry of Jesus Begins

CHAPTER FOUR 49
    Jesus Teaches in Galilee

CHAPTER FIVE 55
    The Sermon on the Mount

CHAPTER SIX 71
    Jesus Ministers in Galilee

CHAPTER SEVEN 89
    Christ Teaches in Parables

CHAPTER EIGHT 107
    The Storm Is Stilled

CHAPTER NINE 111
    The Gadarene Demoniac

CHAPTER TEN 117
    The Daughter of Jairus Is Raised

CHAPTER ELEVEN 123
    The Blind Are Made To See, the Dumb To Speak

CHAPTER TWELVE 127
    Jesus Is Rejected Again at Nazareth

CHAPTER THIRTEEN 131
    The Twelve Sent Forth

CHAPTER FOURTEEN 139
    Herod Beheads John

CHAPTER FIFTEEN 143
    The Five Thousand Are Fed

CHAPTER SIXTEEN 149
    Jesus Discourses Upon Cleanliness

CHAPTER SEVENTEEN 153
    Three Significant Miracles

CHAPTER EIGHTEEN 161
    Jesus Speaks Again of Signs

CHAPTER NINETEEN 165
    Peter Testifies of the Christ

CHAPTER TWENTY 171
    The Mount of Transfiguration

CHAPTER TWENTY-ONE 177
    Ministering Along the Way

CHAPTER TWENTY-TWO 195
    Jesus Ministers Again in Judea

CHAPTER TWENTY-THREE 223
    Jesus Ministers in Perea

CHAPTER TWENTY-FOUR 233
    A Series of Parables and Discourses

CHAPTER TWENTY-FIVE 245
    The Savior's Final Journey to Jerusalem

CHAPTER TWENTY-SIX 267
    Prelude to the Final Events

CHAPTER TWENTY-SEVEN 297
   The Final Events

CHAPTER TWENTY-EIGHT 331
   Events Following the Resurrection

CHAPTER TWENTY-NINE 347
   Jesus Appears and Ministers in America

INDEX 407

CHAPTER ONE

The Awakening

The Spiritual Famine Ends

The Prophet Amos, writing near 750 B.C., predicted there would be a famine in the land, "not a famine of bread nor a thirst for water but of hearing the word of the Lord" (Amos 8:11). From the days of Malachi in 430 B.C. and onward until a few months before the birth of Jesus Christ, the word of the Lord through His prophets in Palestine was not heard. The heavens were silent. Israel was left to exist upon the words of the prophets uttered before the famine began. During this drought, the Jews continued to implore their God for guidance and to perform the rites and ordinances of their religion in holy edifices, the Temple of Herod being the one in use at the time of Christ's birth.

The rites and ordinances in the Temple of Herod in Jerusalem were administered by a large cadre of Jewish priests who lived in communities in relatively close proximity to the temple. Twice annually they would be assigned to work in the temple for a period of six days and two Sabbaths, performing various administrative tasks as well as assignments involving the rites and ordinances of the temple. During these periods, the priests lived in the temple. The most significant of these rites and ordinances, and the one most sought after by the priests, was the burning of incense in the Holy Place near the Holy of Holies. This entailed sprinkling incense upon burning coals, thereby creating clouds of smoke wafting upward, which symbolized the prayers of all Israel ascending to the Almighty to expedite the reign of Jehovah upon the earth. The large number of Jewish priests who could perform this sacred ordinance and the fact assignments were made by lot greatly minimized the chance of one having that honor bestowed upon him. Thus, this was something very special to the one selected.

On the day of which we speak, Zacharias, an aged, faithful priest, had the honor of burning incense in the Holy Place. He had come from his home, believed to have been in Hebron, some twenty miles from the temple. He lived there with his faithful wife, Elisabeth, who was childless and aged or, as the record states, "well stricken in years." Caught up in the honor which had come to him to burn incense in the Holy Place, and given the centuries during which there had been no communication from heaven, it is doubtless true that Zacharias had no hint as to what was about to happen to him. In this state of oblivion, he entered the Holy Place in company with another priest who carried hot coals taken from the altar of sacrifice. These were laid upon the altar of incense. Having done this, he departed, leaving Zacharias alone in the Holy Place. As the incense was sprinkled on the hot coals and as the smoke wafted upward, "there appeared unto him an angel of the Lord standing on the right side of the altar of incense" (Luke 1:11). Because Zacharias was the only one present in the Holy Place, it is apparent that he provided the narrative upon which Luke relied. That being so, it is telling that he remembered and reported the exact place where the angel stood.

It is understandable Zacharias was "troubled and fear fell upon him" by the sudden appearance of this heavenly being. Observing his reaction, the angel sought to calm him saying:

> Fear not, Zacharias: for thy prayer is heard; and thy wife Elisabeth shall bear thee a son, and thou shalt call his name John.
>
> And thou shalt have joy and gladness; and many shall rejoice at his birth.
>
> For he shall be great in the sight of the Lord, and shall drink neither wine nor strong drink; and he shall be filled with the Holy Ghost, even from his mother's womb.
>
> And many of the children of Israel shall he turn to the Lord their God.
>
> And he shall go before him in the spirit and power of Elias, to turn the hearts of the fathers to the children, and the disobedient to the wisdom of the just; to make ready a people prepared for the Lord. (Luke 1: 13-17)

It is apparent Zacharias had been praying about his lack of seed, and here was a heavenly being declaring he not only would have seed, but that this son would be a mighty man capable of bringing many people to a knowledge of the truth. And not only that, he would go "before him" to prepare a people ready to receive the Lord.

One would think in the face of such unusual promises, not only of a son but also of the significance of his mission, that the mind of Zacharias would have been focused upon these things. Instead, what do we hear from him? "Whereby shall I know this? For I am an old man and my wife well stricken in years" (Luke 1:18).

Obviously Gabriel, whom Joseph Smith has identified as Noah (*Teachings of the Prophet Joseph Smith*, p. 157), was displeased with the response and with the questioning attitude it reflected. To emphasize his role and status and the importance of his message, the angel told Zacharias, "I am Gabriel that stands in the presence of God; and I am sent to speak unto thee and to show thee these glad tidings" (Luke 1:19). Then in consequence of

Zacharias's questioning attitude he added: "Behold thou shalt be dumb and not able to speak, until the day that these things shall be performed, because thou believest not my words which shall be fulfilled in their season" (Luke 1:20).

This interview delayed the emergence of Zacharias from the Holy Place so that the waiting throng "marveled that he tarried so long in the temple" (Luke 1:21). When he finally appeared, the audience "perceived that he had seen a vision in the temple: for he beckoned unto them and remained speechless" (Luke 1:22).

This extraordinary event marked the end of the long spiritual famine that had engulfed Israel for centuries. It also marked the beginning of an era of spiritual refulgence when the windows of heaven were thrown open for the blessing of all mankind.

Elisabeth and Mary

We can only surmise Elisabeth's reaction when her speechless husband returned from his temple assignment with the world-shaking news. The record says only "after those days his wife Elisabeth conceived, and hid herself five months, saying, Thus hath the Lord dealt with me in the days wherein he looked on *me,* to take away my reproach among men" (Luke 1:24-25). A month later the scene shifts to Elisabeth's cousin Mary, to whom the angel Gabriel had another significant assignment. Luke reports it thus:

> And in the sixth month the angel Gabriel was sent from God unto a city of Galilee, named Nazareth,
> To a virgin espoused to a man whose name was Joseph, of the House of David; and the virgin's name *was* Mary.

> And the angel came in unto her, and said, Hail, *thou that art* highly favoured, the Lord *is* with thee: blessed art thou among women.
> And when she saw *him*, she was troubled at his saying, and cast in her mind what manner of salutation this should be. (Luke 1:26-29)

Seeing the young woman was shaken by his pronouncement, the angel hastened to add:

> Fear not, Mary: for thou hast found favour with God.
> And, behold, thou shalt conceive in thy womb, and bring forth a son, and shall call his name JESUS.
> He shall be great, and shall be called the Son of the Highest: and the Lord God shall give unto him the throne of his father David:
> And he shall reign over the house of Jacob for ever; and of his kingdom there shall be no end. (Luke 1:30-33)

After processing this startling information in her mind, young Mary asked the logical question; "How shall this be, seeing I know not a man?" (Luke 1:34) Then came the shocking answer:

> The Holy Ghost shall come upon thee, and the power of the Highest shall overshadow thee: therefore also that holy thing which shall be born of thee shall be called the Son of God.
> And behold, thy cousin Elisabeth, hath also conceived a son in her old age: and this is the sixth month with her, who was called barren.
> For with God nothing shall be impossible. (Luke 1:35-37)

Mary's brief response to this news is testament enough of the poise and graciousness of this young woman, destined to play a role unlike that of any woman before or after her. She simply said, "Behold the handmaid of the Lord; be it unto me according to thy word" (Luke 1:38). At that the angel departed.

Angelic Ministrations

The significant role of Gabriel in ending the heavenly famine that had extended for so many centuries focuses upon the role of angelic messengers in the eternal scheme of things. The Prophet Joseph Smith taught there are two general classes of heavenly beings, first, "Angels, who are resurrected messengers, having bodies of flesh and bones—" (D&C 129:1) and second, "the spirits of just men made perfect, they who are not resurrected, but inherit the same glory" (D&C 129:3). It is clear at the time Gabriel appeared to Zacharias and Mary, he was of the latter category. It is assumed the following personages who appeared to the Prophet Joseph Smith in the course of the restoration of the gospel—The Father and The Son; Moroni; John the Baptist; Peter, James, and John; Moses; Elijah; and others—were resurrected beings. Whatever their category, each brought either a message from heaven or an authority to speak and to act in the name of God. The means has been clearly defined by which one can discern whether a heavenly visitor is of one category or the other (see D&C 129:4-7).

A view held by many is that there are "guardian angels" assigned to protect, instruct, or comfort specific individuals. There is no scriptural authority either to sustain or to disprove this belief. Some point to the experience of Alma the Younger to suggest there may be substance to it. This Alma was a rowdy, undisciplined young man, whose life changed suddenly when an angel appeared to him and his friends (see Mosiah 27:11). Such was their astonishment that they fell to the earth. Later Alma was stricken dumb and became paralyzed. He remained in this condition for two days and two nights while his family and friends prayed for him. At the end of that period, he was restored to health. He then bore witness of the miraculous change that had taken place in him. He said:

> My soul hath been redeemed from the gall of bitterness and the bonds of iniquity. I was in the darkest abyss; but now I behold the marvelous light of God. My soul was racked with eternal torment; but I am snatched, and my soul is pained no more. (Mosiah 27:29)

This experience set Alma on a new course in life. For the next ten years he was imbued with a burning desire to help others avoid the deathly trap into which he had fallen. So successful and notable was he, that he ultimately became the head of both the civil and the ecclesiastical government of Zarahemla. There came a time, however, when he wished to devote all his energies to his church duties, and so he relinquished the judgment seat. He then undertook a speaking tour among the leading cities of the kingdom, preaching faith and repentance. He had success in the cities of Zarahemla, Gideon, and Melek, but at Ammonihah he encountered serious opposition. Indeed, the people there totally rejected him, essentially saying he had no authority over them, as he had given up the judgment seat, and they didn't believe what he said. He was terribly dejected on leaving Ammonihah, traveling toward the city of Aaron. Being weighed down with sorrow, an angel of the Lord appeared to him, saying: "Blessed art thou, Alma; therefore, lift up thy head and rejoice, for thou hast been faithful in keeping the commandments of God from the time thou received thy first message from him." Then came the astonishing revelation: "Behold, I am he who delivered it unto you" (Alma 8:15). It is unclear whether this unnamed angel had a permanent assignment in dealing with Alma. What is clear is that he had these two significant assignments to visit him. We do not know how the priesthood line is structured and directed in administering angelic assignments to earth. We do know that Michael, who is Adam, is the Archangel, suggesting that he directs such assignments. (HC 3:386)

Results of Gabriel's Visitations

At the time Mary conceived, she was espoused to a man named Joseph, of the House of David. She, too, was of that kingly lineage. An espousal was merely a contract to marry, so that at the time of her conception, she was a virgin, the marital relationship with Joseph never having been consummated. When Mary advised Joseph of her condition, his world crumbled. He knew of only one means of procreation, so he had difficulty accepting her explanation of what had happened. His initial and logical reaction was that another man was involved. This scenario led him to consider the possibility of pursuing a formal nullification of the espousal contract according to Jewish law. There is much in the record to suggest that it was at this juncture Mary decided to travel to Hebron to seek solace from her cousin Elisabeth, who was now well along in her pregnancy.

It was no small thing for Mary, thought to have been about fifteen years of age at the time, to make a trip from Nazareth to Hebron, near Jerusalem, a distance of about a hundred miles. The path was well marked and frequently traveled, so there was no concern about becoming lost. But the terrain was rough, and the distance made it certain it would be a difficult trip of several days. Moreover, there was the danger of encountering thugs and robbers. For these and other reasons, there can be little doubt that Mary's family arranged a traveling group to accompany her for both protection and sociality, or that she traveled with a group already organized.

Walking was a common mode of travel at the time. It is easy then to envision fifteen-year-old Mary, walking in the open air and enjoying the sights, the sounds, and the fragrances of this fabled land where her Jewish ancestors had dwelled for centuries. Should she become weary of walking, there doubtless would have been a donkey or a handcart in the company on which she could ride. And can there be any question that intermittently during this journey, Mary reflected upon the visit from Gabriel, his announcements, and the surprising event that followed. She treasured these sacred things in her heart throughout life, reflecting on them often while seeking to understand more about their meaning.

At journey's end, Mary was welcomed into the home of Zacharias, who doubtless showed his pleasure at her arrival with silent gestures and a beaming countenance. Mary must have reciprocated with heartfelt greetings, for:

> when Elisabeth heard the salutation of Mary, the babe leaped in her womb; and Elisabeth was filled with the Holy Ghost:
> And she spake out with a loud voice, and said, Blessed *art* thou among women, and blessed *is* the fruit of thy womb. (Luke 1:41-42)

Here is the first testimony, borne of the Holy Ghost, of the exalted status of the Savior and His mother. Then followed the testimony that the child Mary carried in her womb was the Lord Jesus Christ: "And whence *is* this to me," said Elisabeth, "that the mother of my Lord should come to me?" (Luke 1:43)

While still caught up in the marvel of what had happened to her, Elisabeth rejoiced in what lay in store for her young cousin, saying of Mary: "blessed is she that has believed: for there shall be a performance of those things which were told her from the Lord"

(Luke 1:45). In response, Mary uttered a hymn of praise of the Almighty, which was later incorporated in the musical ritual of churches as the Magnificat. Said she:

> My soul doth magnify the Lord,
> And my spirit hath rejoiced in God my Saviour.
> For he hath regarded the low estate of his handmaiden: for, behold, from henceforth all generations shall call me blessed.
> For he that is mighty hath done to me great things; and holy *is* his name.
> And his mercy *is* on them that fear him from generation to generation.
> He hath shewed strength with his arm; he hath scattered the proud in the imagination of their hearts.
> He hath put down the mighty from *their* seats, and exalted them of low degree.
> He hath filled the hungry with good things; and the rich he hath sent empty away.
> He hath holpen his servant Israel, in remembrance of *his* mercy;
> As he spake to our fathers, to Abraham, and to his seed for ever. (Luke 1:46-55)

The spiritual elevation these words suggest continued for a period of three months while Mary stayed with Elisabeth and Zacharias (see Luke 1:56). We can imagine that during those days they discussed over and over again the minutest detail of the appearances of Gabriel to Zacharias and Mary and of the implications these held for them personally and for all Israel throughout the generations of time. It was amazing to them, and perhaps from time to time even caused them to wonder whether these things actually happened; or could they have been dreaming?

This pleasing respite was exactly what Mary needed to prepare her to face the grave issue between her and Joseph. She departed from Hebron about the time Elisabeth gave birth to her baby John. Throughout the return journey she was stressed by a new element of concern in her relationship with Joseph. Now her condition was becoming visible. How would Joseph react to this? And what did the future hold for her were he to opt for a public nullification of the espousal?

Joseph Is Instructed in a Dream

Arriving at Nazareth, Mary learned the problem she feared had been resolved by a revelation from God. However, this was not accomplished without serious upset to Joseph. For a time he wavered between pursuing a public or a private nullification. Matthew advises us of the outcome of this dilemma: "Then Joseph her husband, being a just *man*, and not willing to make her a publick example, was minded to put her away privily" (Matthew 1:19). This procedure would achieve two important objectives. It would save Mary, whom he dearly loved, from the embarrassment of public disgrace and the cutting gossip that would inevitably follow; and it would protect the reputation of the noble Davidic line. Yet after making the decision, Joseph was not entirely comfortable with it, as the record shows:

> But while he thought on these things, behold, the angel of the Lord appeared unto him in a dream, saying, Joseph, thou son of David, fear not to take unto thee Mary thy wife: for that which is conceived in her is of the Holy Ghost.
> And she shall bring forth a son, and thou shalt call his name JESUS: for he shall save his people from their sins.

> Then Joseph being raised from sleep did as the angel of the Lord had bidden him, and took unto him his wife:
>
> And knew her not till she had brought forth her firstborn son: and he called his name JESUS. (Matthew 1: 20-21, 24-25)

In preparing his summary, Matthew added this commentary:

> Now all this was done, that it might be fulfilled which was spoken of the Lord by the prophet, saying,
>
> Behold, a virgin shall be with child, and shall bring forth a son, and shall call his name Emmanuel, which being interpreted is, God with us. (Matthew 1:22-23)

The prophet referred to here is Isaiah, who predicted: "Therefore the Lord himself shall give you a sign; Behold, a virgin shall conceive, and bear a son, and shall call his name Immanuel" (Isaiah 7:14). Repeatedly in the four gospels and especially in Matthew, the writer seeks to associate events in the life of Jesus with the utterances of the ancient prophets. It is almost made to appear that the Savior was following a script written by the holy prophets ages before.

John Is Born

When "Elisabeth's full time came . . . she brought forth a son" (Luke 1:57). It was an occasion of great jubilation among "her neighbors and his cousins," who were amazed that one as old as she could bear a child. In accordance with Abrahamic law, they came on the eighth day to circumcise the newborn. This ancient ritual had been performed among the Jews with exactness since the time the Lord appeared to Abraham when he was ninety-nine years old. "I am the Almighty God" Abraham was told, "walk before me, and be thou perfect" (Genesis 17:1). One of the laws the Jews thought led to perfection was this: "He that is eight days old shall be circumcised among you" (Genesis 17:12). The consequence of failure to observe this law was dire: "That soul shall be cut off from the people; he hath broken my covenant" (Genesis 17:14).

On the solemn occasion of John's circumcision, "They called him Zacharias, after the name of his father" (Luke 1:59). When Elisabeth corrected them saying his name was John, they were surprised, saying, "There is none of thy kindred that is called by this name" (Luke 1:61). They then "made signs" to Zacharias, asking him the name to be given his son. "And he asked for a writing table and wrote, saying, His name is John. And they marvelled all" (Luke 1:63). Some have speculated that Zacharias was deaf also because they made signs to him. It is possible they merely thought he was deaf.

After Zacharias had written that his son was to be named John:

> his mouth was opened immediately, and his tongue *loosed*, and he spake and praised God.
> And fear came on all that dwelt around about them; and all these sayings were noised about throughout all the hill country of Judaea.
> And all they that heard them laid them up in their hearts, saying, what manner of child shall this be! And the hand of the Lord was with him. (Luke 1:64-66)

Zacharias, then being moved upon by the Holy Ghost, uttered a moving prophecy called the Benedictus, which was later set to music and sung in many Christian churches:

> Blessed *be* the Lord God of Israel; for he hath visited and redeemed his people,

> And hath raised up an horn of salvation for us in the house of his servant David;
>
> As he spake by the mouth of his holy prophets, which have been since the world began:
>
> That we should be saved from our enemies, and from the hand of all that hate us;
>
> To perform the mercy *promised* to our fathers, and to remember his holy covenant;
>
> The oath which he swear to our father Abraham,
>
> That he would grant unto us, that we being delivered out of the hand of our enemies might serve him without fear,
>
> In holiness and righteousness before him, all the days of our life.
>
> And thou, child, shalt be called the prophet of the Highest: for thou shalt go before the face of the lord to prepare his ways;
>
> To give knowledge of salvation unto the people by a remission of their sins,
>
> Through the tender mercy of our God; whereby the dayspring from on high hath visited us,
>
> To give light to them that sit in darkness and *in* the shadow of death, to guide our feet in the way of peace. (Luke 1:68-79)

After the happening of these supernal events, the record is silent as to the first thirty years of John's life, except for this terse statement: "And the child grew, and waxed strong in spirit, and was in the deserts till the day of his shewing unto Israel" (Luke 1:80). We are left to speculate as to the privations he endured and the sources of the vast knowledge he acquired of Jewish theology and history. He doubtless had access to historical scrolls and was schooled in spiritual things through the ministrations of the Holy Ghost, which he enjoyed from the moment of his birth. So thorough was his preparation that from the moment he burst upon the scene, he drew large crowds who gathered to hear him speak, to observe his quaint, rustic attire, and to feel the spiritual impact of his discourse. He soon attracted a large following. Included among his disciples were two men, Andrew and John, who later became members of the original Quorum of the Twelve Apostles (see John 1:35-42). Jesus himself attested to John's power and influence, saying there was no greater prophet than he (see Matthew 11:7-11).

Jesus Is Born

Although his wife Mary was "great with child" (Luke 2:5), Joseph planned a trip to Bethlehem in the spring of the year. This small pastoral village, located some five miles from Jerusalem, was the birthplace of King David, Joseph and Mary's ancestor, and was the predicted site where Israel's Savior was to be born. However, this historical coincidence is not what motivated the trip. Rather it was compelled by a decree from Caesar Augustus "that all the world should be taxed" (Luke 2:1). This imperial decree was aimed at a census that would form the basis for an equitable tax levied on the entire Roman Empire. Ordinarily this census would have been taken at the taxpayers' residence. However, Rome yielded to Jewish custom and allowed the census to be taken at the taxpayers' ancestral home. So here at His earthly beginnings we see evidence of the Savior's scripted life. He was to be born in Bethlehem of the lineage of David as the holy prophets had predicted.

The housing crush in Bethlehem was severe, as members of King David's numerous progeny gathered there for the census. By the time Joseph and Mary arrived, all the commercial facilities had been taken. In these dire circumstances, Joseph had no option but to provide a place for them to sleep in a stable. It was here that

Mary "brought forth her firstborn son, and wrapped him in swaddling clothes, and laid him in a manger; because there was no room for them in the inn" (Luke 2:7). How fitting it was that the One destined to become the Savior of all mankind was born in such humble and unpretentious circumstances. Obviously the pathetic circumstances of the Savior's birth did not imply that Joseph was in poverty, for he was a well-known and successful builder in Nazareth. He was caught in a dilemma.

At the time of the birth:

> "There were in the same country shepherds, abiding in the field, keeping watch over their flock by night.
>
> And, lo, the angel of the Lord came upon them, and the glory of the Lord shone about them: and they were sore afraid.
>
> And the angel said unto them, Fear not: for behold I bring you good tidings of great joy, which shall be to all people.
>
> For unto you is born this day in the city of David a Saviour, which is Christ the Lord.
>
> And this *shall be* a sign unto you; Ye shall find the babe wrapped in swaddling clothes lying in a manger.
>
> And suddenly there was with the angel a multitude of the heavenly host praising God, and saying,
>
> Glory to God in the highest and on earth peace, good will toward men. (Luke 2:8-14)

As the heavenly host and the angel departed, the shepherds talked excitedly among themselves about the amazing thing that had happened to them. At length they decided to go to Bethlehem:

to see this thing which is come to pass, which the Lord has made known unto us.

And they came with haste, and found Mary and Joseph, and the babe lying in a manger.

And when they had seen *it*, they made known abroad the saying which was told them concerning this child.

And all they that heard it wondered at those things which were told them by the shepherds. (Luke 2:15-18)

After eight days, the child was circumcised according to the law, and "his name was called JESUS, which was so named of the angel before He was conceived in the womb" (Luke 2:21). After forty days, the period of Mary's purification, His parents took Jesus to the temple "to present *him* to the Lord" (Luke 2:22). At the temple they encountered a man named Simeon, a man "just and devout, waiting for the consolation of Israel: and the Holy Ghost was upon him. And it was revealed unto him by the Holy Ghost, that he should not see death before he had seen the Lord's Christ" (Luke 2:25-26). And when His parents brought Jesus into the temple, Simeon:

took he him up in his arms, and blessed God, and said,

Lord, now lettest thou thy servant depart in peace, according to thy word.

For mine eyes have seen thy salvation,

Which thou hast prepared before the face of all people;

A light to lighten the Gentiles and the glory of thy people Israel.

And Joseph and his mother marvelled at those things which were spoken of him.

And Simeon blessed them, and said unto Mary his mother, "Behold, this *child* is set for the fall and rising again of many in Israel; and a sign which shall be spoken against;

(Yea, a sword shall pierce through thy own soul also,) that the thoughts of many hearts may be revealed. (Luke 2:28-35)

There was an aged prophetess named Anna, a widow who "served *God* with fastings and prayer night and day. And she coming in that instant gave thanks likewise unto the Lord, and spake of him to all them that looked for redemption in Jerusalem" (Luke 2:36-38).

The pronouncements of Simeon and Anna in the temple were the first known testimonies of Christ's Messianic mission uttered after His birth. These, added to the testimony of Elisabeth, uttered while He was yet in the womb, were a wonderment to the young mother. It was difficult for her to grasp the reality that this infant, so helpless and so dependent on her for His every physical need, was destined to fulfill the dominant role predicted for him.

Leaving the temple, the young couple went to the place where they then resided to prepare for the return journey. Presumably they had moved there from the stable after the crush of the census taking had subsided. "And when they had performed all things according to the law of the Lord, they returned unto Galilee, to their own city Nazareth" (Luke 2:39).

The Magi and a New Star

Some time after the birth of Jesus in the stable,

there came wise men from the east to Jerusalem,
Saying, Where is he that is born King of the Jews? for we have seen his star in the east, and are come to worship him.

When Herod the king had heard *these things,* he was troubled, and all Jerusalem with him. (Matthew 2:1-3)

King Herod, an Edomite and a descendant of Esau and Ishmael, had married a Jewish woman, Mariamne, of a noble Maccabbean family; had converted to Judaism; and had rebuilt the temple all as a means of ingratiating himself with his Jewish subjects. The strategy did not work. He was hated by them from the beginning. Part of the feeling was tribal, tracing back to the birthright disputes between Isaac and Ishmael and Jacob and Esau. More than that, however, King Herod was hated and feared because he was a jealous, violent, wicked, and unstable man, guilty of killing his wife and one of his sons, and also, as we shall see, ordering the killing of innocent babies in a fruitless effort to do away with the Savior.

Against this background, it is plain to see why Herod was troubled. If this baby were indeed "the king of the Jews," Herod's kingdom could be in jeopardy. He immediately went into crisis mode and assembled:

> all the chief priests and scribes . . . [and] demanded of them where Christ should be born.
> And they said unto him, In Bethlehem of Judaea: for thus it is written by the prophet,
> And thou Bethlehem, *in* the land of Juda, art not the least of the princes of Juda; for out of thee shall come a Governor that shall rule my people Israel. (Matthew 2:4-6)

Being satisfied that this baby was the Christ, Herod summoned the wise men and "inquired of them diligently what time the star appeared" (Matthew 2:7). Then showing the duplicity for which he was well known, "he sent them to Bethlehem and said, Go and search diligently for the young child; and when ye have found *him,* bring me word again, that I may come and worship him also" (Matthew 2:8). When the wise men left the king's presence:

> lo, the star which they saw in the east, went before them, till it came and stood over where the young child was.
>
> When they saw the star, they rejoiced with exceeding great joy.
>
> And when they were come into the house, they saw the young child with Mary his mother and fell down and worshiped him: and when they had opened their treasures, they presented unto him gifts; gold, frankincense and myrrh. (Matthew 2:9-10)

The identity of these wise men is unknown. We know only that they came from the east, they were wealthy—judging from the quality of the gifts they offered, and they were knowledgeable about the significance of the new star. That such knowledge was global in extent is suggested by the fact "a new star did appear" in the Western Hemisphere (see 3 Nephi 1:21).

Once the wise men had presented their gifts and had paid their respects to the newborn and His mother, they left, "being warned of God in a dream that they should not return to Herod, they departed into their own country another way" (Matthew 2:12).

The Slaughter of the Babes

When Herod discovered that he had been mocked of the wise men, he was "exceeding wroth, and sent forth, and slew all the children that were in Bethlehem, and in all the coasts thereof from two years old and under, according to the time when he had diligently enquired of the wise men" (Matthew 2:16). At this point in his narrative, Matthew added this commentary showing his perception that this gruesome event was part of a pre-ordained script:

> Then was fulfilled that which was spoken by Jeremy [that is Jeremiah] the prophet, saying,
> In Rama was there a voice heard, lamentation, and weeping, and great mourning, Rachel weeping *for* her children, and would not be comforted, because they are not. (Matthew 2:17-18)

The Sojourn in Egypt

At the time of the departure of the wise men:

> the angel of the Lord appeared to Joseph in a dream, saying, Arise, and take the young child and his mother, and flee into Egypt, and be thou there until I bring thee word: for Herod will seek the young child to destroy him.
> When he arose he took the young child and his mother by night and departed into Egypt. (Matthew 2:13,14)

It is noted that Matthew is the only one of the gospel narrators to mention this incident. All of the four gospels were written some thirty years following the crucifixion. It seems obvious the four narrators had different materials with which to work. And the preferences and perceptions of the writer dictated which materials were to be used and which ignored. It seems unlikely that the other three narrators would have deliberately ignored an incident of such dramatic import. All this suggests that the documentation upon which Matthew relied in writing his narrative, for some unexplained reason, did not fall into the hands of either Mark, Luke, or John.

That being said, we are left to wonder about the route followed in going to Egypt, the place where they stayed, the conditions they found there, and the length of the sojourn. We know only that once Herod was dead, "an angel of the Lord appeared in a dream to Joseph in Egypt, saying, Arise and take the young child and his mother and go into the land of Israel: for they are dead which sought the young child's life" (Matthew 2:19-20). Joseph did as he was directed:

> But when he heard that Archelaus did reign in Judea in the room of his father Herod, he was afraid to go thither: notwithstanding, being warned of God in a dream, he turned aside into the parts of Galilee:
> And he came and dwelt in a city called Nazareth. (Matthew 2:22-23)

Here again we find Matthew referring to the script: "that it might be fulfilled which was spoken by the prophets, He shall be called a Nazarene" (Matthew 2:23). Thus differing from the account of Luke, Matthew brings the child into Nazareth by the circuitous route of Egypt.

CHAPTER TWO

From Infancy to the Temptation

What Manner of Child Is This?

The historian Josephus wrote this of Jesus Christ: "Now there was about this time Jesus, a wise man, if it be lawful to call him a man" (Antiquities 18.3.3). He was a man in that, through His mother Mary, He acquired all of the human traits of mankind. He had the physical body of a man. He had all of the normal passions and appetites of a man. Through His mother He inherited the characteristics of His Jewish ancestors, extending back to King David, and beyond. And as part of that physical legacy, His body was subject to death and disintegration. But on His Father's side, He inherited all of the qualities and powers of a God. So notwithstanding His physical disabilities acquired through Mary, He had the power to lay down His life and to take it up again acquired from His Father. Thus we see in Jesus Christ the only true human hybrid that has ever existed or that will ever exist upon earth. He was both God and man wrapped in one. This reality imposes upon anyone who seeks to write about Him an imponderable burden. How do you write about someone who had no precedents? It is a very daunting thing and one that induces serious feelings of incompetence and humility and of reliance upon a higher power.

The Savior's Early Life

The record of the early life of the Savior is paper thin. It consists of this: "And the child grew and waxed strong in spirit, filled with wisdom: and the grace of God was upon him" (Luke 2:40). It is curious that from these few words has emerged a vast library of writings about the Savior's early life. But it is all based upon inference and conjecture. Against this background this writer takes license to add this: Jesus was a most precocious child. He had the innate ability to grasp and understand things and concepts and to accomplish unusual things without seeming effort. We have seen similar aptitudes reflected in the lives of so-called child prodigies like Mozart. Confirming evidence of this in the life of the Savior is found in this experience He had at age twelve:

He went to Jerusalem with His parents and a large company of relatives and friends to celebrate the feast of the Passover. This was an annual affair for the family and an altogether joyous and carefree occasion for all. Given the large size of the group and those of the age of Jesus, there was little supervision given to them and they were free to move about at will. Thus it was that:

> when they had fulfilled the days, as they returned, the child Jesus tarried behind in Jerusalem; and Joseph and his mother knew not *of it*.
>
> But they, supposing him to have been in the company, went a day's journey; and they sought him among *their* kinfolk and acquaintance.
>
> And when they found him not, they turned back again to Jerusalem, seeking him". (Luke 2:43-45)

One can imagine the anxiety of the parents as they looked for the boy. Jerusalem was a dangerous place. True, there were many pious and harmless people who resided there. Mixed among these, however, were many thieves, cutthroats and others of low repute of the kind who dwelled in ancient, populous cities like Jerusalem. They hunted feverishly for the boy for three days, which means that, counting the two days they had lost in travel, Jesus had been separated from His parents for five days. By this time they might well have been in a panic. And so it fell out that at the end of the fruitless three-day search, "they found him in the temple, sitting in the midst of the doctors, both hearing them, and asking them questions" (Luke 2:46). It is clear from the record that He not only was asking questions, but He was expounding, since "all that heard him were astounded at his understanding and answers" (Luke 2:47). It must be remembered these "doctors" were mature men, some perhaps aged, who had devoted themselves to a detailed study of the scriptures and rabbinical lore and whose main joy and activity in life was to gather at the temple to talk about the holy writ, sometimes, perhaps, regaling each other with chapters' long quotations from the scriptures.

Seeing their son in this unusual setting, they "were amazed" by His poise and eloquence and the depth of His scriptural knowledge. Yet this amazement was alloyed with a sense of annoyance that they had been put through this five-day ordeal of anxiety. So Mary, instead of expressing amazement and perhaps motherly pride at the son's performance, uttered words of mild reproach. "Son, why hast thou thus dealt with us? behold, thy father and I have sought thee sorrowing" (Luke 2:48). Then came the boy's unexpected answer: "How is it that you sought me? wist ye not that I must be about my father's business? (Luke 2:49) Luke's commentary about this interchange suggests the parents had no clear understanding of the true identity of the young son who was growing up in their home. Wrote he: "And they understood not the saying which he spake unto them" (Luke 2:50). They then returned to Nazareth where Jesus "was subject unto them: but his mother kept all these sayings in her heart" (Luke 2:51).

The holy record is silent about the Savior's personal progress from this time until His ministry began eighteen years later, except for this: "And Jesus increased in wisdom and stature, and in favor with God and man" (Luke 2:52). The Savior's response to His mother in the temple implies that at age twelve He knew the Eternal God was His real father. What else Jesus knew about Him lies in the realm of speculation. But whatever else He knew clearly did not deter Him from submitting willingly to the direction of Joseph and according him the respect and obedience owing to a father in Israel.

To everyone outside the family, it was made to appear Jesus was the oldest son of Joseph and Mary. As such it was expected of Him to assist Joseph in the conduct of the family business of carpentry. Because most of the buildings in Nazareth were of stone construction, and trees were scarce, some scholars believe Joseph and his sons might have been stonemasons as well. If true, such would have been tough, demanding work, calculated to develop the muscles of the body, especially the arms, the back, and the chest. Handling rough stones could have created thick callouses on the hands, and working outside in the sun could have produced deep tanning, accentuated by the natural olive tint of their complexion. Speculation about His appearance should not ignore these words from Isaiah, "As many were astonied at thee; his visage was so marred more than any man, and his form more than the sons of men" (Isaiah 52:14); or these from the Book of Mormon, "As many were astonished at thee—his visage was so marred, more than any man, and his form more than the sons of men" (3 Nephi 20:44); nor these words, composed by W. W. Phelps in the hymn, *O God, the Eternal Father,* included in the first LDS hymnbook: "With no apparent beauty, That man should him desire—" (*Hymns,* no. 175) Nevertheless, any portrayal of Jesus as weak and effeminate would seem to fly in the face of reality.

There were several younger children in Joseph and Mary's family. Little is known about them. One son named James acquired some prominence later in life (see Josephus, Antiquities 20.9.1), but this was long after He left the family home. Jesus himself, of course, acquired no distinction until He began His ministry. Nor was the family of Joseph and Mary known beyond the confines of the neighborhood. It was a diligent, faithful family like so many others, where the scriptures were taught, prayers were offered, the traditional feasts and festivals were observed, and where they assembled regularly at the synagogue for worship and instruction. Nor could He claim any distinction from His place of residence. Nazareth was a small, inconspicuous town, often held in derision. When Philip told Nathaniel that the Savior had been found in Nazareth, his response was, "Can there any good thing come out of Nazareth?" (John 1:46) Thus as Jesus approached age thirty, there was nothing about Him or His family or His village which even hinted to the outside world of the distinction He was to attain or the mission He would perform.

John's Ministry Begins

John began His ministry in the fifteenth year of the reign of Tiberius Caesar (see Luke 3:1), who became the emperor in 14 A.D. at the death of Augustus Caesar. Thus, being in His thirtieth year, John "came into all the country about Jordan, preaching the baptism of repentance for the remission of sins" (Luke 3:3). The narrator then wrote these words as coming from "Esaias the prophet" which, with some variations, corresponds with Isaiah 40:3-5:

> The voice of one crying in the wilderness, Prepare ye the way of the Lord, make his paths straight.
> Every valley shall be filled, and every mountain and hill shall be brought low; and the crooked shall be made straight, and the rough way shall be made smooth;
> And all flesh shall see the salvation of God. (Luke 3:4-6)

This set the stage for John's ministry as the forerunner of his cousin Jesus Christ whose ministry would bring about "the salvation of God," which all Israel fervently sought. So John is seen as fulfilling the prophecy of Isaiah uttered centuries before.

John's preaching appears to have been centered near Jericho, a distance of some twenty to twenty-five miles from Jerusalem. It is a testament to his persuasiveness and charisma that "multitudes" came from Jerusalem to hear him. They came over the hill above the Mount of Olives, and down past Bethany, and through the long stretch of barren land unfit for habitation. They came on donkeys or on carts drawn by them, or the fortunate few rode camels. But most of them walked, there being no mass transit system. Life moved at a more leisurely pace then, and the residents in and around Jerusalem probably thought it well worth their time to take a few days off and travel to see and hear this unusual man who had suddenly emerged from the desert, dressed in shabby clothing and speaking with a sharp vehemence. Among the multitude who came were many of the priestly class, Pharisees and Sadducees, who were conversant with the prophecies of Isaiah about the "voice of one crying in the wilderness," but who came with a smug sense of superiority, prepared to make jest of and to deride still another deranged imposter, of whom there were many. John immediately recognized these people of arrogance and had a few pointed things to say to them:

> O generation of vipers, who hath warned you to flee from the wrath to come?
> Bring forth therefore fruits worthy of repentance, and begin not to say within yourselves; We have Abraham to *our* father: for I say unto you, That God is able of these stones to raise up children unto Abraham.
> And now also the axe is laid unto the root of the tree: every tree therefore which bringeth not forth good fruit is hewn down, and cast into the fire. (Luke 3:7-9)

John's teaching was clear and direct. Those who did not live worthily and did not produce "good fruit," were to be cut off and cast into the fire. His persuasive words and his dire prediction of the fate of the disobedient moved many to ask, "What shall we do then?" (Luke 3:10) The answer sounded a note of compassion for the needy, a quality that characterizes those who are truly charitable: "He that hath two coats, let him impart to him that hath none; and he that hath meat, let him do likewise" (Luke 3:11). To the publicans who asked the same question, he answered: "Exact no more than that which is appointed you" (Luke 3:13). And to the soldiers who asked, He said, "Do violence to no man, neither accuse *any* falsely: and be content with your wages" (Luke 3:14). The wisdom of John's discourse, his intelligent answers to questions, and the energizing effect of his personality caused some to speculate whether he was the promised Messiah. John acted promptly to lay this flattering suggestion to rest. Said he:

> I indeed baptize you with water; but one mightier than I cometh, the latchet of whose shoes I am not worthy

to unloose: he shall baptize you with the Holy Ghost and with fire:

Whose fan *is* in his hand, and he will thoroughly purge his floor, and will gather the wheat unto his garner; but the chaff he will burn with fire unquenchable. (Luke 3:16-18)

By some unexplained means, whether through the Holy Ghost or by word of mouth emanating from the excitement at the Jordan River, Jesus learned of John's work and traveled there from Nazareth. And so it was that Jesus was baptized in the Jordan River by His second cousin, John; and:

being baptized, and praying, the heaven was opened,

And the Holy Ghost descended in a bodily shape like a dove upon him, and a voice came from heaven, which said, Thou art my beloved son; in thee I am well pleased. (Luke 3:21-22)

In this clear language, Luke, the narrator, delineates the separate identity of the Father, speaking from heaven, the Holy Ghost, descending like a dove, and the Savior who had just been immersed in the water. It is incredulous that many in the Christian world today accept the garbled description of the Godhead which came out of a committee at Nicaea in preference to this description by one who was well acquainted with the surrounding circumstances and who wrote his narrative some three decades after the event. Even more incredulous is that those who accept the Nicene Creed brand as "unchristian" those who accept Luke's description.

Much has been written about why the Savior felt the need to be baptized. Was it a vain act since He was sinless? Certainly not. He said it was necessary "to fulfill all righteousness" (2 Nephi 31:5). Over the centuries, linguists have argued over these words.

Nephi provides a clear explanation in the Book of Mormon as to why the Savior was baptized. "He showeth unto the children of men that, according to the flesh he humbleth himself before the Father, and witnesseth unto the Father that he would be obedient unto him in keeping his commandments" (2 Nephi 31:7). Also, "it showeth unto the children of men the straitness of the path, and the narrowness of the gate, by which they should enter, he having set the example before them"(2 Nephi 31:9).

The narrator, John, places the site of the baptisms at Bethabara beyond Jordan (see John 1:28). Among the throng who witnessed them were certain priests and Levites whom the Jewish fathers in Jerusalem had sent to interrogate John. They said to him, "Who art thou? that we may give an answer to them that sent us. What sayest thou of thyself?" (John 1:22) John answered, "I am the voice of one crying in the wilderness, Make straight the way of the Lord, as said the prophet Esaias" (John 1:23). The questioners continued to probe into John's identity, but got only this in response: "I baptize with water: but there standeth one among you, whom ye know not; He it is, who coming after me is preferred before me, whose shoe's latchet I am not worthy to unloose" (John 1:26-27). The day following these interrogations, John saw Jesus among the throng and said:

> Behold the Lamb of God, which taketh away the sins of the world.
> This is he of whom I said, after me cometh a man which is preferred before me: for he was before me.
> And I knew him not: but that he should be made manifest to Israel, therefore am I come baptizing with water. (John 1:29-31)

John then bore testimony about the identity of Jesus, whom he had baptized:

> I saw the Spirit descending from heaven like a dove, and it abode upon him.
>
> And I knew him not: but he that sent me to baptize with water, the same said unto me, Upon whom thou shalt see the Spirit descending, and remaining on him, the same is he which baptizeth with the Holy Ghost.
>
> And I saw, and bear record that this is the Son of God. (John 1:32-34)

The following day, John was standing near the river with two of his disciples amidst the throng that had gathered there. As Jesus walked by, John said: "Behold the Lamb of God!" (John 1:36) When John's disciples heard this, they began to follow Jesus, who, detecting their presence, invited them to the place where He was staying. One of this pair was Andrew, the brother of Simon. The following day, Andrew found Simon and said to him:

> We have found the Messias, which is, being interpreted, the Christ.
>
> And he brought him to Jesus. And when Jesus beheld him, he said, Thou art Simon the son of Jona: thou shalt be called Cephas, which is by interpretation, A stone. (John 1:41-42)

The next day as Jesus prepared to return to Galilee, He encountered Philip, telling him, "Follow me" (John 1:43). Philip, who was of Bethsaida, the same city as Andrew and Simon, obeyed and, finding Nathaniel, said to him:

> We have found him, of whom Moses in the law, and the prophets, did write, Jesus of Nazareth, the son of Joseph.
>
> And Nathaniel said unto him, Can there any good thing come out of Nazareth? Philip saith unto to him, Come and see. (John 1:45-46)

Later, on seeing Nathaniel, the Savior said, "Behold an Israelite indeed, in whom is no guile!" (John 1:47)

And so in the follow-up of His baptism, the Savior found these four men from Galilee, who had traveled the long distance to see and hear John and who would become His faithful disciples. Their attraction to Him seems to have been instinctive. There was nothing about Him physically that would have been especially attractive or distinctive. Here was a mature, bearded, broad-shouldered man, sunburned, with rough hands and a friendly attitude. Their acquaintance with Him would change their lives, and He would change the world.

The Temptation of Christ

Soon after His baptism, Jesus retired to the wilderness for a forty-day period of prayer and reflection. It was to prepare Him for the three-year ministry, which lay ahead, and would culminate with His crucifixion and resurrection. As a means of elevating His spiritual perceptions during this crucial period, He refrained from partaking of food and water. The mortal component of His makeup assured that the Savior would experience intense feelings of hunger and thirst. It was after the fast ended that Satan sought to take advantage of the Savior's weakened condition by posing questions whose answers, in his tortured thought, would in some way demonstrate his superiority.

This encounter between Jesus and Satan was, in effect, the resumption of a contest that had been waged in heaven. That was at a juncture when the Almighty was formulating the plan of happiness for His spirit children, who ultimately would take bodily form, inhabit the earth prepared for them, and there endeavor to prove themselves worthy of an eternal habitation with God. It was foreseen that, separated from Him, God's children would transgress the laws to be given, thereby alienating themselves from Him. Lacking the ability, in that alienated state, to effect a reconciliation with God, a savior, or redeemer, would be necessary, through whose ministrations the disobedient ones could be reconciled with God and returned to Him, clean and pure, cleansed through the atoning blood of a savior. In the process of selecting this savior, Satan offered himself, declaring that he would save everyone regardless of his or her personal desires and conduct, and that the reward for this service would inure to him personally. The Savior merely said He would be submissive to God's will, without exception, and that the glory would inure to God. When the Savior's plan was accepted, there "was war in heaven" (Revelation 12:7) and Satan or Lucifer "was cast out into the earth, and his angels were cast out with him" (Revelation 12:9).

This background was evident when Satan appeared to Jesus at the end of His fast. The timing presumed the physical component of the Savior's makeup would be at low ebb and therefore more susceptible to the evil one's blandishments. There were three parts of the temptation, all of which are described in Matthew, Mark, and Luke, although in different sequence. John makes no mention of them. The following commentary is based upon Luke's narrative. And that narrative, obviously, is based upon information Jesus provided, since only He and Satan were privy to the conversation.

In the first part of the temptation, Satan said to the Savior, "If thou be the Son of God, command this stone that it be made bread" (Luke 4:3). The statement challenged the legitimacy of the Savior's Messianic role and suggested how Jesus could use His vast power for personal benefit. Not wishing to be led into a debate about these insulting implications, Jesus brushed off the question with the comment, "man shall not live by bread alone, but by every word of God" (Luke 4:4). Then in the setting of a high mountain, Satan, referring to the kingdoms of the world, said: "All this power will I give thee, and the glory of them . . . If thou will worship me" (Luke 4:6-7). Ignoring the arrogant presumption of the statement—that Satan could actually do this—Jesus answered, "Get thee behind me, Satan: for it is written, Thou shalt worship the Lord thy God, and him only shalt thou serve" (Luke 4:8). Finally, we see the Savior in Jerusalem at the pinnacle of the temple where Satan said,

> If thou be the Son of God, cast thyself down from hence: For it is written, He shall give his angels charge over thee to keep thee: And in *their* hands they shall bear thee up, lest at any time thou dash thy foot against a stone." (Luke 4:9-11)

Ignoring the presumptuous challenge of His Messianic role and the childish disconnect between dashing a foot against a stone and falling to the ground from a high place, Jesus answered: "Thou shalt not tempt the Lord thy God" (Luke 4:12).

While this ended the interview, it did not end the harassment the Savior would endure from Satan or his surrogates during the course of His ministry. At almost every juncture would be found satanic influences or interventions intended to thwart or impede the work.

CHAPTER THREE

The Ministry of Jesus Begins

The Miracle at Cana

When Jesus and His four disciples—Andrew, Peter, Philip, and Nathaniel—left the Jordan River, they returned to their homes in Galilee. Then following the Savior's temptation, He and the disciples were invited to a wedding feast at Cana (see John 2:2). This was a village where Nathaniel lived, which was located about four miles from Nazareth. The mother of the Savior was present also and seemed to have some responsibility at the feast, for when the supply of wine was exhausted, she went to Jesus saying, "They have no wine" (John 2:3). In response the Savior said: "Woman, what have I to do with thee? mine hour is not yet come" (John 2:4). This exchange between mother and son is fraught with implied meaning. It implies Mary knew Jesus had the power to remedy the lack of wine, yet He was reluctant to exercise that power under the circumstances. By a means not reported in John's record (and he was the only one of the four narrators who recorded the incident), the Savior's reluctance was overcome, and Mary instructed the servants, "Whatever he saith unto you, do *it*" (John 2:5). Jesus then told the servants to fill stone water pots standing nearby with water. Then when they had done this, He told them to serve the Governor of the feast with liquid from the pots. When the Governor had tasted it, he called to the bridegroom, saying: "Every man at the beginning doth set forth good wine; and when men have well drunk, then that which is worse: *but* thou hast kept the good wine until now" (John 2:10). We are left to wonder what changed the Savior's mind, what words, if any, He used in making the transformation, and what physical process brought about the change. There are no answers to these questions sufficient to satisfy the human mind, any more than there are answers to questions like how was the earth brought into being or how is a dead body resurrected. The intervention of some process or principle we do not understand, creating a result beyond our comprehension, leads us into the realm of miracles. It was in this realm that much of our Savior's ministry was performed. And the event at Cana was the first of the multitude of miracles He would perform during the course of His three-year ministry.

There remains a question of semantics in the words Jesus used in responding to His mother, "Woman, what have I to do with thee." These seem harsh and disrespectful, hardly what we would expect from a person such as he. A significant part of the disconnect could be explained by cultural changes wrought by time. As the Savior hung on the cross, He addressed His mother saying, "Woman, behold thy son." Surely at this crucial time the Savior would not say anything that would add to the exquisite pain she then felt. So it seems likely that at the time these words were uttered, they imparted no sense of rudeness or disrespect, but the contrary.

John completes his account of the feast at Cana observing, "This beginning of miracles did Jesus in Cana of Galilee, and manifested forth his glory; and his disciples believed on him" (John 2:11). There is special significance to the words about the disciples. Before Cana they had had intense feelings about Jesus, a sense that perhaps He was the Messiah. Now, however, they were witnesses of His extraordinary power. From that time forward they saw Him in a different light than before, with a focus and fervor that were transforming.

After the wedding feast at Cana, the Savior went to Capernaum with "his mother, and his brethren, and his disciples" (John 2:12). This was a fishing village on the northern shore of the Sea of Galilee. It also was a place of popular resort where visitors could relax and enjoy the cool breezes that wafted over the water. Nearby to the northeast was Bethsaida, the home of Simon Peter, Andrew, and Philip. After a few days in Capernaum, Jesus traveled to Jerusalem to celebrate the Passover.

Jesus Clears the Temple

This was the first known visit Jesus had made to the temple in Jerusalem since age twelve, when He tarried there as His parents left for Nazareth without him. He was disturbed by what He found on this second visit. Instead of a quiet atmosphere with the rabbis expounding on the scriptures for their enjoyment and for the edification and entertainment of onlookers, He found a scene of bedlam and confusion. In the outer courts of the temple, He found pens of sheep, stalls of oxen, and cages of doves and pigeons, which were used in the temple ceremonies. Adding to the confusion were the loud voices of the owners of these birds and animals proclaiming their suitability for the rites and ordinances. Amidst this array were tables where moneychangers were busy exchanging the currency authorized for use in the temple for currency of commerce used outside. The temple patrons needed this authorized currency, not only for the purchase of sacrificial offerings, but for the payment of the yearly poll tribute of the sanctuary and the ransom offering required of every male in Israel. Incensed at this desecration:

> [Jesus] drove them all out of the temple, and the sheep, and the oxen; and poured out the changers' money, and overthrew the tables;
>
> And said unto them that sold doves, Take these things hence; make not my Father's house an house of merchandise. (John 2:15-16)

When the furor caused by the Savior's cleansing of the temple abated, the Jewish leaders accosted Him saying, "What sign shewest thou unto us, seeing that thou doest these things?" (John 2:18) In essence the Jewish leaders seemed to be asking Jesus by what authority He had done this. His enigmatic answer was: "Destroy this temple, and in three days I will raise it up" (John 2:19). John then added this commentary: "But he spake of the temple of his body" (John 2:21).

The veiled comment of the Savior to the Jewish leaders was the first time He publicly announced His death and resurrection. At the time Jesus made the statement, it is doubtful John and the other disciples understood it. They had been conditioned to the idea that the Messiah would appear as an all-powerful secular leader who would avenge the Jews of all the injustices they had endured over the centuries. The insights into His power gained from the events at Cana gave hope that their expectations would be vindicated. Thus they seemingly were unable to grasp the notion that He would be destroyed then would be resurrected in three days. While John and other of the disciples were unable to grasp this reality at the time of the temple's cleansing, the Savior's later teachings and the fact of His crucifixion and resurrection finally brought them full understanding. So when John wrote his narrative thirty years after the resurrection, all was clear to him.

It seems some of the Jewish leaders had a different take on the Savior's statement at the time He cleansed the temple. Consider that soon after the crucifixion, the chief priests and Pharisees went to Pilate saying,

> Sir, we remember that that deceiver said, while he was yet alive, After three days I will rise again.
>
> Command therefore that the sepulchre be made sure until the third day, lest his disciples come by night, and steal him away, and say unto the people, He is risen from the dead: so the last error shall be worse than the first. (Matthew 27:63-64)

There has been much discussion about the contrast between the benign character of the Savior, reflected in His conduct and teachings, and the aggressive man who cleared the temple. An appraisal of the event must take into account the reality He was His mother's son. Mary was the descendant of a long line of Jewish warriors. Following the exodus, the Jews under Joshua forcibly evicted those who occupied the land, beginning with the victory at Jericho. Thereafter, the cities of the gentiles were systematically conquered and the inhabitants killed, as the Jews reclaimed their promised land. So the Savior's ancestors on the mother's line would have thought little of Him taking a whip to the polluters of the temple. However, given the dominant quality of Christ's makeup acquired from His Father, it is hard to believe His conduct in the temple was actuated by a base or impulsive motive. Indeed, there is much in the surrounding circumstances to suggest that what the Savior did was pre-planned and deliberate. Can there be little doubt that during the Savior's forty days in the wilderness, or on other occasions, He was given heavenly instruction about the mission He was to perform? As Joseph Smith approached his mission, he was given detailed instructions by the angel Moroni that included the citation of ancient scriptures. Joseph Smith was told exactly what was to happen and the role he was expected to play. Is it conceivable that the Savior would have embarked on His mission without similar direction? Thus, it is credible to believe Jesus knew about this event before it happened and was prepared for it in advance. Note John's description of how He prepared: "when he had made a scourge of small cords, he drove them all out of the temple" (John 2:15). This was not one who flew into a rage, but one who deliberately prepared to do what was expected of Him. And the language He used in evicting the polluters was measured and intelligent, not the language of a zealot. Said He, "Take these things hence; make not my Father's house an house of merchandise" (John 2:16).

Several factors endowed this incident with special significance. It came at the threshold of the Savior's public ministry. Before then He was known only to John and the disciples who met Him at the Jordan River and who knew about the events at Cana. It was here, as already noted, that He first announced His death and resurrection. And here was presaged the fulfillment of the Law of Moses, which over the centuries had become burdened with a stifling array of rules, restrictions, and mandates which dominated Jewish life. Ultimately these were to be replaced by the Savior's message of love, mercy, and hope, which He would articulate over the months ahead.

Another important consequence of the cleansing of the temple was that it introduced the Savior to the Jewish world. He became a celebrity almost overnight. People flocked to see Him and to hear him. Later as the number and variety of His miracles increased, the size of the crowds became almost unmanageable. In an apparent effort to reduce the size of them, He sometimes asked those whom He blessed to tell no one about it.

Nicodemus Visits Jesus

In clearing the temple, Jesus incurred the wrath of the Jewish leaders, including the powerful Sanhedrin. This august body included men of the highest academic achievement and political influence. Thus, it was significant that Nicodemus, a Pharisee and a notable member of that body, sought a private interview with the Savior. Given his status, the disrespect in which Jesus was held by the Sanhedrin, and the rancor over the temple clearing, it was not surprising that Nicodemus requested that the meeting be held at night. Because only the two of them were present, it seems apparent that Jesus provided John with a report of the meeting, John being the only one of the four gospel narrators who provided an account of the interview. Because of the significance of this interview and the importance of the subject matter, the transcript, appearing as verses 1-21 of John, Chapter 3, is considered by some to be the first sermon of the Savior's ministry.

The interview began with Nicodemus making this astounding statement: "Rabbi, we know thou art a teacher come from God: for no man can do these miracles that thou doest, except God be with him" (John 3:2). What was astonishing was his respectful salutation, "Rabbi," which acknowledged the Savior's eminent status. He also acknowledged the veracity of Christ's miracles; and his use of the plural "we" suggested there were others in the Sanhedrin who shared his views. The Savior passed over this pleasantry and focused immediately upon a doctrinal theme. Said he: "Verily, verily, I say unto thee, Except a man be born again, he cannot see the kingdom of God" (John 3:3). The response seems unworthy of Nicodemus, who said: "How can a man be born when he is old? Can he enter the second time into his mother's womb and be born?" (John 3:4) Nicodemus knew, for instance, that entrance into the Jewish faith was regarded as a rebirth, so why this needless comment? Ignoring what He could have taken as a sophistry, Jesus elaborated: "Except a man be born of water and *of* the Spirit, he cannot enter into the kingdom of God" (John 3:5).

Jesus went on to say that which is born of the flesh is flesh and that which is born of the spirit is spirit and then likened spirit to the wind passing through the trees, whose origin and destination are unknown. When Nicodemus asked, "How can these things be?" Jesus uttered a mild reproach, saying, "Art thou a master of Israel, and knowest not these things?" (John 3:10) Then came the Savior's chastisement: "We do know, and testify that we have seen; and ye receive not our witness. If I have told you earthly things, and ye believe not, how shall ye believe, if I tell you *of* heavenly things?" (John 3:11-12) Jesus then affirmed His Messianic mission saying,

> And as Moses lifted up the serpent in the wilderness, even so must the Son of man be lifted up:
> That whosoever believeth in him shall not perish, but have eternal life.
> For God so loved the world, that he gave his only begotten Son, that whosoever believeth in him shall not perish, but have everlasting life. (John 3:14-16)

Jesus then spoke of God's condemnation, "that light is come into the world, and men loved darkness rather than light, because their deeds were evil" (John 3:19). He ended by saying that those who do evil hate the light and avoid it lest their deeds be proved, while those who "doeth truth" come to the light, that their deeds be made manifest (see John 3:20-21).

Nicodemus could not have felt comfortable about this interview. Especially troubling to him would have been the Savior's pointed comments about those who veil their misdeeds in darkness. Was he among these because he sought the interview at night so as to shield himself from the criticism or suspicion of his associates? Yet the Savior's forthright and unyielding statements seem not to have turned Nicodemus away. Indeed they seem to have brought him closer, if not to baptism, for after Joseph of Arimathaea obtained Christ's body after the crucifixion, Nicodemus "brought a mixture of myrrh and aloes about an hundred pound weight" (John 19:39) for use in preparing the body for burial.

Through this incident, the Savior made it patently clear that baptism is an essential element of salvation. And through His own example and later pronouncements, to be efficacious a baptism must be by immersion and by one holding the requisite priesthood authority. His reference to being lifted up also was a veiled reference to His crucifixion.

John Testifies of Jesus, Is Imprisoned, Beheaded

Soon after the interview with Nicodemus, "came Jesus and his disciples into the land of Judaea; and there he tarried with them, and baptized" (John 3:22). At the same time, "John also was baptizing in Aenon near to Salim, because there was much water there" (John 3:23). When a question arose between John's disciples and the Jews about purification, they came to John and said, "Rabbi, he that was with thee beyond Jordan, to whom thou barest witness, behold, the same baptizeth, and all *men* come to him" (John 3:26). John then bore witness of the Messianic role of Jesus Christ. Among other things he told the questioners:

> Ye yourselves bear me witness, that I said, I am not the Christ, but that I am sent before him.
> He must increase, but I *must* decrease.

The Father loveth the Son, and hath given all things into his hand.

He that believeth on the Son hath everlasting life: and he that believeth not the Son shall not see life; but the wrath of God abideth on him." (John 3:28, 30, 35, 36)

Later, John was imprisoned by Herod Antipas because he rebuked the king for living with Herodias, the former wife of his brother Philip. Angered by this, Herodias urged Herod Antipas to have John killed. He refused because he feared John's popularity and the unforeseen consequences that would follow his death. Later Herod Antipas was so pleased by the dancing of Salome, daughter of Herodias by Philip, that he promised her whatever she asked, even to half of his kingdom. When she asked her mother what she should ask for, she said, "The head of John the Baptist" (Mark 6:24). When Salome returned, she asked for John's head in a charger.

The king was exceeding sorry; *yet* for his oath's sake, and for their sakes which sat with him, he would not reject her.

And immediately the king sent an executioner, and commanded his head to be brought: and he went and beheaded him in the prison,

And brought his head in a charger, and gave it to the damsel: and the damsel gave it to her mother. (Mark 6:26-28)

The Woman of Samaria

Jesus was prompted to leave Judaea and return to Galilee. The route He followed took Him through Samaria, which was inhabited by a people whom the Jews loathed. They were considered to be unclean, so a Jew would never eat anything prepared by a Samaritan. Fruits and vegetables grown in Samaritan soil were acceptable to a Jew, but once touched by Samaritan hands became polluted and unacceptable. Such was their enmity toward Samaritans and revulsion at their very presence; some Jews in traveling from Judaea to Galilee would bypass Samaria in order to avoid the contamination. Ignoring these perceptions, Jesus and His disciples traveled through the very heart of Samaria. Arriving at Jacob's well, the disciples went to nearby Sychar to purchase food while Jesus waited at the well.

While He waited, a Samaritan woman came to draw water. She was startled when Jesus said, "Give me to drink" (John 4:7). Recovering from the shock, she responded: "How is it that thou, being a Jew, askest drink of me, which am a woman of Samaria? for the Jews have no dealings with the Samaritans." Jesus answered, "If thou knewest the gift of God, and who it is that saith to thee, Give me to drink; thou wouldest have asked of him, and he would have given thee living water" (John 4:9-10). She said, "Art thou greater than our father Jacob, which gave us the well, and drank thereof himself, and his children, and his cattle?" Ignoring this, Jesus answered:

> Whosoever drinketh of this water shall thirst again:
> But whosoever drinketh of the water I shall give him shall never thirst; but that I shall give him shall be in him a well of water springing up into everlasting life."
> The woman saith unto him, Sir, give me this water, that I thirst not, neither come hither to draw. (John 4:13-15)

The Savior told her to call her husband, and when she said she had no husband, He startled her even more, saying: "Thou hast well said, I have no husband: For thou hast had five husbands; and he whom thou now hast is not thy husband: In that saidst thou truly" (John 4:17-18).

This evoked from her the statement "I perceive that thou art a prophet" (John 4:19), and after further discussion, she added, "I know that Messias cometh, which is called Christ: when he is come, he will tell us all things" (John 4:25), to which Jesus said, "I that speaketh unto thee am he" (John 4:26). Suggesting the impact this astonishing statement had upon the woman, she "left her waterpot, and went her way into the city, and saith to the men, Come, see a man, which told me all things that ever I did: is not this the Christ?" (John 4:28-29) This prompted those who heard her to go to Jacob's well. "And many of the Samaritans of that city believed on him for the saying of the woman, which testified, He told me all that ever I did" (John 4:39). At their urgent request, Jesus remained there teaching for two days, following which they told the woman, "Now we believe, not because of thy saying: for we have heard *him* ourselves, and know that this is indeed the Christ, the Saviour of the world" (John 4:42).

This was the first occasion when Jesus unequivocally declared himself to be the Christ. The earlier statement in the temple implying His crucifixion and resurrection was veiled and subject to interpretation. His statement to the woman at the well was direct and unambiguous. No one could doubt or misconstrue His meaning. That the Savior chose this time and place to reveal His true identity seems symbolic. The person involved was a woman whose sins were of the deepest hue and whose society was constantly maligned and disrespected. She and her people, and those of like kind, were the ones who would be the foremost beneficiaries of the redemption He had to offer. He would be the champion of the afflicted, the deprived, and the downtrodden of mankind. He would be a ray of hope in their lives of drudgery and pointless toil. What better symbol of this hope for a brighter tomorrow than this lonely woman who had come to Jacob's well to draw water?

CHAPTER FOUR

Jesus Teaches in Galilee

Healing a Nobleman's Son

Upon His return to Galilee, the Savior went to Cana where He had converted water into fine wine. There a nobleman, whose son was grievously ill at Capernaum, approached Jesus, asking Him "that he would come down, and heal his son: for he was at the point of death" (John 4:47). The Savior then uttered words that on their face seem to be a reproach, "Except ye see signs and wonders, ye will not believe" (John 4:48). Undeterred, the nobleman responded, "Sir, come down ere my child die. Jesus saith unto him, Go thy way; thy son liveth. And the man believed the word that Jesus had spoken unto him, and he went his way" (John 4:48-50). While at first the nobleman seemed to think the presence of the Savior at his son's bedside was necessary for there to be a healing, his faith in the Savior was sufficient to believe the healing could be effected merely by His word. Later as the nobleman traveled toward Capernaum, he met his servants, who told him his son was alive. He asked when the healing had occurred, and they answered: "Yesterday at the seventh hour the fever left him" (John 4:52). Then the father knew *"it was* at the same hour, in which Jesus said unto him, Thy son liveth: and himself believed, and his whole house" (John 4:53). John concluded his narrative of this incident by saying it was "the second miracle *that* Jesus did, when he was come out of Judaea unto Galilee" (John 4:54).

Jesus Testifies at Nazareth

By this time, the knowledge of the Savior's miracles and powerful preaching was widespread. As Luke explains it, "there went out a fame of him through all the region around about. And he taught in their synagogues, being glorified of all" (Luke 4:14-15). It was against this background that He attended the synagogue in Nazareth on a Sabbath day. He had worshiped there numerous times as a boy and young man growing up in the home of Joseph and Mary. He was well known in this closely-knit Jewish community. There apparently was nothing He had done here over a period of thirty years that had portended the fame and notoriety He now possessed. He had burst forth on the public consciousness with the miracle at Cana. And later events at Capernaum, Jerusalem, Samaria, and again at Cana, had geared up the public excitement to fever pitch by the time He took His seat in the Nazareth synagogue. It was the Jewish custom at synagogue to invite visiting dignitaries to read and comment on the scriptures. So when the time in the service arrived for the reading and commentary, the minister called on Jesus, who stood up to read. He was given the book or scroll of Isaiah.

> And when he had opened the book, he found the place where it was written,
> The Spirit of the Lord *is* upon me, because he hath anointed me to preach the gospel to the poor; he hath sent me to heal the brokenhearted, to preach deliverance to the captive, and recovering of sight to the blind, to set at liberty them that are bruised,

> To preach the acceptable year of the Lord. (Luke 4:17-19)

This scripture (see Isaiah 61:1-2) was generally regarded by the Jews to refer to the Messiah, and since Jesus had said the scripture was fulfilled in Him, it is surprising that the audience did not rise in anger at once and accuse Him of blasphemy.

The apparent reason they did not do this was because the further commentary the Savior made of this scripture is not contained in Luke's account. He merely added these words: "And all bear him witness, and wondered at the gracious words which proceeded out of his mouth" (Luke 4:22).

At this point there seems to have been a change in the mood of the audience from admiration of the Savior's eloquence to concern over the implications of what He had said. In the buzz that followed, there emerged the sense, or perhaps some called it out, "Is not this Joseph's son?" (Luke 4:22) The Savior understood the lack of faith and the enmity toward Him these words implied. He also understood their feeling that the miracles He had performed elsewhere should be replicated in Nazareth. He responded first by saying, "No prophet is accepted in his own country" (Luke 4:24). He then cited instances in Jewish history when, first, only one of many widows during a famine was fed and, second, when only one of many lepers was healed. The fact that both the widow and the leper were gentiles made the analogy offensive to the congregation. Because of this and the apparent understanding the congregation finally had of the implications of the Savior's reference to the prophecy of Isaiah, they were enraged:

> And all they in the synagogue, when they heard these things, were filled with wrath,

> And rose and thrust him out of the city, and led him unto the brow of the hill whereon their city was built, that they might cast him down headlong. (Luke 4:28-29)

However, Jesus was able to escape.

It is significant this was the first occasion when the Savior affirmed His Messianic status in a public gathering. He had hinted at it at the temple in Jerusalem, and He had stated it clearly, but privately, to the Samaritan woman at Jacob's well; but this was the first public declaration.

Jesus Ministers at Capernaum

Having escaped death threatened by His neighbors at Nazareth, the Savior went to Capernaum with many of His disciples. There He taught on their Sabbath days, "And they were astonished at his doctrine: for his word was with power" (Luke 4:32). It was there the Savior first encountered evil spirits who had invaded the bodies of men. In the synagogue one day,

> there was a man, which had a spirit of an unclean devil, and cried out with a loud voice,
>
> Saying, Let us alone; what have we to do with thee, thou Jesus of Nazareth? art thou come to destroy us? I know thee who thou art; the Holy One of God.
>
> And Jesus rebuked him, saying, Hold thy peace, and come out of him. And when the devil had thrown him in the midst, he came out of him, and hurt him not. (Luke 4:33-35)

The statement of the one possessed, "I know thee who thou art," is telling. He knew the Savior from His role in the preexistence. He knew Jesus was the one selected by Elohim to serve as the Savior and mediator of mankind upon the earth. So here is the first testimony from the mouth of one of Satan's followers of the preeminent role of Jesus Christ upon the earth.

It is easy to conceive the commotion and the sense of surprise created in the synagogue that day. The man suddenly shouting in a loud voice, the Savior's calm but powerful rebuke, and the tossing about of the one afflicted would have created a scene of awe and suspense.

> And they were all amazed, and spake among themselves, saying, What a word *is* this! For with authority and power he commandeth the unclean spirits, and they come out,
> And the fame of him went out into every place in the country round about. (Luke 4:36-37)

The Savior Heals at Bethsaida

Following the events at Capernaum, Jesus went to the home of Peter. There He found that Peter's mother-in-law was ill with a "great fever." Being bidden to do so, "he stood over her, and rebuked the fever; and it left her: and immediately she arose and ministered unto them" (Luke 4:38-39). The news of the healing spread rapidly, and by sunset, "all they that had any sick with divers diseases brought them unto him; and he laid his hands on every one of them, and healed them" (Luke 4:40). This is the first reported instance of Jesus performing healings by laying on His hands. At Cana, the nobleman's son was healed merely by His word.

At Peter's house in Bathsaida, "devils also came out of many, crying out, and saying, Thou art Christ the Son of God. And he rebuking *them* suffered them not to speak: for they knew that he was Christ" (Luke 4:41). We are left to wonder and speculate why the Savior wished to silence these evil spirits.

Could it be He wished to spare onlookers the trauma of hearing loud, anguished cries like those uttered by the one exorcised at Capernaum? Or could it be He did not wish that the evil spirits be accorded any fame or notoriety because they knew Him of old? Or could it be He wished to tamp down the public excitement, which continued to build.

Following the crush at Bethsaida, the Savior went into the desert, apparently to seek respite and to prepare for the work ahead, but:

> the people sought him, and came unto him, and stayed him, that he should not depart from them.
>
> And he said unto them, I must preach the kingdom of God to other cities also: for therefore am I sent.
>
> And he preached in the synagogues of Galilee. (Luke 4:42-44)

CHAPTER FIVE

The Sermon on the Mount

The four gospels contain the accounts of two major sermons delivered by the Savior during His ministry. The first, the Sermon on the Mount, is recorded in Matthew, Chapters 5-7. The second, the Sermon on the Plain, is recorded in Luke 6:17-49. Both sermons contain much of the same doctrinal and historical matters, although the account in Matthew is more extensive. This difference seems to lie in the fact that Matthew was present at the Sermon on the Mount, which was attended by a select few of the Savior's disciples. The Sermon on the Plain, however, was attended by a vast assembly of persons of different social, economic, and intellectual backgrounds and from different parts of the Holy Land.

Calling of the Twelve

It seems apparent that Matthew's account was based upon remarks the Savior made to a small, select group of disciples following the naming of the Twelve.

> And it came to pass in those days, that he went out into a mountain to pray, and continued all night in prayer to God
> And when it was day, he called *unto him* his disciples: and of them he chose twelve, who also he named apostles;

Simon (whom he also named Peter), and Andrew his brother, James and John, Philip and Bartholomew,

Matthew and Thomas, James the *son* of Alpheus, and Simon called Zelotes,

And Judas *the brother* of James, and Judas Iscariot, which also was the traitor. (Luke 6:12-16)

Thus was taken the first step in the formal organization of Christ's church upon the earth. This vital organizational step having been taken, the Savior provided a broad outline of the scope, the substance, and the content of His ministry and of the Church He organized. Matthew, who was present, later recorded what then transpired. He wrote that when Jesus "was set [seated] . . . he opened his mouth and taught them" (Matthew 5:1-2).

Commentary on the Sermon on the Mount

The Beatitudes (Matthew 5:3-12)

It is not surprising that Jesus began His instruction to the Twelve, and other disciples who were present, referring to the humble and the lowly and to the supernal blessings that awaited them. "Blessed are the poor in spirit, for theirs is the kingdom of heaven" (Matthew 5:3) recorded Matthew; those who mourn are to be comforted; the meek are to inherit the earth. Then followed a litany of the blessings which awaited persons possessed of noble qualities of character: those who hunger and thirst after righteousness shall be filled; the merciful shall obtain mercy; the pure in heart shall see God; peacemakers shall be called the children of God; those who are persecuted for righteousness sake shall inherit the kingdom of heaven. And finally, "Blessed are ye, when men shall revile you, and persecute you, and shall say all manner of evil against you for my sake" (Matthew 5:11). He said those who endured these indignities would rejoice and be exceeding glad, for their reward in heaven would be great, "for so persecuted they the prophets which were before you" (Matthew 5:12).

The Special Role of Disciples

Following His enunciation of the Beatitudes, which were addressed to all believers, Jesus focused on the role of the disciples, especially the newly called members of the Twelve. To these He said, "Ye are the salt of the earth" (Matthew 5:13). Few things are more basic and needful to man than is salt: It flavors and helps preserve our food; it is an important ingredient in many pharmacological compounds; it promotes healing and is indispensable in numerous other ways. The analogy suggests the vital role the Savior expected the disciples to play in helping to establish and promote His church. Yet, He offered a warning lest the disciples lose their focus: "But if the salt have lost his savour, wherewith shall it be salted? It is thenceforth good for nothing, but to be cast out and to be trodden under foot of man" (Matthew 5:13).

The Savior also declared to the disciples, "Ye are the light of the world," adding, "A city that is set on a hill cannot be hid. Neither do men light a candle and put it under a basket but on a candlestick; and it giveth light unto all that are in the house" Matthew 5:14-15). Then by way of admonition He said, "Let your light so shine before men, that they may see your good works, and glorify your Father which is in heaven" (Matthew 5:16). This was a call for the disciples to be active and productive, busily engaged in the Savior's work. They were to be both workers and exemplars.

Christ's Teachings Supersede Mosaic Law

The Savior made it clear that His purpose was to fulfill, not destroy, the law. "Think not that I am come to destroy the law or the prophets: I am not come to destroy but to fulfil" (Matthew 5:17). Lending emphasis He added: "Till heaven and earth pass, one jot or one tittle shall in no wise pass from the law, till all be fulfilled" (Matthew 5:18). Moreover, dire consequences would inure to anyone who broke the law, or taught others to do so, while those who observed or taught the law would "be called great in the kingdom of heaven" (Matthew 5:19). Yet, the Savior emphasized that merely living the law could not bring salvation. Said he, "except your righteousness shall exceed *the righteousness* of the scribes and Pharisees, ye shall in no case enter into the kingdom of heaven" (Matthew 5:20). He then illustrated how His teachings superseded the Law of Moses. For instance, as to the Mosaic Law against killing, He announced, "But I say unto you, That whosoever is angry with his brother without a cause shall be in danger of the judgment" (Matthew 5:22). Moreover, anyone who called his brother a fool "shall be in danger of hell fire" (Matthew 5:22). He urged compromise and reconciliation as the process for resolving personal conflicts. Said He,

> Therefore if thou bring thy gift to the altar, and there rememberest that thy brother hath aught against thee;
> Leave there thy gift before the altar, and go thy way; first be reconciled to thy brother, and then come and offer thy gift. (Matthew 5:23-24)

Citing the Mosaic Law against adultery, the Savior said: "Ye have heard that it was said by them of old time, Thou shalt not commit adultery." By contrast, He announced, "But I say unto you, That whosoever looketh on a woman to lust after her hath committed adultery with her already in his heart" (Matthew

5:27-28). Thus He placed a restraint not only upon a forbidden act, but upon the thought which might lead to that act. He then counseled about the process of forsaking for anyone caught up in adultery, or any other transgression.

> And if thy right eye offend thee, pluck it out, and cast *it* from thee: for it is profitable for thee that one of thy members should perish, and not *that* thy whole body should be cast into hell.
> And if thy right hand offend thee, cut it off, and cast *it* from thee, for it is profitable for thee that one of thy members should perish, and not *that* thy whole body be cast into hell. (Matthew 5:29-30)

Regardless of the cost, the Savior counseled, it is better to forsake misconduct than to lose everything. And the forsaking should be prompt and unequivocal.

The Savior was well aware of the enmity toward Him, His doctrine and His disciples emanating from the Jewish leaders. As a means of avoiding conflicts with them and ensuing interruptions in the work, He discouraged argument and debate in favor of a positive presentation of His teachings. To this end He told them:

> Agree with thine adversary quickly, while thou art in the way with him; lest at any time the adversary deliver thee to the judge, and the judge deliver thee to the officer, and thou be cast into prison.
> Verily I say unto thee, Thou shalt by no means come out thence, till thou has paid the uttermost farthing. (Matthew 5:25-26)

This must not be viewed as condoning laxity toward principle, but as a device to avoid becoming embroiled in meaningless, time-consuming debate or argument.

The Savior also focused on marital relations, alluding to the Mosaic requirement that when a man put his wife away he should "give her a writing of divorcement" (Matthew 5:31). In contrast, He said, "That whosoever shall put away his wife, saving for the cause of fornication, causeth her to commit adultery: and whosoever shall marry her who is divorced committeth adultery" (Matthew 5:32). In its strictness, this teaching was a strong inducement to preserve the marital union.

It is obvious the Savior believed that words had meaning and that there were consequences to the individual for the words he uttered. Referring to the Law of Moses, He said:

> Ye have heard that it hath been said by them of old time, Thou shalt not forswear thyself, but shalt perform unto the Lord thine oaths:
>
> But I say unto you, Swear not at all; neither by heaven; for it is God's throne:
>
> Nor by the earth; for it is his footstool: neither by Jerusalem; for it is the city of the great King.
>
> Neither shalt thou swear by thy head, because thou canst not make one hair white or black.
>
> But let your conversation be, Yea, yea; Nay, nay: for whatsoever is more than these cometh of evil. (Matthew 5:33-37)

Then alluding to the Mosaic law, "an eye for an eye, a tooth for a tooth" (Matthew 5:38), He said:

> whosoever shall smite thee on thy right cheek, turn to him the other also.

> And if any man will sue thee at the law, and take away thy coat, let him have *thy* cloak also.
>
> And whosoever shall compel thee to go a mile, go with him twain.
>
> Give to him that asketh thee, and from him that would borrow of thee turn him not away. (Matthew 5:39-42)

Herein lies Christ's formula for eliminating recurring conflicts and dissensions among men and nations. The Mosaic rule of retaliation breeds only more conflict. The sense of relief or justification felt by one who retaliates against an attack has its counterpoint in the anger generated in the one against whom he has retaliated. And so it goes, back and forth, with no end in sight other than the prospect of interminable conflict and woe. Only observance of the law of Christ can break that vicious cycle. It is difficult to do; but as in all things, He showed the way. As He hung on the cross dying, He asked the Father to forgive them.

The Savior's Moral Mandates

While the Mosaic code decreed love for neighbors, it also decreed hatred for enemies. Now the Savior admonished His disciples to, "Love your enemies, bless them that curse you, do good to them that hate you, and pray for them which despitefully use you, and persecute you" (Matthew 5:44). By this means, the disciples could qualify to become the children of God who, Himself, made no distinction among earth's inhabitants as to who should benefit from the sun and the rain. That being so, why should children distinguish among those who should be beneficiaries of their love? As a means of underscoring the level of excellence expected of the disciples, the Savior said: "For if ye love them which love you, what reward have ye? do not even the publicans the same? And if ye salute your brethren only, what do ye more *than* others? Do not even the publicans so?" (Matthew 5:46-47)

We may wonder about the startled response of the disciples to this revolutionary doctrine, since all of them had been reared under the dark shadow of the Mosaic Code. If that startled them, think of their reaction to the Savior's concluding statement: "Be ye therefore perfect, even as your Father which is in heaven is perfect" (Matthew 5:48).

The Savior was anxious that His disciples not only do the right thing in any given situation, but that they do it for the right reason. So in the matter of almsgiving, their sole focus should be providing aid and sustenance for the needy among them. Therefore, "do not your alms before men, to be seen of them: otherwise ye have no reward of your Father which is in heaven." He cautioned them not to "sound a trumpet before thee, as the hypocrites do in the synagogues and in the streets, that they may have glory of men." Of these He said, "They have their reward." The disciples were to do their alms in secret with the promise that "thy Father which seeth in secret himself shall reward thee openly." (Matthew 6:1-4)

What the Savior said of almsgiving applied to prayer as well. The disciples were not to pray as the hypocrites did, "standing in the synagogues and in the corners of the streets, that they may be seen of men." By contrast, the disciple was to pray in his closet in secret with the promise that the Father, "which seeth in secret shall reward thee openly." Furthermore, the disciples were not to use "vain repetitions" like the heathen who erroneously believed they would be heard for their much speaking. (Matthew 6:5-8)

The Lord then provided a model for the disciples to follow in offering their prayers. It is one of the most frequently memorized and quoted scriptures in the Bible (Matthew 6:9-13). It is addressed to our Heavenly Father, Elohim, the Father of our spirits, with whom we dwelled before taking bodily form. His very name is honored and revered. An earnest appeal is offered that the heavenly kingdom, governed by His holy will, be replicated on earth. Then follows a request for "daily bread," or life's necessities, and for forgiveness from our debts, conditioned upon our forgiving the debts owing to us. The phrase, "lead us not into temptation, but deliver us from evil," seems to have lost something in the translation, a loss which was mitigated by the Prophet Joseph Smith's retranslation, which uses the words, "And suffer us not to be led into temptation." The prayer ends with an affirmation of the kingdom, the power and the glory of the Almighty. Having given the prayer, the Savior offered these comments: "For if ye forgive men their trespasses, your heavenly Father will also forgive you. But if ye forgive not men their trespasses, neither will your Father forgive you." (Matthew 6:14-15)

In teaching the law of the fast to His disciples, the Savior admonished them to shun the example of hypocrites who, through physical contortions and actions, sought to convey to onlookers the physical discomfort they suffered by fasting. Instead He admonished them:

> But thou, when thou fastest, anoint thine head, and wash thy face;
> That thou appear not unto men to fast, but unto thy Father which is in secret: and thy Father, which seeth in secret shall reward thee openly. (Matthew 6:17-18)

As a means of focusing upon their work, the disciples were admonished to seek for eternal riches, not for earthly wealth: "For where your treasure is," He said, "there will your heart be also" (Matthew 6:19-21). Pursuing the theme of focus, the Savior noted that if the eye, the light of the body, be focused upon the work, "thy whole body shall be full of light," whereas "if thine eye be evil, thy whole body shall be full of darkness" (Matthew 6:22-23). In the same vein, He told the disciples, "No man can serve two masters: for either he will hate the one, and love the other; or else he will hold to the one, and despise the other. Ye cannot serve God and mammon" (Matthew 6:24).

Then the Savior drove home the point that the disciples were a class apart who should be wholly and exclusively devoted to the work of the ministry. And in that devotion they should not concern themselves with what they should eat or wear. As to food, they were reminded of the fowls of the air "who neither reap or gather into barns; yet your heavenly Father feedeth them. Are ye not much better than they?" And as to raiment, the Savior asked the disciples to "Consider the lilies of the field, how they grow; they toil not, neither do they spin: And yet I say unto you, That even Solomon in all his glory was not arrayed like one of these." (Matthew 6:25-30)

By way of summation as to the focus and total dedication the disciples should bring to the work, the Savior said:

> Therefore, take no thought, saying, What shall we eat? or, What shall we drink? or, Wherewithal shall we be clothed?
>
> (For after all these things do the Gentiles seek:) for your heavenly Father knoweth that ye have need of all these things.
>
> But seek ye first the kingdom of God, and his righteousness; and all these things shall be added unto you.
>
> Take therefore no thought for the morrow: for the morrow shall take thought for the things of itself.

Sufficient unto the day *is* the evil thereof. (Matthew 6:31-34)

The counsel and instructions given by the Savior on the Mount were of two general kinds. The first were those given to the disciples, especially the Twelve, in their role of leadership. The second were those intended for all members of the church in their efforts to attain to perfection. The admonition to avoid judging others is of this second category. "Judge not, that ye be not judged," said the Savior, "For with what judgment ye judge, ye shall be judged; and with what measure ye mete, it shall be measured to you again" (Matthew 7:1-2). By way of emphasis, the Savior asked why someone with a beam in his own eye would presume to remove the mote from another's. "Thou hypocrite, first cast out the beam out of thine own eye; and then shalt though see clearly to cast out the mote out of thy brother's eye" (Matthew 7:3-5). Recognizing that many lacked the temperament, the capacity, or the good intentions with which to understand or process them, the Savior warned His followers not to share their spiritual knowledge or experiences with such as these: "Give not that which is holy unto the dogs, neither cast ye your pearls before swine," said He, "lest they trample them under their feet, and turn again and rend you" (Matthew 7:6). As a means of enabling His followers to find safe passage through a complex and threatening world, the Savior offered this counsel:

> Ask and it shall be given you; seek and ye shall find; knock, and it shall be opened unto you. For every one that asketh receiveth; and he that seeketh findeth; and to him that knocketh it shall be opened." (Matthew 7:7-8)

By way of illustration, He observed that the man whose son asked him for bread or a fish would not bestow a stone and a serpent in response. "If ye then, being evil know how to give good gifts unto your children, how much more shall your Father which is in heaven give good things to them that ask of him." The Savior then cited the ancient law of reciprocity: "Therefore all things whatsoever ye would that men should do to you, do ye even so to them: for this is the law and the prophets." (Matthew 7:9-12)

The Savior defined two pathways in life available to mankind. One was entered through a strait gate and followed a narrow way, leading to "life." The other was entered through a wide gate and followed a broad way, which led to "destruction." The first was the way of the few; the second, the way of the many. The first was the way of obedience and discipline; the second, of negligence and disobedience. Given these alternatives, the Master's mandate to His followers was clear: "Enter ye in at the strait gate. . . . Because strait *is* the gate, and narrow is the way which leadeth unto life, and few there be that find it" (Matthew 7:13-14).

The Master warned His disciples about false prophets, men who came in sheep's clothing, but inwardly "are ravening wolves." He said they would recognize them by their fruits. "Do men gather grapes of thorns, or figs of thistles?" He asked. Of course not. "A good tree cannot bring forth evil fruit, neither can a corrupt tree bring forth good fruit." Jesus concluded saying, "Wherefore by their fruit ye shall know them." (Matthew 7: 15-20)

Here the Savior reflected a characteristic of practicality and common sense evident throughout His teachings, especially in the parables and in the principles He wished to emphasize, which were illustrated with things or events with which all were familiar.

The Savior ended His Sermon on the Mount by drawing a distinction between the hearers and the doers of the word. "Not everyone that saith unto me, Lord, Lord, shall enter into the kingdom of heaven; but he that doeth the will of my Father which is in heaven" (Matthew 7:21). Anticipating the assertion that performing good works equated with doing the will of the Father, He said: "Many will say to me in that day, Lord, Lord, have we not prophesied in thy name? and in thy name have cast out devils? and in thy name done many wonderful works?" His answer to such as these was succinct and unambiguous: "I never knew you: depart from me, ye that work iniquity" (Matthew 7:22-23).

The Master then likened the hearers and doers of the word to the wise man who built his house upon a rock whose stability would withstand the winds and the storms of life. By contrast, he who heard the word and failed to observe it was likened unto a foolish man who built his house upon sand, which was eroded away by the winds and the storms of life, causing the house to fall; "and great was the fall of it." (Matthew 7:24-27)

When the Savior had finished His sermon, His disciples "were astonished at his doctrine: For he taught them as *one* having authority, and not as the scribes" (Matthew 7:28-29). It is unknown whether the Sermon on the Mount contains all that Christ said on that occasion. Nor is it known whether the wording and phraseology correspond exactly with the spoken words as they fell from His lips. Moreover, it is impossible to know whether the various translations the Sermon has undergone have altered the speaker's intentions in any way. Despite these and any other technical uncertainties, there can be no credible doubt that the Sermon contains the essence of the thoughts expressed by the Savior, recorded by one who was present at the time. And the sweet, confirming spirit that attends the reading of the Sermon, even to this day, attests to its divine origin and import.

The Sermon is the founding document of the Christian religion. That the Savior repeated the substance of it on the plain the following day, and to the Nephites following His resurrection, suggests the importance He attached to it.

The Sermon on the Plain

Luke recorded that after the Savior had called the Twelve on the mount, "he came down with them, and stood in the plain." So, unlike His procedure on the mount where He sat while speaking, here He stood on His feet. That He did so is understandable, given the size of His audience, which, according to Luke, included "the company of his disciples, and a great multitude of people out of all Judea and Jerusalem, and from the sea coast of Tyre and Sidon, which came to hear him, and to be healed of their diseases." (Luke 6:17)

Since the site of the sermon was near Capernaum in Galilee, consider the vast distances many of the members of His congregation would have traveled, most of them by foot, in order to hear and hopefully to be healed by the Savior. And so it is recorded that those "vexed with unclean spirits . . . were healed" (Luke 6:18). Moreover, "the whole multitude sought to touch him: for there went virtue out of him, and healed *them* all" (Luke 6:19). Unlike the situation at Cana when the nobleman's son, who was in Capernum, was healed by the word of Christ, here the healing occurred because of the presence of the Savior and of the "virtue" which emanated from Him.

Following this remarkable instance of mass healing, the Savior undertook to address the multitude. He began with language similar to that of the beatitudes: He uttered words of blessing upon the poor and upon those who hunger, "for ye shall be filled," and upon those who weep, "for ye shall laugh" (Luke 6:21). Then followed these significant words:

> Blessed are ye when men shall hate you, and when they shall separate you *from their company*, and shall reproach *you*, and cast out your name as evil, for the Son of man's sake.
>
> Rejoice ye in that day, and leap for joy: for behold, your reward *is* great in heaven: for in the like manner did their fathers unto the prophets. (Luke 6:22-23)

Unlike the Sermon on the Mount, the Savior then had words of reproach for a select few: "Woe unto ye that are rich! for ye have received your consolation. Woe unto you that are full! for ye shall hunger. Woe unto you that laugh now! for ye shall mourn and weep." And finally, "woe unto you, when all men shall speak well of you! for so did their fathers to the false prophets" (Luke 6:24-26).

The Savior then admonished His hearers to love their enemies; to bless them who cursed them; to pray for those who despitefully used them; to offer the other cheek when smitten; to offer the coat to him who took the cloak; to give to everyone who asked; and to refrain from asking the return of goods taken away (see Luke 6:27-30). The Savior told the multitude to treat others as they wished to be treated, and "to love ye your enemies, and do good, and lend, hoping for nothing again" (Luke 6:31-35).

The Savior then uttered what are known as the reactive commandments:

> Judge not, and ye shall not be judged; condemn not, and ye shall not be condemned: forgive, and ye shall be forgiven; Give, and it shall be given unto you . . . for with the same measure that ye mete withal it shall be measured to you again. (Luke 6:37-38)

After reciting the parable, "Can the blind lead the blind? Shall they not both fall in the ditch," He condemned the hypocrisy of trying to remove the mote from a neighbor's eye while ignoring the beam in one's own. "Cast out first the beam out of thine own eye, and then shalt thou see clearly to pull out the mote that is in thy brother's eye" (Luke 6:41-42). Alluding to the physical reality that trees produce after their kind, He drew an analogy to men, noting that a good man "bringeth forth that which is good" and the evil man "bringeth forth that which is evil" (Luke 6:45).

In conclusion, the Savior observed that those who heard and obeyed His word were likened unto those who built their house upon a rock, while those who heard and obeyed not were likened unto those who built their house upon the soil.

When the Savior appeared to the Nephites in the Western Hemisphere following His resurrection, He called twelve apostles as He had done in the holy land. At the time of the call of the Nephite Twelve, He taught them, and a multitude that were gathered together, the principles and concepts contained in the Sermon on the Mount and the Sermon on the Plain. These are recorded in Third Nephi, Chapters 12-14, in the Book of Mormon. When the Savior had finished this teaching,

> he cast his eyes round about on the multitude, and said unto them: Behold, ye have heard the things which I taught before I ascended to my Father; therefore, whoso remembereth these sayings of mine and doeth them, him will I raise up at the last day. (3 Nephi 15:1)

CHAPTER SIX

Jesus Ministers in Galilee

A Mighty Draught of Fish

Luke recorded that Jesus once "stood by the lake of Gennesaret" amidst a large group of people who "pressed upon him to hear the word of God." This was an area in the northwest part of the Sea of Galilee, off shore from the land of Gennesaret, a fertile plain, a mile wide and two and a half miles long, which was five hundred feet below the level of the Mediterranean. Fishing was the major industry here, and pickled fish from the area were marketed throughout the Roman Empire. The Savior saw two fishing boats anchored nearby, whose crews were off the boats washing their nets. He boarded one of these boats, which was owned by Simon, and asked him to, "thrust out a little from the land." Simon happily complied, whereupon the Savior "sat down, and taught the people out of the ship." When Jesus had finished speaking, He said to Simon: "Launch out into the deep, and let down your nets for a draught." Simon seemed to remonstrate with the Savior, explaining they had toiled all night and had taken nothing. However, he said, "at thy word I will let down the net." When he did this, Simon caught "a great multitude of fishes," the weight of which broke the net. Simon called for help to his partners, James and John, the sons of Zebedee, who were on the other boat. In the end, after James and John came to help, both boats were so laden with fish they began to sink. Seeing the magnitude of the draught of fish, Simon, betraying the charming quality of his effervescent character, "fell down at Jesus' knees, saying, Depart from me; for I am a sinful man, O Lord." In response, Jesus said to him: "Fear not; from henceforth thou shalt catch men. And when they had brought their ships to land, they forsook all, and followed him." (Luke 5:1, 3-11)

It was no small thing for these disciples to abandon their fishing business and to follow him. It meant turning their backs on the valuable assets they had acquired over the years and the steady stream of income that had sustained them and their families. It represented an enormous leap of faith into a future that was fraught with uncertainty and peril. They were well aware of the revolutionary nature of the Master's teachings and of the enmity these had aroused on the part of the ruling classes toward Him and His followers. At the time they had no inkling how this would all turn out, that within a few short months Jesus would suffer a horrible death and that the principal responsibility for carrying on the work He had commenced would rest upon them. All these and many other uncertainties, which lay in the dim future, were of no apparent concern to them. All they knew was that this unusual, charismatic man had called them to work with Him, and this alone was sufficient for them. All else was encompassed in this reality.

A Leper Is Healed

Leprosy was prevalent among the Jews in Jesus' day. Indeed, this loathsome disease existed from ancient times and Moses himself was temporarily afflicted with it (Exodus 4:6-9). Leprosy being highly contagious, one afflicted with it was forbidden to enter a walled city and was required to utter the word "unclean" to anyone approaching him on the street. A leper approached Jesus one day in a certain city, "who seeing Jesus fell on *his* face, and besought him, saying, Lord, if thou wilt, thou canst make me clean." Jesus then "put forth *his* hand, and touched him, saying, I will: be thou clean. And immediately the leprosy departed from him." The Savior then charged the man "to tell no man," but to go to the priest and make an offering as required by the law. (Luke 5:12-14)

The apparent reason for the request of silence was to tamp down the publicity attending His ministry, which had increased the size of the crowds to the point they were almost unmanageable. St. Mark recorded how the cured leper treated the request:

> But he went out, and began to publish *it* much, and to blaze abroad the matter, insomuch that Jesus could no more openly enter into the city, but was without in desert places: and they came to him from every quarter. (Mark 1:45)

One With Palsy Is Healed

At Capernaum, while Christ spoke in a house filled to overflowing, four men brought one with palsy on a bed to be healed. Unable to get through the crowded entry, they carried the man to the roof, broke open the tiling, and let him down in front of the Savior. Seeing their faith, Jesus said "Man, thy sins are forgiven thee" (Luke 5:20). Certain scribes and Pharisees who were present criticized this statement within their minds, concluding it was blasphemous, since only God can forgive sins. Perceiving their thoughts, Jesus said, "What reason ye in your hearts? Whether is easier, to say, Thy sins be forgiven thee; or to say, Rise up and walk?" (Luke 5:22-23) Then to make plain to the questioners who He was and the power He possessed, He added:

> But that ye may know that the Son of man hath power upon earth to forgive sins, (he said unto the sick of the

palsy,) I say unto thee, Arise, and take up thy couch, and go unto thine house. (Luke 5:24)

The man then took up his bed and left. Those who witnessed this extraordinary incident were "amazed, and they glorified God, and were filled with fear, saying, We have seen strange things today" (Luke 5:26). Perhaps one source of their fear was Christ's ability to perceive the thoughts of others. It is noted that both Matthew (9:2-8) and Mark (2:1-12) recorded this incident, but Matthew makes no reference to the infirm man being lowered through the roof. This illustrates again the differences in the narratives of the writers of the four gospels resulting from discrepancies in the records available to them when they wrote.

Jesus Discourses on Fasting

Some of the disciples of John came to Jesus to ask: "Why do we and the Pharisees fast oft, but thy disciples fast not?" (Matthew 9:14) Employing a device He used often, Jesus answered by asking a question: "Can the children of the bridechamber mourn, as long as the bridegroom is with them?" Then responding to His own question, He said: "but the days will come, when the bridegroom shall be taken from them, and then shall they fast" (Matthew 9:15). Here the Savior adroitly taught the purpose of the fast, sharpening our spiritual perceptions by controlling our physical needs and appetites, thus bringing us closer to God. But if God is already present in the person of Jesus Christ, fasting is a vain, unnecessary thing. The Savior then took the occasion to engage in some parabolic teaching. He said you don't put new cloth into an old garment, nor do you put new wine into old bottles. He wished to make it patently clear that His doctrine and teachings were new and different, not to be confused with or intermixed with the old.

Plucking Corn on the Sabbath

The officious Pharisees accused the disciples of violating the Sabbath because they ate corn while passing through the fields. Ever resourceful, Jesus first defended the disciples by challenging the Pharisees vaunted knowledge of the law: "Have ye not read what David did when he was an hungered and they that were with him?" (Matthew 12:3) This was an allusion to 1 Samuel 21:3-6, when David and his friends were hungered and entered the temple, eating the holy shewbread intended only for the priests. Further challenging their supposed superior knowledge of the law, He asked: "Or have ye not read in the law, how that on the sabbath days the priests in the temple profane the sabbath, and are blameless?" (Matthew 12:5)

Then passing over the rabbinical lore which so much obsessed the Pharisees, Jesus offered this practical defense: "The sabbath was made for man, and not man for the sabbath" (Mark 2:27). Having confounded the Pharisees with His detailed knowledge of the law and its application, Jesus took occasion to assert His divine nature and mission: In reference to the temple He said, "In this place is *one* greater than the temple" (Matthew 12:6). Then putting an end to the whole matter He added: "For the Son of man is Lord even of the sabbath day" (Matthew 12:8). With such an overwhelming defense, we may wonder how the Pharisees ever again found the courage to challenge Him.

A Healing on the Sabbath

Not long after the incident of the disciples eating corn in the field on the Sabbath, Jesus was faced with another issue involving Sabbath activity. Here on the Sabbath in the synagogue was a man with a withered hand. Present were Pharisees who "watched him, whether he would heal him on the sabbath day; that they might accuse him" (Mark 3:2).

Jesus was well aware of their cat and mouse game, but He was unwilling to play it, except on His own terms. So He asked the man to stand, and then, addressing the Pharisees, He asked "Is it lawful to do good on the sabbath days, or to do evil? to save life, or to kill?" St. Mark reported that Jesus, being grieved at the hardness of the hearts of the Pharisees and at their failure to respond to His questioning, "looked round about on them with anger." He then said to the man, "Stretch forth thine hand. And he stretched *it* out: and his hand was restored whole as the other." (Mark 3:3-5)

It came as no surprise that the Pharisees immediately left the synagogue and "straightway took counsel with the Herodians against him, how they might destroy him" (Mark 3:6). The blindness of the Pharisees is astonishing, ignoring the grandeur of the miracle while focusing only on the technical violation of the law.

While the conduct of the Pharisees was no surprise, the magnitude of the crowd that followed Him afterward was astonishing. According to St. Mark:

> Jesus withdrew himself with his disciples to the sea: and a great multitude from Galilee followed him, and from Judea,
> And from Jerusalem, and from Idumaea, and *from* beyond Jordan; and they about Tyre and Sidon, a great multitude, when they had heard what great things he did." (Mark 3:7-8)

The Centurion's Servant Is Healed

A centurion in the Roman Army commanded up to a hundred men. Sixty centurion units comprised a Roman Legion. These disciplined soldiers were garrisoned throughout the Roman Empire to induce unity and control and to quell any uprising. More often than not, the centurion created a friendly rapport with the local Jewish leaders. A certain centurion in Capernaum, of whom we now speak, had endeared himself to the local Jewish leaders by building a synagogue for them. When the centurion's servant became gravely ill, he went to the Jewish leaders and asked them to intercede in seeking a blessing from the Savior. They responded immediately, going to Jesus saying the centurion was worthy, "For he loveth our nation, and he hath built us a synagogue" (Luke 7:5). Jesus went with them toward the centurion's house, but they were intercepted by a messenger who said the centurion felt himself unworthy to receive the Savior in his home, "but say in a word, and my servant shall be healed. For I also am a man set under authority, having under me soldiers" (Luke 7:7-8). On hearing this, Jesus said to those with him, "I say unto you, I have not found so great faith, no, not in Israel" (Luke 7:9).

When the messenger returned to the centurion's home, he found the servant had been healed. Jesus uttered no express words of healing, His laudatory comments about the centurion's faith being sufficient to accomplish it. The New Testament contains several other references to Roman centurions, the most prominent one being that of Cornelius, whose spiritual experiences and involvement with Peter ultimately resulted in extending the gospel to the gentiles (see Acts 10:1-35). This incident illustrates that not all Jewish leaders were at war with the Savior. Many were friendly and cooperative. And many were secret believers.

It is noted that Matthew's account of the incident (Matthew 8:5-13) has the centurion making a direct approach to the Savior about his ailing servant. Matthew's account also adds this significant commentary: "And I say unto you, That many . . . shall sit down with Abraham, and Isaac, and Jacob, in the kingdom of heaven" (Matthew 8:11). This is another illustration of how an incident in the life of the Savior was treated differently by different narrators with different emphases, which necessarily reflect differences in the data available to them when they wrote their narratives some three decades following His resurrection.

Raising the Son of the Widow of Nain

The day following the healing of the centurion's servant, Jesus, followed by "many" disciples and "much" people, approached the walled city of Nain. Nearing the gate of the city, "behold, there was a dead man carried out, the only son of his mother, and she was a widow: and much people of the city was with her" (Luke 7:12). Moved by compassion at this sorrowful scene, Jesus told the mother, "Weep not." He then approached the bier and, touching it, said, "Young man, I say unto thee, Arise. And he that was dead, sat up and began to speak. And he delivered him to his mother" (Luke 7:14-15). The consequences of this startling event were predictable:

> And there came a fear on all: and they glorified God, saying, That a great prophet is risen up among us; and, That God has visited his people.
> And this rumour of him went forth throughout all Judea, and throughout all the region round about. (Luke 7:16-17)

John the Baptist Learns of the Raising

John the Baptist was informed of the raising at Nain by his disciples as he languished in the dungeon of Machaerin. He had been imprisoned there as a result of his criticism of Herod Antipas for his improper relationship with Herodias, the former wife of his brother Philip. It was a time of deep disappointment and foreboding for John. Deprived of the wild freedom he cherished and the simple diet of the desert, which had sustained him over the years, he chafed under the restrictions and the indignities now imposed upon him. Nor did he hold out significant hope for his future, being aware of the deep animus Herodias held toward him and of the evil influence she exerted upon Herod, an influence that ultimately led to John's beheading. These dire circumstances may help to explain the action John took on learning of the raising at Nain: "And John calling *unto him* two of his disciples sent *them* to Jesus, saying, Art thou he that should come? or look we for another?" (Luke 7:19) How could it be that John, who baptized Jesus at Jordan, who saw the spirit descend upon Him in the form of a dove, and who heard the voice of God declaring Christ to be His son, could now question His identity? Moreover, he later declared Jesus to be the chosen One and expressed his inferiority to him. Aside from the depressing, discouraging circumstances of his imprisonment already described, another explanation of John's disconnect was the imperfect understanding he and others had of Christ's purpose and mission. These had accepted the idea that the Messiah would be a powerful secular leader who would lead the nation to a position of dominance. When the meek and gentle Jesus failed to meet their preconceived notion of His identity, they wandered and waffled and wondered as John had done when he sent the disciples to Jesus with the doubtful inquiry: "Art thou he that should come? or look we for another?" (Luke 7:20) Luke reported that at the very hour John's disciples asked these questions, the Savior "cured many of *their* infirmities and plagues, and of evil spirits; and unto many *that were* blind he gave sight" (Luke 7:21). Only after these events did Jesus undertake to answer their questions. He said to them:

> Go your way, and tell John what things ye have seen and heard; how that the blind see, the lame walk, the lepers are cleansed, the deaf hear, the dead are raised, to the poor the gospel is preached.
> And blessed is *he*, whosoever shall not be offended in me. (Luke 7:22-23)

Following the departure of his disciples, Jesus lauded John as the messenger chosen to prepare the way before Him and said that, "Among those that are born of women there is not a greater prophet than John the Baptist" (Luke 7:28).

There is no scriptural account of John's reaction on hearing the report of his two disciples. Given the significance of John's prophetic mission, the nobility of his character and the importance of his role in restoring the Aaronic Priesthood in the latter days, it is assumed John was completely accepting of the Savior's role and status. Christ's final comment to John's disciples about the blessed state of those who are not offended by Him would have been a strong inducement to reach this conclusion.

John was beheaded not long after this event. It occurred following a birthday celebration for Herod Antipas. At the feast Herod was so pleased with the dancing of Salome, the daughter of Herodias by Philip, he promised to give her anything she asked, even to half of his kingdom. When she asked for John's head in a charger, he complied for the oath's sake although he did so reluctantly, being an admirer of John. Accounts of John's beheading are found in both Matthew 14:6-12 and Mark 6:21-29. The two accounts are essentially the same, except in Matthew the daughter asked immediately for John's head, while in Mark's account she went to her mother Herodias first to inquire what she should ask for.

Jesus Anointed by a Sinful Woman

Jesus accepted the invitation of a Pharisee named Simon to dine at his home. The host failed to accord Him the usual amenities extended to special guests, water to bathe His feet and ointment for His hair and beard. Nor did Simon bestow a friendly kiss upon the cheek of his guest despite it being a widespread custom of the day. The Savior, always sensitive and alert, could not have failed to note these glaring omissions of social courtesy, although He remained silent about them. According to the customs of the day, it was not unusual for strangers to enter homes like Simon's at mealtime as long as their presence was respectful and not disruptive. So on this occasion, an uninvited woman, bearing an alabaster box of ointment, entered the room and positioned herself near the feet of the Savior. Luke identified this person as a woman "which was a sinner"(Luke 7:37).

In an apparent attempt to obtain some relief from the burden of the sins she bore, this woman began to bathe the feet of the Savior with her tears and then to dry them with locks of her abundant hair. That being accomplished, she applied to His feet the fragrant ointment from the alabaster box she had brought with her. While all this transpired, Jesus remained silent except for conversation at the dinner table. Simon, well aware of what was going on, said nothing about it, since his guest seemed not to object. However, while Simon's tongue was still, his thoughts were active, and "he spake within himself, saying, This man, if he were a prophet, would have known who and what manner of woman *this is* that toucheth him: for she is a sinner." Perceiving his thoughts, Jesus said to Simon, "I have somewhat to say to thee." He then told the parable of the two debtors, one who owed five hundred pence and the other fifty. The creditor having forgiven both debts, He asked Simon which of the two debtors would love the creditor the most. Simon answered, "*he*, to whom he forgave most" (Luke 7:39-43).

Saying Simon had judged rightly, Jesus proceeded to teach him several valuable lessons. He called attention to his glaring failures as a host. He noted Simon had failed to give Him water with which to wash His feet, while the woman had washed His feet with her tears, drying them with her hair. Simon had not bestowed a welcoming kiss upon Him while the woman had not ceased to kiss His feet. Simon had failed to anoint His head with oil, while the woman had poured the fragrant ointment she had brought upon His feet. Then to make it plain to Simon that contrary to his judgmental thoughts, Jesus knew precisely who this woman was, saying "Her sins which are many, are forgiven; for she loved much: but to whom little is forgiven, *the same* loveth little." Other people who were at the table hearing this said within themselves, "Who is this that forgiveth sins also?" To make it clear to them He was not exercising His inherent power of forgiveness, but was stating a fact that resulted from the woman's faith, He said to her, "Thy faith hath saved thee: go in peace." (Luke 7:44-50)

Mary Magdalene

Mary of Magdala (a town on the western shore of the Sea of Galilee) is often referred to as Mary Magdalene. This Mary, "out of whom went seven devils" (Luke 8:2), was a close friend of the Savior. She was near the cross at the time of His crucifixion (Matthew 27:56; Mark 15:40; John 19:25), was at the burial (Matthew 27:61; Mark 15:47), was at the tomb in the morning (Matthew 28:1; Mark 16:1; Luke 24:10; John 20:1), and was the first one to see the Savior after His resurrection (Mark 16:9; John 20:14-18).

Without any scriptural authority to support it, some have equated this Mary with the unnamed fallen woman who appeared and ministered to the Savior at the house of Simon the Pharisee. Moreover, because of this imputation, the name Magdalene has become a generic designation for any woman who has fallen and then repented. This is patently unfair to the Savior's friend and supporter. While in the court of history this would appear to be an injustice without remedy, it is to be hoped she will be vindicated by the scales of eternal justice.

Blind and Dumb Man Is Healed

There was brought to the Savior a man possessed with a devil, who was both blind and dumb, "and he healed him insomuch that the blind and dumb both spake and saw" (Matthew 12:22) and the devil was expelled. There were credible witnesses to this triple healing, something unheard of in the annals of Jewish history. The novelty and the significance of it spread like electricity throughout the region, "And all the people were amazed, and said, Is this not the son of David?" (Matthew 12:23)

As events such as this multiplied, and as the large number of the followers and disciples of Jesus grew apace, there was mounting concern among the Pharisees, which bordered on panic. It was in this context, "the Pharisees went out, and held a council against him, how they might destroy him" (Matthew 12:14). These people were focused and determined. They were highly educated according to the norms of the day and they had the means and the will to carry out any plan they might devise. And what was the plan they came up with after hours of animated debate? "This *fellow* doth not cast out devils, but by Beelzebub the prince of the devils" (Matthew 12:24). It is difficult to conceive of a charge more illogical. Recognizing this, the Savior laid the groundwork for a response that would reveal the absurdity of it. Said he: "Every kingdom divided against itself is brought to desolation; and every city or house divided against itself shall not stand" (Matthew 12:25).

With that grounding established, which the Pharisees could not deny or refute, came the unassailable conclusion: "And if Satan cast out Satan, he is divided against himself; how shall then his kingdom stand?" (Matthew 12:26) This actually ended the debate because there was no logical answer the Pharisees could advance. But Jesus, wishing to add emphasis to His conclusion, did so by assuming He acted by the Spirit of God. In that event said He, "the kingdom of God is come unto you" (Matthew 12:28). Finally, the Savior wished to demonstrate that His act of casting out devils—far from being an illustration of His subordination to Satan, as the Pharisees claimed—in reality was an illustration of His dominance over Satan, "Or else how can one enter into a strong man's house, and spoil his goods, except he first bind the strong man? and then he will spoil his house" (Matthew 12:29). In other words, how could Christ liberate one possessed of an evil spirit without first dominating the one who initiated the possession?

In their contest with the Savior, the Pharisees had sought to picture Him as a tool of Satan, when in reality they were Satan's tools. In that contest there was no position of neutrality. You were either for or against the Savior. Jesus made this plain: "He that is not with me is against me; and he that gathereth not with me scattereth abroad" (Matthew 12:30).

The self-righteous Pharisees apparently did not comprehend that they were tools of Satan. How could that be when they were the descendants of Father Abraham? And in that bubble of self-aggrandizement, they did not grasp that a larger issue here was not merely a contest between them and Jesus, but was, in the final sense, an issue between God and Satan. Thus Jesus said to them: "And whosoever speaketh a word against the Son of man, it shall be forgiven him: but whosoever speaketh against the Holy Ghost, it shall not be forgiven him, neither in this world, neither in the *world* to come" (Matthew 12:32). And again, "Wherefore I say unto you, All manner of sin and blasphemy shall be forgiven unto men: but the blasphemy *against* the *Holy* Ghost shall not be forgiven unto men" (Matthew 12:31).

It is likely true that the Pharisees had little if any understanding about the meaning or import of these words. They had rejected the Savior's teachings and wanted to kill him. They were wedded to the Law of Moses and the performance of endless tasks and duties that law imposed. On the other hand, these words had deep meaning for the Savior and His disciples. They raised a dire warning against any word disrespectful of or demeaning to deity. Moreover, they were warned that, "every idle word that men shall speak, they shall give account thereof in the day of judgment. For by thy words thou shalt be justified, and by thy words thou shalt be condemned" (Matthew 12:36-37).

Jesus Speaks of Signs

Certain Pharisees and scribes came to Jesus saying, "Master, we would see a sign from thee" (Matthew 12:38). Implied in the statement was the idea they would believe Him if only He would perform some marvelous act. John explained the mindset of such as these: "What sign showest thou then, that we may see, and believe thee?" (John 6:30)

Jesus knew there was nothing He could say or do that would cause these men to believe in him. They were well aware of the miracles He had already performed; He had caused the blind to see, the deaf to hear, the dumb to speak, the lame to walk, and the leper to become clean. None of these miracles had caused the Pharisees and scribes to believe in Him. Quite the contrary, they had only accelerated their efforts to destroy Him. So Jesus treated their request with the contempt it deserved. Said He: "An evil and adulterous generation seeketh after a sign" (Matthew 12:39). The Savior, having aligned the Pharisees and the scribes with the evil and adulterous generation, promised to give them a sign after all:

> there shall no sign be given to it [the evil and adulterous generation], but the sign of the prophet Jonas:
> For as Jonas was three days and three nights in the whale's belly; so shall the Son of man be three days and three nights in the heart of the earth. (Matthew 12:39-40)

This is the Savior's first allusion to His burial. The statement made at the first cleansing of the temple alluded only to His death and resurrection. The two statements read together provided His disciples with a clear picture of the end of His earthly ministry. But none of them fully comprehended it.

After giving the sign of His burial through the experience of Jonah, the Savior undertook to condemn the Pharisees and scribes and to reaffirm His supremacy through two historical incidents. He said the men of Nineveh would rise up in judgment against them, "because they repented at the preaching of Jonas; and, behold, a greater than Jonas *is* here" (Matthew 12:41). He then said the Queen of the South [Sheba] would rise up in judgment against them, because "she came from the uttermost parts of the earth to hear the wisdom of Solomon; and, behold, a greater than Solomon *is* here" (Matthew 12:42). In these illustrations, the Savior condemned the Pharisees and scribes for their failure to repent and change like the men of Nineveh had done, and their failure to seek wisdom like the Queen of Sheba had done.

The Savior then chastised the Pharisees and scribes for their inconstancy and lack of purpose in life through a fictitious story He related. The story began with the eviction of an unclean spirit from a person who then felt isolated and unable to find rest. As a remedy he decided to return to his former residence and took with him "seven other spirits more wicked than himself." Thus the last state of this man was worse than the first. "Even so shall it be also unto this wicked generation," said He. (Matthew 12:43-45)

Who Is My Brother?

While in conversation with others, Jesus was told that His mother and His brethren were without, wishing to speak with Him. Not wanting to interrupt the conversation, and assuming the family's request did not involve an urgent matter, He used the occasion to teach a lesson. Speaking rhetorically He asked, "Who is my mother? and who are my brethren?" (Matthew 12:48) Answering His own question, He said, stretching His hand toward His disciples, "Behold my mother and my brethren! For whosoever shall do the will of my Father which is in heaven, the same is my brother, and sister, and mother" (Matthew 12:49-50). Here is defined the criterion to be met by anyone wishing to be considered a brother, or a sister of the Lord Jesus Christ, that is, one who does the will of the Father in all things. At the same time, these words of the Savior on this occasion seem to have a deeper meaning, implying that the disobedient are forever barred from the family or the presence of God, who does not regard transgression with the least degree of allowance.

CHAPTER SEVEN

Christ Teaches in Parables

During the first period of His earthly ministry, a period of about twenty months, the Savior's teaching was clear and direct, free of all uncertainty or ambiguity. During that period, the opposition of the priestly class, the scribes and Pharisees, mounted dramatically until it had become solidified into a determined effort to kill him. These enemies were thwarted in their design to do away with Him because of Christ's phenomenal and ever-increasing popularity among the people. Thousands upon thousands swarmed around Him wherever He went, seeking to be healed by Him, to listen to His inspiring discourse, or simply to be near Him to feel His energizing presence, or, perhaps, merely to touch His garments. Such was the crush created by this phenomenon, that the disciples had fitted out a small craft, which could be anchored a short distance off shore, and from which He could speak to the throng without interruption.

By the end of this initial twenty-month period, the enemies of Jesus, unable to gainsay or to explain His remarkable healings and miracles, had settled upon the idea that He was an agent of Satan. In an effort to foment this idea, the priestly class undertook to monitor His every move and to critically assess His every public pronouncement. It was within the context of this intense scrutiny that Jesus began to teach in parables.

Parables Defined

A parable is a short narrative that describes a scene or circumstance in which certain persons, elements, or concepts are intermixed. The purpose of the narrative is to evoke in the mind of the reader or the listener an understanding of spiritual or intellectual truths or concepts that the narrative implies or suggests. A special value of the parable is that it provides a means of inculcating eternal truths in a manner consistent with every level of intellectual understanding or attainment. So the grade school student can understand it as well as the college professor. Moreover, this teaching mode has a reactive value, as when one sees an element of the narrative, i.e. a sower planting seeds, which brings back the memory of the parable.

The parable was an invaluable instrument for the Savior in His ongoing warfare with the scribes and Pharisees. When He first began to teach in parables, "the disciples came and said unto him, why speakest thou unto them in parables?" (Matthew 13:10) In answer, He said it was given to the disciples to understand these things, but it was not given to the scribes and Pharisees to do so because they had rejected Him and His teachings. He added that those who understood would be given more, but those who understood not would lose what they had: "Therefore speak I to them in parables: because they seeing see not, and hearing they hear not, neither do they understand" (Matthew 13:13). The Savior added, "In them is fulfilled the prophecy of Esaias, which saith, By hearing ye shall hear, and shall not understand; and seeing ye shall see, and shall not perceive" (Matthew 13:14). Thus the enemies could see the words when written or could hear them when spoken, but would be unable to understand their deeper meanings.

Rabbinic Parables Distinguished

At the time of the Savior's earthly ministry, the priestly class of the Jews used the Rabbinic parables frequently. However, this practice among them does not seem to have been of ancient origin, since the Old Testament contains only two parables. The first is the parable of the poor man's ewe lamb found in 2 Samuel 12:1-7, 13. The second is the story of the vineyard found in Isaiah 5:1-7. The function of the Rabbinic Parables at the time of the Savior's earthly ministry was to teach the Mosaic Law to the Jews. Wrote Edersheim:

> Perhaps no other mode of teaching was so common among the Jews as that by Parables. Only in their case, they were almost entirely illustrations of what had been said or taught; while, in the case of Christ, they served as the foundation for His teaching. . . . Jewish writers extol Parables, as placing the meaning of the Law within range of the comprehension of all men" (*The Life and Times of Jesus the Messiah*, Edersheim, Book 3, Chapter 23, pp. 400-401).

Other Parabolic Distinctions

The scriptures contain examples of other literary devices writers used in their narratives, which are to be distinguished from the Evangelical Parables used by the Savior. These include *the allegory*, which is the statement of a proposition under the guise of some other subject; *the apologue*, which is a fable or moral tale, especially one in which animals or inanimate objects speak or act; *the fable*, a brief story, legend, or myth embodying a moral concept, which sometimes uses animals or inanimate objects as speakers or actors; *the myth*, a fictitious narrative, presented as historical, but which lacks any basis of fact; and *the proverb*, a brief pithy saying embodying a familiar and widely known and popular saying.

The First Series of Parables

The Sower of the Seed – Matthew 13:3-9, Mark 4:26-29

The setting of the first groundbreaking parable Jesus uttered was not unusual. It was on the same day His mother and brethren had sought to speak with Him while He was involved teaching a large group inside a building. He left there and went to the seashore, with the usual large crowd following Him. Several of His disciples cleared the way for Him and helped Him board a small boat, which was tied to the dock. Presumably this was the craft His followers had built for Him and which He used from time to time at various locations on the Sea of Galilee. The Savior's friends maneuvered the craft a distance from the shoreline and dropped anchor. The enormous crowd then gathered at the shoreline facing the ship, standing rank after rank, waiting expectantly and growing in size by the minute as word spread that Jesus was about to speak.

This vast audience, which had gathered from various villages in Galilee and Judea and places in between, including from Tyre and Sidon on the Mediterranean coast, was, generally speaking, divided into two groups, believers and unbelievers. Among the former were those who had been drawn by the hope of being cured of the diseases or disabilities which afflicted them, the blind, the deaf, the dumb, the lame and the leprous. Intermixed with these were other believers who sought relief from mental or emotional ills or, still others, who were attracted by the Savior's analytical and inspirational treatment of doctrinal subjects. All these were energized and excited by the reports of the numerous healings Jesus had performed and of the raising of the widow's son at Nain. Among all these there was found nothing but love, respect, and a sense of awe for the man who was about to speak to them. By way of sharp contrast, there were among the unbelievers present a large number who feared and hated Jesus and who sought to kill Him. These were the scribes and Pharisees and their clients, who now charged that Jesus was an agent of Satan. Their purpose there was not to be taught by Him, but to find in His words further ammunition for their relentless campaign to do away with Him. It must be assumed that not all of the unbelievers had this murderous intent toward Him and perhaps were there to learn more about Him and His doctrine.

Jesus faced this large and diverse audience from a chair on the deck of the boat. The apparent reason for speaking while seated was to avoid unsteadiness on His feet as the small craft moved with the rise and fall of the tides. The Sea of Galilee was well known for its sudden bursts of turbulence. Even in a seated posture, the Savior would have presented an impressive image to the audience. The loose fitting robe He wore could not have concealed His heavily muscled arms, shoulders, and chest, developed over the years working in stone construction at Nazareth. His bronzed appearance, derived from long hours in the Galilean sun, would have conveyed an image of strength and virility. And His calm, self-confident demeanor, enhanced by a full, well-trimmed beard, would have imparted an essential quality of maturity and authority.

Having spent a year and a half speaking to large audiences throughout Palestine, the Savior's voice would have developed remarkably in strength and range so that the first words of the sermon riveted the attention of all:

"Behold, a sower went forth to sow," He declared (Matthew 13:3). Few, if any, in that vast audience would have misunderstood what Jesus had just said. Most, if not all of them, would either have seen a sower at work, or would have been a sower, or would have read about or heard discussions about those who sowed. So, by this simple statement, a prelude to what He would say later, He had brought everyone into the conversation. It was the mark of a skilled and able public speaker. With everyone focused on the subject, and perhaps with examples of sowers then at work in the nearby fields, He told the simple story that when a sower sowed,

> some *seeds* fell by the wayside, and the fowls came and devoured them up:
> Some fell upon stony places, where they had not much earth: and forthwith they sprung up, because they had no deepness of earth:
> And when the sun was up, they were scorched; and because they had no root, they withered away.
> And some fell among thorns; and the thorns sprung up, and choked them:
> But other fell into good ground, and brought forth fruit, some an hundredfold, some sixtyfold, some thirtyfold.
> Who hath ears to hear, let him hear. (Matthew 13:4-9)

When the disciples came to Him afterward, astonished that He had spoken in parables, He gave the explanation previously stated, which in essence was that unbelievers would understand the physical process of planting and the consequences of planting in different kinds of soil, but would have no comprehension of the deeper, spiritual meaning of the parable. Thus the unbelievers are they who see but see not and who hear but hear not.

After delivering the parable of the sower to the multitude, the Savior met apart with His disciples. It was then they asked why He had taught in parables. As part of His explanation about the unbelievers inability to understand what they saw and heard, He said: "But blessed *are* your eyes, for they see: and your ears, for they hear" (Matthew 13:16). He added that many prophets and righteous men had yearned to see and hear the things they had seen and heard, but had been deprived of the privilege.

Without any urging from the disciples, the Savior then undertook to explain the parable of the sower to them. He began, "Hear ye therefore the parable of the sower" (Matthew 13:18). What followed was a discourse on the effect of sowing the seed, or the word, in four different kinds of soil. The sower is likened unto the Savior; the seed is likened unto the word; and the soil is likened unto the spiritual or mental preparedness of the hearer. The seed sown by the well-traveled wayside was likened to the word being taught to one who, lacking spiritual depth, did not understand it: "Then cometh the wicked *one*, and catcheth away that which was sown in his heart" (Matthew 13:19). The seed sown in stony places was likened to the word being received with joy by one with only meager spiritual depth who, after a while, became offended when troubled by tribulation or persecution (Matthew 13:20-21). The seed sown among thorns was likened to the one who received the word, but the cares of the world and the deceitfulness of riches choked the word, "and He becometh unfruitful" (Matthew 13:22). He that received the word in good soil is likened to him that hears and understands the word, who then bears fruit, "some an hundredfold, some sixty and some thirty" (Matthew 13:23).

Some commentators profess to see a philosophy of fatalism expressed in this parable. Such as these infer that those who are lacking in spiritual depth cannot become fruitful, like those described in Matthew 13:23. This view seems at variance with the concept of the perfectibility of man, who is the offspring of God, through faith, repentance, obedience to the laws and ordinances of the gospel, and through persistence.

Before the Savior voluntarily explained the parable of the sower, He told the disciples, "it is given unto you to know the mysteries of the kingdom of heaven, but to them it is not given" (Matthew 13:11). This being so, one wonders why the Savior felt the need to explain the parable without being asked to do so. While the full answer lies in the realm of speculation, it is notable that He attached importance to the explanation, else He would not have uttered it. The Savior knew His remaining time on earth was limited to a few months, and that when He was gone the full responsibility for proclaiming the gospel to the world would rest upon the disciples, especially upon the Quorum of the Twelve Apostles. It was important, therefore, that these should understand the diverse circumstance of those to be taught and of the special limitations surrounding them. Such understanding would enable the disciples to adjust their proselytizing strategies to accommodate the particular conditions of those to be taught. His apparent purpose was to reinforce that understanding, hence His explanation of the meaning of the parable.

Parable of the Seed Growing Secretly

Of the four gospel narrators, only Mark recorded this parable. Jesus said the kingdom of God is likened to a man who "cast seed into the ground" (Mark 4:26). Once the act of planting, or sowing, is accomplished, the planter goes about his other chores, oblivious of the miraculous process of growth going on out of sight underground. That process continues quietly, consistently night and day, until the outer shell of the seed is breached and there springs forth elements of the plant which is the fruit of the seed, "first the blade, then the ear, after that the full corn in the ear" (Mark 4:28). Then when the incomprehensible process of growth from seed to plant has been completed, "he putteth in the sickle, because the harvest is come" (Mark 4:29). The disciples, who understood the spiritual significance of parables, recognized this as a narrative that taught of one of the mysterious, incomprehensible aspects of the kingdom of God. How is it possible that a full-grown plant can emerge from a small seed? The mystery lies in the miraculous process by which the Almighty brings about this result.

Parable of the Wheat and the Tares

The gospel narrator recorded that "The kingdom of heaven is likened unto a man which sowed good seed in his field" (Matthew 13:24). Then while the man slept, his enemy sowed tares among the wheat and left. When the blade of the wheat appeared along with that of the tares, the man's servants came to him and said accusingly: "Sir, didst not thou sow good seed in thy field? from whence then hath it tares?" (Matthew 13:27) When the man explained that an enemy had done this, the servants asked whether they should go and gather up the tares. Declining to follow this zealous but unwise action, the man said:

> Nay; lest while ye gather up the tares, ye root up also the wheat with them.
> Let both grow together until the harvest: and in the time of harvest I will say to the reapers, Gather ye together first the tares, and bind them in bundles to burn them: but gather the wheat into my barn." (Matthew 13:29-30)

Later the disciples came to Jesus and asked for an explanation of the parable. In answer He said,

> He that soweth the good seed is the Son of man;

The field is the world; the good seed are the children of the kingdom; but the tares are the children of the wicked *one*;

The enemy that sowed them is the devil; the harvest is the end of the world; and the reapers are the angels.

As therefore the tares are gathered and burned in the fire; so shall it be in the end of the world

The Son of man shall send forth his angels, and they shall gather out of his kingdom all things that offend, and them which do iniquity;

And shall cast them into a furnace of fire; There shall be wailing and gnashing of teeth.

Then shall the righteous shine forth as the sun in the kingdom of their Father. Who hath ears to hear, let him hear. (Matthew 13:37-43)

Supplement to the Parable of the Wheat and Tares

On December 2, 1832, the Prophet Joseph Smith received a revelation identified as Section 86 of the *Doctrine and Covenants*. This revelation was received during the time the Prophet was reviewing and editing the manuscript of the translation of the Bible. In reference to the parable, it is stated, "the apostles were the sowers of the seed" (D&C 86:2). This is at variance with the account of the parable in Matthew, which reads: "He that soweth the good seed is the Son of man" (Matthew 13:37). An explanation of this variance is found in D&C 86:3. There it appears that after the apostles had "fallen asleep," the church was driven into the wilderness because the tares "choke the wheat." This implies the sowing of the apostles was performed after the death of the Savior and at a time when they were responsible for the promulgation of the gospel worldwide. From this it is posited that the parable of the wheat and the tares recorded in Matthew 13 and in Doctrine and Covenants 86 should be read together. So, reading from D&C 86,

> But behold, in the last days, even now while the Lord is beginning to bring forth the word . . .
> . . . the angels are crying unto the Lord day and night, who are ready and waiting to be sent forth to reap down the fields. (D&C 86:4-5)

In that day, the angels will, "first gather out the wheat from among the tares, and after the gathering of the wheat, behold and lo, the tares are bound in bundles and the field remaineth to be burned" (D&C 86:7). The account in Matthew 13 then records the consequences of the angels reaping down the fields:

> they shall gather out of his kingdom all things that offend, and them which do iniquity;
> And shall cast them into the furnace of fire: there shall be wailing and gnashing of teeth.
> Then shall the righteous shine forth as the sun in the kingdom of their father. Who hath ears to hear, let him hear. (Matthew 13:41-43)

It is tragic to consider the disappointment of those found among the tares at the last day, wailing and gnashing their teeth while contemplating their lost opportunities. Few things are more conducive to repentance than the image of this baleful scene. The remedy lies in removing from personal conduct all things that would be offensive to a celestial community and to renounce all iniquitous conduct.

Parable of the Mustard Seed

The Savior spoke still another parable, likening the kingdom of heaven to a grain of mustard seed, "which a man took, and sowed in his field." Notwithstanding the smallness of the seed, called by Matthew the least of all seeds, "when it is grown it is the greatest among herbs, and becometh a tree, so that the birds of the air come and lodge in the branches thereof" (Matthew 13:31-32). Matthew's characterization of the mustard seed as the smallest of all seeds is an exaggeration, since other seeds like the rue and the poppy are smaller. However, at the time of the Savior, the term, "'small as a mustard seed,' had become proverbial, and was used, not only by our Lord (Matthew 17:20), but frequently by the Rabbis, to indicate the smallest amount" (Edersheim, Book 3, Chapter 23, p. 408-409).

Picturing the kingdom of God as growing from the smallest of all seeds to a mighty tree was difficult for many disciples to grasp, who had been taught from childhood that the Messiah would come suddenly as a powerful political and military leader who would reestablish the house of David to a place of dominance. The idea that Christ's kingdom would grow incrementally from the smallest of seeds to a place of worldwide influence escaped them until taught by such as the parable of the mustard seed.

The Prophet Joseph Smith provided a compelling interpretation of the parable of the mustard seed. Wrote he:

> Now we can discover plainly that this figure is given to represent the Church as it shall come forth in the last days. Behold, the Kingdom of Heaven is likened unto it. Now, what is like unto it?
>
> Let us take the Book of Mormon, which a man took and hid in his field, securing it by his faith, to spring up in the last days, or in due time; let us behold it coming forth out of the ground, which indeed is counted the least of all seeds, but behold it branching forth, even towering with lofty branches, and God-like majesty until it, like the

mustard seed, becomes the greatest of all herbs. And it is truth, and it has sprouted and come forth out of the earth, and righteousness begins to look down from heaven, and God is sending down His powers, gifts and angels to lodge in the branches thereof.

The Kingdom of Heaven is like unto a mustard seed. Behold, then is not this the Kingdom of Heaven that is raising its head in the last days in the majesty of its God, even the Church of the Latter-day Saints. (*Teachings of the Prophet Joseph Smith*, pp. 98-99)

Parable of the Leaven

The Savior taught His disciples, "The kingdom of heaven is like unto leaven, which a woman took, and hid in three measures of meal, till the whole was leavened" (Matthew 13:33). According to Jewish standards, three measures of meal equaled an Epah, "of which the exact capacity . . . According to the so-called 'wilderness,' or original Biblical, measurement, it was supposed to be a space holding 432 eggs" (Edersheim, Book 3, Chapter 23, p. 409). The Jewish mind would have had a clear understanding of how the leaven, or yeast, within that quantity of meal would cause it to rise. So also the disciples, endowed with spiritual insight, would comprehend how the leaven, or the word, would quietly, silently, and inexorably extend its elevating influence, not only throughout the entire mass of an Epah of meal, but by implication throughout the entire world.

Parable of the Hidden Treasure

When the Savior had finished teaching the parable of the leaven to the multitude, He and His disciples repaired to a house in Capernaum. It was there, in the comfort and privacy of this dwelling, that He explained the meaning of the parable of the wheat and the tares. Having explained the parable of the wheat and the tares, the Savior then taught the disciples three additional parables: the parable of the hidden treasure, the parable of the pearl of great price, and the parable of the gospel net.

In the first of these additional parables, the kingdom of God is symbolized by a hidden treasure, which a man accidentally found while examining a piece of property he apparently hoped to purchase. According to Matthew, this treasure was "hid in a field; the which when a man hath found, he hideth, and for joy thereof goeth and selleth all that he hath, and buyeth that field" (Matthew 13:44). At the threshold of the interpretation of this parable is the interesting twist that the man found the valuable hidden treasure in a field he did not own, but was thinking of buying. He then hid the treasure, apparently to prevent anyone else from finding it, sold all the property he owned, and with the proceeds, purchased the field. Since under the law of the treasure trove existing in Palestine at the time, the man violated no law in acquiring the treasure trove (see Edersheim, Book 3, Chapter 23, pp. 410-411). He gave good value for the purchase and apparently violated no personal covenant in concluding the transaction. There remains the question of whether the act of hiding the treasure, once he had found it, thus precluding others from claiming the treasure trove, was morally wrong. The answer to this query depends upon the level of moral sensibility possessed by the reader. The answer, whatever it is, cannot affect the validity, or the powerful impact, of the lesson that the parable teaches, that is, that once a true believer finds and understands the word of Christ, he will give all he has to possess it and to retain it.

Parable of the Pearl of Great Price

This simple story likens the kingdom of heaven to a "merchant man seeking goodly pearls" (Matthew 13:45). Here was a professional, the object of whose business was to search for and to find gems of superior quality. When he found what he considered to be the most rare and exquisitely beautiful gem he had ever seen, he "went and sold all that he had, and bought it" (Matthew 13:46). This result was not an accident. He did not stumble upon this priceless gem by chance while looking for something else. This was the object of his search. And when he had found it, he sold all he had and purchased it. It was priceless because there was no way of affixing a monetary value to it. We may infer the magnitude of its temporal value by considering the various assets a gem dealer could have accumulated over the years — other valuable gems, houses, paintings, statuary, stocks, bonds, bank account, and other assets of value ordinarily acquired over the years by a successful professional.

The disciples readily understood the spiritual application of the parable. They knew the cost of true discipleship was the total, unqualified investment of themselves and of everything they owned in the cause of the Savior. They knew half measures or querulous performance of duty were unacceptable if they hoped to attain exaltation.

Parable of the Gospel Net

This is the final one of the first group of parables taught by the Savior. It likened the kingdom of heaven unto a draw net, or seine, "that was cast into the sea, and gathered of every kind" (Matthew 13:47). When the net was full,

> they drew to shore, and sat down, and gathered the good into vessels, but cast the bad away.
> So shall it be at the end of the world: the angels shall come forth, and sever the wicked from among the just,
> And shall cast them unto the furnace of fire; there shall be wailing and gnashing of teeth. (Matthew 13:48-50)

The disciples understood the analogy that the church contained some who were good and some who were bad, some who were wicked and some who were just. The Apostle Paul recognized this reality when he wrote to the saints at Rome: "For they *are* not all Israel, which are of Israel" (Romans 9:6). It is doubtful the disciples, logically, could have expected a result different from this. In the proselyting process, the gospel net was spread wide to embrace people of diverse backgrounds and of different levels of understanding and motivation. Not all of them were focused upon the ultimate goals of perfection, or of becoming like the Savior, or of divesting themselves of every habit or propensity that would render them offensive to a godly habitation. Some may have entered the church as a means of gaining social, business, or political advantage. Some may have seen in the church a guarantee of personal succor or protection, while others may have seen church membership as a satanic means of striking at the Savior from inside His domain. Still others may have joined the church with good intentions, but, through sloth or disobedience, had failed to retain a remission of their sins. On account of these and other deviations from the principles Christ enunciated, there will be a separation at the last day of those who have failed to measure up, who are cast out and face the furnace of fire with wailing and gnashing of teeth. Who knows but that this furnace of fire represents the realization of lost opportunities.

When Jesus had finished this the last of the first group of parables, He said to His disciples: "Have ye understood all these things?" When they answered yes, He said, "Therefore every scribe *which is* instructed unto the kingdom of heaven is like unto a man that is an householder, which bringeth forth out of his treasure *things* new and old" (Matthew 13:51-52). Here was implicit direction for the disciples to use the new knowledge learned from the parables, and previously acquired knowledge, in their ministry to the world.

CHAPTER EIGHT

The Storm Is Stilled

Matthew 8:18-27, Mark 4:35-41, Luke 8:22-25

In the evening of the day when the Savior first began to teach in parables, there were "great multitudes about him." Apparently weary from the exertions of a long day, "he gave commandment to depart unto the other side" (Matthew 8:18). The "other side" referred to here was the eastern or the Perean side of the lake or the Sea of Galilee. Suggesting this was a decision made on the spur of the moment, Mark reported, "they took him even as he was in the ship" (Mark 4:36). As the disciples cleared the way for Him as He proceeded toward the ship, He was accosted by two individuals who wished to offer their services to Him. The first was a scribe of the priestly class who said, "Master, I will follow thee whithersoever thou goest" (Matthew 8:19). This appears to be the first time during the Savior's ministry when someone of this prestigious class had openly expressed discipleship. Detecting that this man had no conception of the implications of his offer, the Savior answered: "The foxes have holes, and the birds of the air *have* nests; but the Son of man hath not where to lay *his* head" (Matthew 8:20). The record is silent about the scribe's reaction to this statement. He likely was sobered by the reality that the Savior's life was not one of constant, exciting glamor with adoring crowds constantly about to laud and to extol him, but actually was a life of loneliness and uncertainty, one of constant movement and instability. Was he prepared to abandon his life of ease and security for this? And how would he fit in, given the enmity and the murderous intentions of his family and associates toward Jesus? It was not a good fit, and the scribe knew or should have known this.

The second man who accosted Him on the way to the seclusion of the ship said to him: "Lord, suffer me first to go and bury my father." The Savior's succinct answer was, "Follow me, and let the dead bury the dead" (Matthew 8:21-22). It is easy to read into this comment a hint of irritation uttered by one who was bone tired and anxious for a little rest and to be off the stage for a while.

If this man wished to be a special disciple, would he have had any valid question as to the priority between service to the Savior and participation in a funeral? If not, why bother Him at this crucial moment? Moreover, the status of a special disciple derives from the Savior's choice, not the whim of a volunteer.

On board, Jesus went to the stern of the ship, where He laid down on a bench with a pillow beneath His head and immediately fell asleep. Mark recorded "there were also with him other little ships" (Mark 4:36), presumably carrying the more intrepid members of His following. As the ship carrying the Savior approached the Perean side of the lake, it was buffeted by violent winds, which descended on the lake through mountain passes to the east. The driving force of the gale caused the ship to toss and heave as angry waves cascaded over its decks. The passengers were terrified when the waves swamped the ship, which seemed about to founder. Fearful for their lives, the disciples, in a frenzy, awakened the Savior, saying "save us: we perish," while others were heard to say accusingly, "carest thou not that we perish?" According to Matthew's account, the Savior, when awakened, first said, "Why are ye fearful, O ye of little faith?" who then arose "and rebuked the winds and the sea; and there was a great calm" (Matthew 8:26). On the other hand, the record of the event by both Mark and Luke say the Lord first rebuked the storm and then chided His followers for their lack of faith. Here again is illustrated the fact that the accounts of the gospel narrators differ from time to time depending upon the factual sources upon which the narrative is based. In this case, Matthew was aboard the ship, while Mark and Luke relied on hearsay accounts.

The sudden cessation of the storm at the rebuke of Jesus was a source of great amazement to the disciples. "What manner of man is this, that even the winds and the sea obey him!" they asked (Matthew 8:27). There were still many things about this unusual man the disciples and the world were yet to learn. They would not have been surprised about how He quelled the storm had they known that in His pre-mortal state, Jesus, subject to the over-all direction of the Almighty, was the chief architect and builder of the earth upon which they stood. Thus He knew every intricate detail of how it came into being, knew how every aspect of it functioned in time, and knew the levers of power and influence by which its various movements and phenomena were activated and controlled. Those living in the 21st century are not surprised by the various voice-controlled devices developed by science. Marvelous as these are, they are mere child's play compared to the Lord's intricate and mysterious creations, which He controls by means far beyond our power to comprehend. What to His disciples and to us was and is a miracle was to Him merely the performance of a simple act, which lay within the realm of His special knowledge and competence.

The two distinct components of the Savior's makeup derived from His mother Mary and from the Almighty were on dramatic display in this incident of the stilling of the storm. In His weariness and fatigue, His desire for seclusion and rest, we see the consequence of His mortality and humanity. He was Mary's son in every sense of the word. He required daily food and rest in order to function in a normal way. When deprived of either, His body reacted like any other human being, becoming tired and hungry. So at the end of a busy day during which He was under intense pressure as He spoke from the boat to the multitude on shore, laying out His new method of teaching through parables, and as He counseled with the disciples in the home in Capernaum, explaining what He had spoken from the boat and adding other parables, He was tired and needed rest. So when He boarded the ship and was away from the press of the multitude, His sole purpose was to get some sleep. Then when He was abruptly awakened and after His faculties were fully alerted, He heard the anguished pleadings of His disciples and saw the perilous condition of the ship. It was then the godly, eternal component of His being came to the fore with the results already noted. It was no wonder the disciples marveled. They would continue to marvel throughout the remainder of His earthly ministry, with only a vague understanding of who He was, until all was made clear following His death and resurrection.

CHAPTER NINE

The Gadarene Demoniac

Sometime after the Savior stilled the storm, the ship that carried Him anchored near the town of Gerasa in the country of the Gadarenes, "And when he went forth to land, there met him out of the city a certain man, which had devils long time, and ware no clothes, neither abode in *any* house, but in the tombs" (Luke 8:27). As a means of providing some context for this remarkable story, reference is made to the origin of devils upon the earth, some of whom inhabited the body of the man who met the Savior when He landed near Gerasa.

In the pre-existence when the plan of earth life for the spirit children of the Almighty was being formulated, there was discussion about the need for a redeemer who would offer himself as a willing sacrifice for the sins of all mankind, thereby making it possible for all to return to God, conditioned upon obedience and diligence, washed clean and pure through the redeemer's atoning blood. In the process of discussion, Lucifer offered himself as the redeemer with the understanding he would redeem everyone, regardless of personal choice, and that the honor would inure to him personally. In contrast, the Savior offered himself with the understanding He would execute the will of the Father in all things and that the honor and glory would inure to the Father. When Jesus was selected as the redeemer instead of Lucifer,

> There was war in heaven: Michael and his angels fought against the dragon; and the dragon fought and his angels,
>
> And prevailed not; neither was their place found any more in heaven.
>
> And the great dragon was cast out, that old serpent, called the Devil, and Satan, which deceiveth the whole world: he was cast out into the earth, and his angels were cast out with him. (Revelation 12:7-9)

The rebellion of Lucifer and his followers prevented them from taking bodily form, thereby depriving them of the opportunity of being exalted in the presence of the Father. This disability seems to have imbued the angels of Satan, or at least some of them, with the inordinate desire to inhabit earthly bodies. So it was that the body of the demoniac who met the Savior's ship as it anchored near Gerasa had been inhabited by multiple angels of Satan. Thus when the demoniac saw the Savior step ashore near Gerasa, "he cried out, and fell down before him, and with a loud voice said, What have I to do with thee, Jesus, *thou* son of God most high? I beseech thee torment me not" (Luke 8:28).

These words evidently were spoken by one of the evil spirits that inhabited the man's body. And these invading spirits exerted such an evil and violent influence upon him that he was bound in chains and fetters, yet through super human strength could break free from them. So dangerous and fearsome was he that residents of the area gave wide berth to the tombs where he stayed, hoping to avoid any contact with him.

The words of the evil spirit, "Jesus, thou son of God most high," revealed a recognition of the Savior's pre-eminent status extending back to the preexistence and the plea that Jesus not "torment" him suggests a recognition that He had judgmental powers over him. When Jesus asked the name of the evil one, he answered, "Legion: because many devils were entered into him" (Luke 8:30). Since a Roman legion was comprised of from three thousand to six thousand foot soldiers, plus supporting cavalry, some have estimated the number of evil spirits within this poor man to be in the thousands. This of course is a speculation, but given the large number of swine involved in the episode that followed, it is apparent the actual number was very large.

Because the Savior had commanded the evil spirits to come out of the man, "they besought him that he would not command them to go out into the deep" (Luke 8:31). This statement may be interpreted to mean either the depths of the lake or the vast depths of the universe. Whatever the intended meaning, the evil spirits promptly asked that He suffer them to enter into "an herd of many swine feeding on the mountain . . . And he suffered them" (Luke 8:32). Luke then recorded the consequences of the Savior's sufferance: "Then went the devils out of the man, and entered into the swine: and the herd ran violently down a steep place into the lake, and were choked" (Luke 8:33). Illustrating the narrow interpretation given by some to the actions of Jesus, it has been suggested He incurred legal liability for His mere sufferance, which caused the death of the swine.

The topography of the area where this incident occurred lends credence to the narrative.

> About a quarter of an hour to the south of Gersa [Gerasa] is a steep bluff, which descends abruptly on a narrow ledge of shore. A terrified herd running down this cliff could not have recovered its foothold, and must inevitably have been hurled into the Lake beneath. Again, the whole country around is burrowed with limestone caverns and rock-chambers for the dead, such as those that were the dwelling of the demonised. Altogether the scene

forms a fitting background to the narrative. (Edersheim, Book 3, Chapter 25, p. 418-419)

When those responsible to herd the swine witnessed what had happened, they rushed to Gerasa to report. With a sense of disbelief, the residents went to the site "and found the man, out of whom the devils were departed, sitting at the feet of Jesus, clothed, and in his right mind: and they were afraid" (Luke 8:35).

The fear these people felt was not an uncommon reaction to the Savior's miracles. They were so at variance with the normal rhythms of life that those who witnessed them, or the results of them, were surprised and shocked with an anxiety bordering on fear. And in this case, they were appalled by the loss of their property in the drowning of the swine. It possibly was true that the anxiety they showed later to have Him leave the area was dictated as much by the desire to get Him away from their animals as anything else.

The word of what had happened to the swine spread rapidly throughout the entire country. And when a multitude had gathered, the swineherds rehearsed the manner in which the demoniac had been relieved of the burden of the evil spirits and restored to his normal self. At that, "the whole multitude of the country of the Gadarenes round about besought him to depart from them; for they were taken with great fear" (Luke 8:37). Here was reflected an astonishing spiritual blindness, which often was evident among those who witnessed the Savior's miraculous powers. Instead of marveling at these powers and the source from which they came, they focused instead on the physical consequences of their having been exercised.

The narratives of the demoniac at Gerasa found in Matthew, Mark, and Luke are essentially the same, except Matthew wrote that there were two men possessed of evil spirits. However, nothing is said about the second man other than to note his presence. John makes no mention of the episode. All three of the narrators who recorded the incident were uniform in reporting the obvious anxiety of the locals that Jesus leave the area. Matthew wrote "they besought *him* that he would depart out of their coasts" (Matthew 8:34). Mark recorded "they began to pray him to depart out of their coasts" (Mark 5:17). And Luke explained that the whole multitude "besought him to depart from them; for they were taken with great fear" (Luke 8:37). The fact the community reportedly lost some two hundred swine in the incident would not seem to account fully for the urgency of the requests that He leave. It seems likely the miracle of the demoniac's healing played more directly and feelingly into the fears and uncertainties that beset them. Their minds could process and ultimately come to grips with the loss of their swine. But the great mystery of how their death occurred as the result of evil, unseen spirits that emanated from the demoniac was something they could not comprehend. And their inability to do so filled them with fear and apprehension. In this state of ignorance and suspicion, the only remedy they could conceive was to be rid of the one whom they considered to be responsible for what had happened.

As the Savior prepared to abide by the wishes of the multitude and board His ship, the man out of whom the evil spirits had fled pleaded to go with him. But Jesus sent him away, saying, "Return to thine own house, and shew how great things God hath done unto thee. And he went his way, and published throughout the whole city how great things Jesus had done unto him" (Luke 8:39).

The narrator Mark identified Decapolis (Mark 5:20) as the home of the demoniac, where he was to report what had happened to him. Decapolis was part of a large district of ten confederate cities. It became the "life-work" of this man to publish in the ten confederate cities the miracle that Jesus had performed at Gerasa. "And presently, Jesus Himself came back into that Decapolis, where the healed demonised had prepared the way for Him" (Edersheim, Book 3, Ch. 25, p. 423). Many look upon the work of the healed demoniac in Decapolis as the first missionary called to serve in a specific place.

CHAPTER TEN

The Daughter of Jairus Is Raised

Leaving the anchorage near Gerasa, the little ship carrying the Savior sailed to "the other side" and dropped anchor near Capernaum. Here "much people gathered unto him." Among the throng was a man named Jairus, one of the rulers of the synagogue. When Jairus saw Jesus, "he fell at his feet, And besought him greatly, saying, My little daughter lieth at the point of death: *I pray thee*, come and lay thy hands on her, that she may be healed; and she shall live" (Mark 5:22-23). Matthew, who with Luke also related this incident, reported the little girl was already dead. It was unusual that the Jewish Rabbi would prostrate himself at the feet of Jesus. Perhaps more unusual were the words of absolute faith in the healing power of Jesus which he uttered. Undoubtedly, Jairus had heard of the event at Cana, of the healing of the nobleman's son who presumably was a member of his synagogue, of the raising of the widow's son at Nain, and of other miraculous happenings that attested to the Savior's unusual spiritual powers. Now that his tender young daughter was on the verge of death, he cast aside all pretense of his position of power and influence in the Jewish community and humbly pleaded for Jesus to save her.

Heeding this urgent plea, Jesus accompanied the Rabbi to his house amid the press of the large crowd, which thronged the area and impeded their progress.

Among this vast throng was a woman who had been afflicted for twelve years with an issue of blood. She "had suffered many things of many physicians, and had spent all that she had, and was nothing bettered, but rather grew worse" (Mark 5:26). When this woman heard of the many miracles being performed by Jesus, she had the sense she would be healed of her malady were she able merely to touch His garment. So on the day when the Savior was accompanying Jairus to his house, she had joined the throng surrounding Jesus and, having worked herself near to him, she "came in the press behind, and touched his garment" (Mark 5:27). The effect of this touching on the woman was profound because "straightway the fountain of her blood was dried up; and she felt in *her* body that she was healed of that plague" (Mark 5:29). The effect of the touching on the Savior was equally profound, for at that moment "Jesus, immediately knowing in himself that virtue had gone out of him, turned him about in the press, and said, Who touched my clothes?" (Mark 5:30) The disciples standing nearby were surprised by this question and in an almost flippant manner responded: "Thou seest the multitude thronging thee, and sayest thou, Who touched me?" (Mark 5:31) Ignoring this impertinence, Jesus looked about, seeking to identify the one who had touched His clothing with such electrifying effect. The woman, fearful and trembling, now came forward and fell down before him, confessing what she had done and why. With great compassion and understanding, the Savior then said to the woman, "thy faith hath made thee whole; go in peace, and be whole of thy plague" (Mark 5:34).

Judging from the Savior's reaction to the touching, some energy, or holy influence, which He called "virtue" passed from Him into the woman that was the agent of healing. No effort was made to define this virtue or holy influence. Yet, while lacking definition, the effect or impact of it was apparent, for the woman was healed immediately, and she felt and knew she had been healed. The reason given by the Savior for the healing, that the woman had faith to be healed, made it plain that the garment itself was not the agent of healing.

Unlike the incident involving the demoniac, the Savior did not instruct the woman to broadcast what had happened to her, perhaps because of the sensitive nature of her ailment. Nor did He ask her to keep it secret, something impossible to do given the large number who had witnessed the healing.

Even as the incident involving the woman was in progress, messengers came from the house of Jairus with word that his daughter had died, adding, "Why troublest thou the Master any further?" The Savior overheard this comment, which implied it was useless for Jairus to take Jesus to his house because, after all, the daughter was dead, and what could the Savior do about that? Turning to Jairus, Jesus said only, "Be not afraid, only believe" (Mark 5:35-36).

When Jairus first approached Jesus for help, he understood the little girl was only ill, and so he sought a healing at His hand. Now with the word of her death, the faith of Jairus was shaken, being replaced by a fearfulness that Jesus apparently saw in his countenance. His admonition not to fear but to believe seemingly imbued Jairus with new self-confidence as they continued the journey toward his house.

At this juncture, the Savior made a decision that had significant implications for the future governance of His earthly church, for "he suffered no men to follow him, save Peter, and James, and John the brother of James" (Mark 5:37). This is the first instance when the Savior showed special preference among the twelve apostles and the many other disciples who followed him. These three staunch friends and disciples, fishermen from Bethsaida near Capernaum, had been close to Him since His baptism. It will be remembered, too, that one of His early healings was that of Peter's mother-in-law.

It is assumed Jesus knew exactly what would take place at the home of Jairus and that He desired these three chosen disciples to observe and to learn from the miracle which would be performed. Other special opportunities for training would be provided for this chosen three in the future, as, for instance, when they were privileged to be present when the Savior was transfigured on the mount.

It seems likely considerable time elapsed between the notification by the messengers that the daughter was dead and the Savior's arrival at the home of Jairus. This would explain the fact that He found the house was in a tumult, filled with professional mourners who "wept and wailed greatly." Entering the house amidst this chaos, Jesus said, "Why make ye this ado, and weep? the damsel is not dead, but sleepeth" (Mark 5:39).

At this, the professional mourners "laughed him to scorn." They had seen many dead bodies before and they knew this young girl was dead, and they had been invited to perform their acts of remorse and condolence. However, at the insistence of the Savior, the house was cleared of the bedlam. He then entered the room where the young girl lay, accompanied by her parents and Peter, James, and John. Walking to the bedside, "he took the damsel by the hand, and said unto her, Talitha cumi, which is, being interpreted, Damsel, I say unto thee arise." At this, the young girl, thought to be age twelve, arose and walked about amidst, we must assume, the joyful and tearful embraces of her parents, who "were astonished with a great astonishment." Jesus then "went out from thence, and came unto his own country; and his disciples follow him," after He had "charged them straitly that no man should know it." (Mark 5:40-43; 6:1)

Some have pondered the status or condition of the daughter during the period she was "asleep." According to the Savior, she was not dead, yet, presumably she was not breathing nor was there a heartbeat, else the mourners would not have been summoned. All that can be said with any degree of certainty is that while the daughter "slept," her spirit was out of her body, but was returned by the Savior's command Talitha cumi. Where her spirit was during this period is unknown and is only a matter of speculation. The experience of President Lorenzo Snow in calling back the spirit of Ella Jensen, a young girl who had died, is instructive and is relevant to the incident of the Savior and the daughter of Jairus (see *Lorenzo Snow, Spiritual Giant, Prophet of God* by Francis M. Gibbons, pp. 192-196). There President Snow administered to the young girl who had been dead for several hours, commanding her to "Come back, come back," that her life on earth was not finished. Ella Jensen, who later wrote an account of her experience, said when her spirit left her body, she saw members of her family mourning her departure. Later she was so pleased with the place where she was taken she didn't want to heed President Snow's call, but ultimately did so. Some time after returning to her body, Ella Jensen married and bore several children, living until age 86.

CHAPTER ELEVEN

The Blind Are Made To See, the Dumb To Speak

As Jesus left the house of Jairus after raising the young daughter, He made His way along one of the streets of ancient Capernaum. Matthew, who is the only narrator who reported the incident, failed to mention whether anyone accompanied Him. It is hard to believe He walked alone. Nor do we know His destination. He had many friends in Capernaum, any one of whom would have been honored to provide shelter and food for Him. Who knows but that He was on His way to the home of the nobleman whose son He had cured by His word. Because of the itinerant nature of His work, Jesus had to depend upon His friends and disciples for daily sustenance. Perhaps His destination was the home of one of these. He assuredly had no home of His own in Capernaum, or elsewhere, as He had told the eager young Jewish nobleman who had wished to join Him. He was told the foxes had holes and the birds had nests, but the Son of man had nowhere to lay His head.

As Jesus pursued His course along the street in Capernaum, two blind men began to follow him, "crying, and saying, *Thou* Son of David, have mercy on us" (Matthew 9:27). At first, the Savior seemed to ignore these pleas, not because He was unwilling to acknowledge His ancestry through His mother, Mary. It may be because He was tired and hungry, as He had every right to be. Since He boarded the little ship that took Him to the Perean side of the lake, He had been caught up in a series of stressful incidents that would have been enervating to His physical being. He had calmed the raging sea at the insistence of His disciples, and had expelled the evil spirits from the demoniac near Gerasa, afterward dealing with the angry and frightened townspeople who had lost valuable swine. Then soon after His ship dropped anchor after returning from 'Gerasa, He became involved in the lengthy and tiring episode involving the raising of the daughter of Jairus. And, of course, there was the intervening incident when the Savior felt virtue leaving Him as the woman with an issue of blood was healed. With the memory of all this weighing on Him and with the two blind men following, He reached His destination, where He entered a building. The fact that the two blind men followed Him into the building suggests it was a public establishment. Inside, the two blind men "came to him," presumably repeating their cries uttered on the street. Then for the first time, Jesus responded to them, saying: "Believe ye that I am able to do this?" When they answered "Yea, Lord," He touched their eyes, saying, "According to your faith be it unto you." Instantly their eyes were opened, and the Savior charged them, "See *that* no man know *it*." Ignoring this admonition, they "spread abroad his fame in all that country." (Matthew 9:28-31)

Insofar as the Savior's earthly narrative can be accurately unraveled, this is the first instance in which He caused the blind to see. There would be others. In each instance, the words of healing were accompanied by some form of physical touching. So as to the two blind men who sat by the wayside, He touched their eyes as He had done here; in healing the blind indigent in Jerusalem, He placed clay upon the man's eyes; and to another He anointed the blind man's eyes with saliva (Matthew 20:30-34; John 9:6; Mark 8:23). It is apparent that the physical manifestations of these healings played no part in the miraculous consequences that followed. These were the result of the coincidence of the Master's healing power and the faith of the recipient. Why the Savior used these physical devices in performing the miracles was never made plain and remains unknown. Perhaps it was a means of focusing the mind of the recipient, or of the reader, upon the subject of the miracle.

As Jesus left the house where the two blind men were given sight, "they brought to him a dumb man possessed with a devil." And when the devil had been cast out of the man, "the multitude marvelled, saying, It was never so seen in Israel." But the Pharisees, unable to gainsay or to deny the reality of what He had done, asserted that, "He casteth out devils through the prince of the devils." (Matthew 9:32-34)

Criticism such as this seemed to have no adverse effect upon the belief and the faith in Him of His followers as He "went about all the cities and villages, teaching in their synagogues and preaching the gospel of the kingdom, and healing every sickness and every disease among the people" (Matthew 9:35).

CHAPTER TWELVE

Jesus Is Rejected Again at Nazareth

In the process of teaching in all the cities and villages, Jesus came at length to His home village of Nazareth. Bright in memory was the treatment He had received at the hands of His townspeople the last time He was there. Then they had tried to kill Him. They had been offended, then enraged, because after reading the scripture from Isaiah which all understood referred to the coming Messiah, He had declared that scripture was fulfilled in Him. This to them was gross blasphemy. They all knew who He was. He was the oldest son of Mary and Joseph the carpenter. They had seen Him grow up in their midst. Over the years they had seen Him at synagogue, week after week, seated with His parents and siblings. Yes, He was a dutiful son, exemplary in His conduct, a good neighbor and friend. But the Messiah? Such presumption! And so they had taken Him to the brink of the hill, intending to cast Him to His death among the jagged rocks below. But heavenly influences, never fully explained, had intervened to save Him. He was to suffer a brutal and ignominious death, but not at that time and in that manner.

When Jesus arrived in Nazareth, He was not alone. His entourage included many of His disciples, fishermen from Bethsaida and Capernaum. He also brought with Him a notable reputation engendered by the many healings He had performed, by the raisings of the son of the widow of Nain and the daughter of Jairus, and by His skillful and perceptive teaching capabilities.

It was difficult for the townspeople of Nazareth to reconcile this spectacular reputation, which He had garnered in only a matter of months, with the Jesus who had grown up among them over a period of thirty years. During all that time they had never seen or heard anything about Him that remotely resembled the celebrity that now surrounded Him. The news of the miraculous events which had occurred in Bethlehem near the time of His birth and of the happenings at Jerusalem when, as a mere boy, He was found contending with the learned doctors of the law, seemingly had not been known outside the family. Or if they had been, the neighbors had ascribed little significance to them or had completely forgotten them. So when the residents of Nazareth now saw Jesus on the streets or in the synagogue surrounded by His loyal disciples, the tendency was to ask themselves, "Is not this the carpenter, the son of Mary, the brother of James, and Joses, and of Juda, and Simon? and are not his sisters here with us? And they were offended at him" (Mark 6:3). And when He began to teach them in the synagogue, they were astonished, saying, "From whence hath this *man* these things? and what wisdom *is* this which is given unto him, that even such mighty works are wrought by his hands?" (Mark 6:2) In assessing the source of the Savior's wisdom and powers, the townspeople at Nazareth seemed to reject the idea these derived from His family. After all, Mary and her children were quite ordinary, the Savior's brothers never having achieved anything of note, and the sisters apparently had married and were living there in anonymity. Nor had Mary and Joseph, who apparently was then deceased, ever asserted any claim to fame or distinction. So to the townspeople at Nazareth, Jesus was an inexplicable anomaly. And yet, they seemed incapable of grasping that He was what He proclaimed Himself to be when previously He had spoken in their synagogue. It was this reticence of the townspeople, this refusal to believe

Jesus, which precluded Him from performing any miracles or other mighty works among them. His ministrations among them were limited to laying "his hands upon a few sick folk" and healing them (Mark 6:5).

Notwithstanding the cool reception Jesus received in Nazareth on this occasion, the difference between it and the earlier visit is dramatic. Here there was no accusation of blasphemy. The people of Nazareth now seemed to acknowledge without question the reality of Christ's miracles. Their refusal to acknowledge the divine source of His powers and wisdom may have been influenced wholly or in part by the persistent accusations of the Judean rabbis that He accomplished these things as an agent of Satan or that He was Satan incarnate.

The Savior summed up His second Messianic visit to His hometown with the oft-quoted statement, "A prophet is not without honour, but in his own country, and among his own kin, and in his own house" (Mark 6:4).

CHAPTER THIRTEEN

The Twelve Sent Forth

As Jesus pursued His ministry among the cities and villages of Galilee, He lamented about the enormity of the work to be accomplished and the scarcity of the laborers with which to do it. Said He to His disciples, "The harvest truly *is* plenteous, but the labourers *are* few," adding wistfully, "Pray ye therefore the Lord of the harvest, that he will send forth labourers into his harvest" (Matthew 9:37-38). These earnest yearnings for help in the ministry foreshadowed what took place soon afterward. Then, for the first time, the Savior named the twelve men who would comprise His key leadership cadre, men who could help do the work now and upon whom, following His ascension, would fall the major responsibility for performing and supervising the work of salvation which He had begun.

We have seen before this time how He had extended calls to Peter and Andrew, James and John (Matthew 4:18-22), and to Matthew (Matthew 9:9-13). Now He named these seven additional disciples to be included among "the twelve apostles": Phillip and Bartholomew; Thomas; James, the son of Alpheus; Lebbaeus, whose surname was Thaddaeus; Simon the Canaanite; and Judas Iscariot, "who also betrayed him" (Matthew 10:2-4). Eleven of these chosen ones were Galileans. Only one, Judas Iscariot, was from Judea.

These chosen apostles, some of whom had been with Him from the time of His baptism, had been witnesses of the Savior's enormous power and authority, had seen Him heal the sick, causing the blind to see, the deaf to hear, and the lame to walk, while Peter, James and John had witnessed the daughter of Jairus raised from the dead. The apostles also had seen the Savior cast out evil spirits, quell the raging elements, and convince multitudes with His powerful discourse. Moreover, they had profited from instructions He had given them in intimate settings where they had heard Him discuss sensitive matters and had heard His response to questions about a variety of subjects. No one of their generation, indeed, no one in the history of Christianity had been better trained and instructed in matters pertaining to the eternal salvation of mankind than had these twelve apostles. Now was the time for them to begin to share their knowledge and wisdom with others and to exercise the vast authority that He would confer upon them.

The apostles were sent out two by two. This procedure of teaching in pairs is followed in the Church of Christ, even to this day. Its purpose is to provide companionship as well as protection against physical harm and worldly enticements and to provide a dual witness of the truth of their message. The apostles were restricted in the scope of the audience they were authorized to teach, being precluded from teaching among the gentiles and the Samaritans. Thus their ministry was limited to "the lost sheep of the house of Israel." They were to preach that "The Kingdom of heaven is at hand," and that "men should repent" (Matthew 10:6-7; Mark 6:12).

To enable the apostles to preach effectively and with observable results, "he gave them power *against* unclean spirits, to cast them out, and to heal all manner of sickness and all manner of disease" (Matthew 10:1). By way of final admonition, the Savior said to the apostles as they departed: "Heal the sick, cleanse the lepers, raise the dead, cast out devils: freely ye have received, freely give" (Matthew 10:8).

The sole focus of the apostles was to be upon their work of teaching and baptizing, of healing the sick and the oppressed, and of casting out evil spirits. Therefore, they were to leave all of their earthly wealth behind, their gold, silver, and brass. Nor were they to take scrip or money with them, relying entirely upon the liberality of friends and associates and the blessings of the Lord for their daily sustenance. Nor were they to concern themselves about food, housing, and raiment, traveling light with only the clothing they wore. They were assured all necessities would be provided for them, "for the workman is worthy of his meat" (Matthew 10:10). They were to be selective about their residence in a new city or town, staying only in homes of the "worthy." Once having located this place by inquiry, they were told, "there abide till ye go thence" (Matthew 10:11).

The reward of a liberal host was the "peace" an apostle would leave upon the home as he departed. In the event an apostle was not received or listened to in a new city, the consequences were dire. In such a case they were told, "when ye depart out of that house or city, shake off the dust of your feet." (Matthew 10:13-14)

Although this was a practice designated for apostolic use, over the years many Christian missionaries followed it. In the summer of 1942, residents of Cedar Key, Florida, on the Gulf of Mexico, told this writer and his missionary companion that several decades before, a devastating hurricane struck that area. Long-time residents ascribed this event to the actions of two Mormon missionaries who, reacting to their rejection by the community, brushed the dust from their feet as they departed.

The Savior warned that the apostles would be like sheep in the midst of wolves, admonishing them, therefore, to be "wise as serpents, and harmless as doves" Matthew 10:16). So when they were brought before the councils, or scourged in the synagogues through the betrayal of false men, they were to take no thought about their defense, "for it shall be given you in that same hour what ye shall speak; For it is not ye that speak, but the Spirit of your Father which speaketh in you" (Matthew 10:19-20).

Christ also warned that the apostles would be "hated of all *men*" for their defense of Him, but in the end would gain salvation and exaltation through their faith and endurance. Upon encountering persecution in one city, they were to flee to another; "for verily I say unto you, Ye shall not have gone over the cities of Israel, till the Son of man be come." (Matthew 10:22-23)

As it appears in the New Testament, the term "Son of man" is used by the Savior to identify Himself, but is never used by others to describe Him. In using the term in his narrative several decades after the Savior's death, Matthew obviously was not alluding to the master's second coming, when He will return to rule and reign upon the earth. The assumption is that he was instead referring to Christ's appearance to the apostles following His crucifixion and resurrection.

Having observed the Master's benign conduct and recognizing Him as a man of peace, the apostles may have been surprised by this statement He made about himself: "Think not that I am come to send peace on earth: I came not to send peace, but a sword. For I am come to set a man at variance against his father, and the daughter against the mother" (Matthew 10:34-35). The Savior followed up this shocking statement with these words: "He that loveth father or mother more than me is not worthy of me: and he that loveth son or daughter more than me is not worthy of me" (Matthew 10:37). While initially the apostles may have been shocked by these statements, reflection would have convinced them of their reasonableness and verity. To have greater love, and hence loyalty, for any living person than for the living Son of the living God, defies logic and implies a serious lack of understanding. Of course, the Savior and His divine being and eternal principles must take precedence over any human being or agency. And it is precisely this point of precedence that explains and underscores the Savior's statement that He did not bring peace but a sword, a sword that would sever all previous relationships and loyalties and would cause Him to become the very center of the lives and loyalties of His disciples.

Near the end of the instructions Jesus gave the apostles as they undertook their ministry, He expounded ideas which were beyond the scope of their apostolic duties and which had significance for all mankind.

As He counseled the apostles not to fear, He noted that two small sparrows could be purchased for a farthing, the equivalent of a halfpenny. Yet not one of these small, insignificant creatures could fall to the earth without God's knowledge. "Fear ye not, therefore," He told them, "ye are of more value than many sparrows." Moreover, He said, "the very hairs of your head are all numbered." (Matthew 10:30-31)

Herein the apostles were instructed about the omniscience of God and about the Almighty's awareness of the minutest part of His creation. And if the hairs of their head are numbered, what about the rest of their bodies? Does this imply that these bodies have a continuing existence as identifiable beings? Is this a hint about a resurrection for them, as the Savior had hinted about His own resurrection? And what about the myriad of God's other spirit children who had inhabited or would inhabit earthly bodies? These were supernal issues for these first apostles to ponder, issues which would be elaborated by Paul in his apostolic letters and more fully by the Prophet Joseph Smith in Section 76 of the Doctrine and Covenants.

The Savior promised the apostles they would find their lives as they lost themselves in the work of redemption for the lost sheep of the house of Israel. He gave assurance that those who received them also received both Him and the Father. He then contrasted the status of those who followed or relied upon others than the Father and the Son. Said He: "He that receiveth a prophet in the name of a prophet shall receive a prophet's reward; and he that receiveth a righteous man in the name of a righteous man shall receive a righteous man's reward" (Matthew 10:41). The Savior then made it plain that acts of human kindness are recognized and lauded, regardless of the identity of the person in whose name the acts are performed. "And whosoever shall give to drink unto one of these little ones a cup of cold *water* only in the name of a disciple, verily I say unto you, he shall in no wise lose his reward" (Matthew 10:42). Herein is implied the diversity that exists among various individuals and groups who perform acts of human kindness. All are to be lauded and encouraged in their endeavors. Such recognition, however, should not deter the effort to bring these generous, good-hearted persons within the ambit of Christ's kingdom.

Having received these instructions and admonitions, the twelve apostles then proceeded to perform their assigned ministry among the villages and cities of the Holy Land.

The Twelve Return and Report

The duration, the scope, and the substance of the apostles' first apostolic mission are unknown. Because there were six pairs of them, and assuming they divided up the work so as to avoid overlapping and duplication, they likely visited all of the main cities and villages of Galilee, Perea, and Judea, even, perhaps, communities on the Mediterranean coast. Their core message would have been cogent and direct — the kingdom of heaven is at hand in the person of Jesus Christ, and people are to repent and to adhere to the teachings of Jesus. All along the route of their ministry, the apostles would have exercised the authority conferred upon them by the Savior, healing the sick, causing the lame to walk, the deaf to hear, and casting out evil spirits. It is easy to see how these earnest, energetic young men, filled with the spirit of their apostolic calling and performing numerous miraculous healings, would have created excitement and curiosity throughout all the land of Palestine.

Through pre-arrangement, or by instruction given to the six pairs of apostles, they were assembled at the same time at a place not far from Capernaum where they reported to the Master "all things, both what they had done and what they had taught" (Mark 6:30). Anyone who has attended a missionary report meeting has some inkling as to what occurred here as the apostles, filled with the spirit and having a sense of awe, spent several hours, sharing their experiences and bearing testimony. It is unfortunate we have no record of what the Savior said on this occasion. He assuredly was pleased with the chosen twelve who had been raised up to help share the load.

Observing that the apostles were weary from their extensive travels and enervating labors, the Savior said to them following the report meeting, "Come ye yourselves apart into a desert place, and rest a while" (Mark 6:31).

CHAPTER FOURTEEN

Herod Beheads John

Following his baptism of Jesus Christ, John the Baptist preached and baptized in many parts of the Holy Land. Wherever he went, he attracted large crowds who were impressed by the power and sincerity of his discourse, by his rustic appearance, and by the spiritual influences his words and actions generated. As John ministered in Perea, Herod Antipas, one of the sons of Herod the Great, came under his influence. Herod Antipas greatly admired John, an admiration not shared by his wife, Herodias. Indeed, Herodias hated John and wanted to have him killed; but her husband would not hear of it, not only because he liked John, but he was fearful of doing so due to John's popularity among the people. However, Herod later ordered that John be imprisoned in the dungeon at Machaerus because he publicly denounced Herod for his marital relationship with Herodias who was the former wife of his brother, Philip. Machaerus was an ancient prison located on the northern shore of the Dead Sea, the rubble of which is evident to this day. The dungeon at Machaerus is not mentioned by name in the New Testament, but was identified by the historian Josephus as the place where John was beheaded (Antiquities 18.5.1-2).

It was while John was imprisoned in the dungeon at Machaerus that he received word of the raising by the Savior of the son of the widow at Nain. On learning this, John summoned two of his disciples and asked them to contact the Savior and to ask him: "Art thou he that should come? or look we for another?" (Luke 7:19) It seems incredulous that John would now raise the question whether Jesus Christ was the promised Messiah. After all, when he performed the baptism he saw the Spirit of the Lord descend upon Jesus in the form of a dove and heard a voice from heaven declaring this was His son. How then could he now raise a question about the Savior's identity? The answer lies wholly in the realm of speculation. There is nothing in the holy record indicating John ever explained his words. But there is much there to suggest an explanation for them. John, for instance, was raised during a time when the general perception in Israel was that the Messiah would come as a mighty secular figure who would return the house of David to a place of political and military prominence. Jesus did not fit that perception. He was mild-mannered and soft-spoken, preaching love and conciliation, not warfare. It is true He told the apostles He did not bring peace but a sword. But in the context in which He uttered these words and against the background of his entire earthly ministry, the sword to which He referred doubtless was the sword of love and holy principles, not of munitions and armaments of physical warfare.

When John's disciples found the Savior, He was ministering to the people according to His usual pattern, healing the sick, causing the blind to see, the deaf to hear and the dumb to speak, while cleansing the lepers and raising the dead. When John's disciples were given an audience with the Master, they said to him: "John Baptist hath sent us unto thee, saying; art thou he that should come? or look we for another?" (Luke 7:20) In answer, the Savior merely said, "Go your way, and tell John what things ye have seen and heard; how that the blind see, the lame walk, the lepers are cleansed, the deaf hear, the dead are raised, to the poor the gospel is preached." Then by way of mild reproof, He added, "blessed is *he*, whosoever shall not be offended in me" (Luke 7:22-23).

Once the messengers from the Machaerus prison had departed, the Savior lauded John the Baptist to the throng standing nearby who had heard His comments to the messengers. The Master then said of John: "I say unto you, Among those that are born of women there is not a greater prophet than John the Baptist: but he that is least in the kingdom of God is greater than he" (Luke 7:28). The holy record is silent about John's reaction to the Savior's answer to his impertinent questions. It is inferred that he was subdued by it and perhaps embarrassed by the doubt and lack of faith the questions implied.

A large and glittering gathering assembled at the palace near the Machaerus prison to celebrate the birthday of Herold Antipas. Among the distinguished guests were "his lords, high captains, and chief *estates* of Galilee" (Mark 6:21). As with other regal events like this birthday celebration, an air of sumptuous gaiety overlay the ornate dining hall. The entertainments of the evening included a dance performed by Salome, the alluringly beautiful daughter of Herodias. The stunning impact of her performance is suggested by Herod's comments to her afterward. Said he," Ask of me whatever thou wilt, . . . and I will give *it* thee, unto the half of my kingdom" (Mark 6:22-23). Given the magnitude of this offer, Salome sought the advice of her mother before responding. Seeing the opportunity, at last, to silence John's public criticism of her marriage to Herod Antipas, Herodias answered immediately, "The head of John the Baptist" (Mark 6:24).

When Salome adopted this suggestion and relayed it to Herod, he was saddened because he admired John, even as he feared him. However, because of the oath he had made in the presence of his court, Herod Antipas promptly "sent an executioner, and commanded his head to be brought: and he went and beheaded him in the prison" Mark 6:27). John's head in a charger was then given to Salome, and she gave it to her mother, Herodias. John's disciples took the body and reverently buried it (Mark 6:29). This is the last we hear of John the Baptist in holy writ until May 15, 1829, when, as a resurrected being, he appeared to Joseph Smith and Oliver Cowdery on the banks of the Susquehanna River. There he conferred upon them the priesthood of Aaron, "which holds the keys of the ministry of angels, and of the gospel of repentance, and of baptism by immersion for the remission of sins" (D&C 13:1). Following this ordination, Joseph Smith baptized Oliver Cowdery, and he in turn baptized Joseph Smith. Since then, over thirteen million persons have been baptized as members of the Church of Jesus Christ of Latter-day Saints pursuant to the authority of the Aaronic Priesthood.

At the time of his appearance on the banks of the Susquehanna River, the resurrected John the Baptist explained he was acting under the direction of Peter, James, and John, the ancient apostles, who held the keys of the higher or Melchizedek Priesthood. The promise was given to Joseph and Oliver that in due time, the Priesthood of Melchizedek would be conferred upon them.

Later, Herod Antipas heard about the fame of the Savior in His miraculous work among the people. Perhaps feeling guilty for having ordered John's beheading, or maybe being fearful, he said to his servants, "This is John the Baptist; he is risen from the dead; and therefore mighty works do shew forth themselves in him" (Matthew 14:1-2; see also Mark 6:14-16 and Luke 9:7-9). The incident reflects the existence of a belief in a resurrection from the dead, a belief held by many at the time, although the Sadducees rejected it.

CHAPTER FIFTEEN

The Five Thousand Are Fed

Following their first missionary endeavor, the Twelve were exhausted from the constant and demanding efforts the work entailed. So when they had reported to the Savior, He said to them: "Come ye yourselves apart into a desert place, and rest a while: for there were many coming and going, and they had no leisure so much as to eat. And they departed unto a desert place by ship privately" (Mark 6:31-32). This desert place, called Bethsaida Julias, was near the city of Bethsaida, the home of Simon Peter and his brother, Andrew. It being the spring of the year, this site was covered with a carpet of green grass. Since only about four miles separated Bethsaida and Capernaum, this was a populous area, notwithstanding the chosen site was considered to be a desert. By some unexplained means, word leaked about their destination, so when the people saw the Twelve depart by ship, they "ran afoot thither out of all cities, and outwent them, and came together unto him" (Mark 6:33). When the Savior beheld the throng which had gathered, He "was moved with compassion toward them, because they were as sheep not having a shepherd: and he began to teach them many things" (Mark 6:34). Along with the teaching He also healed many of their infirmities during the remainder of the day. As the afternoon waned, some of the apostles urged the Savior to dismiss the congregation and to send them into neighboring villages where they could obtain sustenance. Jesus declined this suggestion and instead asked

Philip where bread could be purchased with which to feed the throng. In his narrative of the event, John expressed the belief that the Savior knew from the beginning what He would do to solve the dilemma, and that He put the question to Philip in order "to prove him" (John 6:6). Andrew who was standing nearby said he knew of a boy among the multitude who had five barley loaves and two small fishes, "but what are they among so many?" Jesus asked for the loaves and fishes and, according to Luke, then directed that the multitude be seated in companies of fifty (Luke 9:14). When this had been done,

> he took the five loaves and two fishes, and looking up to heaven, he blessed them, and brake, and gave to the disciples to set before the multitude.
>
> And they did eat, and were all filled: and there were taken up of fragments that remained to them twelve baskets. (Luke 9:16-17)

The significance of this miracle is suggested by the fact that all of the gospel narrators recorded it. This occurred only infrequently. There had been miraculous manifestations of creative power in the past involving food and drink, as when God provided daily manna for the Israelites, when Elisha multiplied the oil in the widow's cruse, and when Jesus effected a qualitative change in the water at Cana. Here, however, there was a quantitative increase in the five barley loaves and two small sardines to the extent that five thousand were fed, and the amount that remained exceeded by far the initial quantities. It is noted parenthetically that the number fed actually exceeded the reported five thousand, Matthew noting, "they that had eaten were about five thousand men, beside women and children" (Matthew 14:21).

The overwhelming magnitude of this miracle caused some among the multitude to say, "This is of a truth that prophet that should come into the world" (John 6:14), and sought by force to make Him a king. Detecting their intent, Jesus departed alone into the mountain while the disciples departed by ship.

It is far beyond human capacity to comprehend, or to assess accurately, this extraordinary miracle. It speaks of the omnipotence of the Almighty God. And it speaks of His love and concern for the meek and the lowly among us and of His willingness to provide succor for them. That the simple fare for this meal was barley loaves and sardines stands in sharp contrast with the sumptuous meal served at the birthday party for Herod Antipas which culminated in the death of the beloved John the Baptist.

Consequences of the Miracle

After the Savior went alone upon the mountain to pray and the apostles had departed by ship, the multitude that had participated in the feast in the desert slowly melted away, returning to their daily employments. Some of them, however, sought to reconnect with the Savior immediately, and, finding Him in Capernaum, asked: "Rabbi, when camest thou hither?" The Savior uttered a profound truth in response: "Verily, verily, I say unto you, Ye seek me, not because ye saw the miracles, but because ye did eat of the loaves, and were filled" (John 6:25-26). Here the Savior chided His questioners for what has been called the chronic myopia of the masses, which is the failure to perceive the spiritual power and influences that produce extraordinary physical phenomena. Such as these dwell on the surface of life, uninstructed in or unconcerned about the mighty spiritual forces being exerted below the surface. Following this reproach, Jesus continued His conversation with the Jews (see John 6:29). In reference to the meal in the desert, He said to them: "Labour not for the meat which perisheth, but for that meat which endureth unto everlasting life, which the Son of man shall give unto you" (John 6:27). As the conversation continued back and forth, Jesus clearly identified the meat that would endure forever. Said He: "I am that bread of life. Your fathers did eat manna in the wilderness, and are dead. This is the bread which cometh down from heaven, that a man may eat thereof, and not die" (John 6:48-50). Then to make His meaning crystal clear He added: "I am the living bread which came down from heaven: if any man eat of this bread, he shall live forever: and the bread that I will give is my flesh, which I will give for the life of the world" (John 6:51).

The Jews were astonished at this and said among themselves, "How can this man give us *his* flesh to eat?" (John 6:52) And some of the disciples said, "This is an hard saying; who can hear it?"(John 6:60) These scriptures, taken with the scriptures pertaining to the Samaritan woman and the "living waters" at Jacob's well, form the basis for the belief in transubstantiation. Later revelation makes it plain that the sacramental emblems of the flesh and blood of the Savior are taken "in remembrance," not in actuality.

Because of misunderstanding about the meaning of the holy sacrament, "Many of the disciples went back and walked no more with him." Observing this, Jesus said to the Twelve, "Will ye also go away?" to which Peter replied, "to whom shall we go? thou hast the words of eternal life." (John 6:66-68)

Jesus Walks on the Sea

When Jesus left the desert place where the five thousand were fed, "he went up into a mountain apart to pray: and when the evening was come, he was there alone" (Matthew 14:23). These moments of prayer and seclusion were necessary for Him to commune with His Father, thereby renewing His faith and commitment and receiving comfort, solace, and instruction for the challenges that lay ahead. It is easy to ignore or to minimize the impact of Mary's ancestral imprint upon the life and activities of the Savior. Being part human in His makeup, He needed these moments of reflection and renewal like the rest of us.

When the Savior left His mountain retreat and returned to the Sea of Galilee, He found the ship carrying the apostles "was tossed with waves: for the wind was contrary" (Matthew 14:24). In the fourth watch of the night, Jesus sought to join the apostles aboard ship, and "went unto them, walking on the sea." When the disciples saw Him, "they were troubled, saying, It is a spirit; and they cried out for fear. But straightway Jesus spake unto them, saying, Be of good cheer; it is I; be not afraid" (Matthew 14:25-27).

Hearing these words, Peter, the irrepressible one, said "Lord if it be thou, bid me to come unto thee on the water." Receiving the Lord's permission, Peter left the ship and began to walk toward Jesus. Then, troubled by the wind and the angry sea, he lost confidence and began to sink. Fearful of drowning, he called out, "Lord, save me," whereupon Jesus caught Peter by the hand, chiding him gently, "O thou of little faith, wherefore didst thou doubt?" When Jesus boarded the ship, the wind ceased and the disciples worshipped him, saying, "Of a truth thou art the Son of God." (Matthew 14:28-33)

Here again, the Master's control over the physical world and its various components is dramatically illustrated. His ability to walk upon the surface of the sea without sinking seems to have suspended the law of gravity. For a brief moment, that immunity applied as well to Peter until he lost confidence in his ability to walk on the water. Thus when doubt crept in, he began to sink, crying out for help to be saved. Herein is convincingly demonstrated the reality that faith is a principle of power which can be eroded and diminished by doubt and fear.

In its broadest sense, this incident is a metaphor for anyone who has embarked with confidence and faith on a course of action and who then is deterred by doubt and fear created by difficult obstacles and opposition. For any and all caught in that dilemma comes Jesus Christ's reproachful question to Peter, "wherefore didst thou doubt?"

CHAPTER SIXTEEN

Jesus Discourses Upon Cleanliness

Not long after Jesus walked upon the sea, He was at Capernaum. There He was accosted by several Pharisees and scribes from Jerusalem, they being among the large cadre who kept Him under almost constant surveillance. Their purpose was to find aught against Him, which would justify putting Him to death. At this stage of their conspiracy against Jesus, these conspirators considered Him to be an agent of Satan. Later this gross insult would morph into the outrageous assertion that He was Satan incarnate.

At this time in Capernaum, their strategy was to attack Him in the hope His response would provide additional evidence for the case they were building against Him. With this apparent motive in mind, they said to Him, "Why do thy disciples transgress the tradition of the elders? for they wash not their hands when they eat bread" (Matthew 15:2). Over the centuries, the Rabbis had developed a staggering body of "tradition" which governed the conduct of the Jews and locked them into a maze of rules and regulations pertaining to the cleanliness of their bodies and of the food they ate. Such was the emphasis the Rabbis placed upon these traditions that in some instances a tradition was deemed to supersede or to overshadow the law itself.

In responding to the criticism that the disciples did not wash their hands before eating, Jesus charged the critics with hypocrisy, alluding to the way in which one of their traditions had superseded the Law of Moses: "ye say, If a man shall say to his father or mother, *It is* Corban" (Mark 7:11), he is thereby freed from the duty to parents imposed by the law. Corban was a sacrifice or offering to God whose effect was to prevent its use by anyone except God, although the one who made the sacrificial offering could continue to use it. Of this violation of Mosaic Law Jesus said: "And ye suffer him no more to do ought for his father or his mother, Making the word of God of none effect through your tradition, which ye have delivered: and many such like things do ye" (Mark 7:12-13). The scribes and Pharisees had no answer for this stinging rebuke that exposed their hypocrisy and sophistry for all to see. This public embarrassment may have been the catalyst that eventually caused the Rabbis to assert Jesus was not merely the agent of Satan, but was Satan incarnate.

Following this rebuke of the scribes and Pharisees, Jesus turned to the multitude and said: "Not that which goeth into the mouth defileth a man; but that which cometh out of the mouth, this defileth a man" (Matthew 15:11). When the disciples told Him later that the Pharisees were offended by this saying, the Savior brushed it off, "Let them alone: they be blind leaders of the blind. And if the blind lead the blind, both shall fall into the ditch" (Matthew 15:14).

However, Peter pushed further, requesting an explanation of the parable. This earned him a mild reproof from Jesus, who answered saying: "Are ye also yet without understanding?" (Matthew 15:16) Then followed the Master's lucid explanation of why the Pharisaical insistence on frequent hand washings was vain and meaningless. He said:

> Do not ye yet understand, that whatsoever entereth in at the mouth goeth into the belly, and is cast out into the draught?

> But those things which proceed out of the mouth come forth from the heart; and they defile the man.
>
> For out of the heart proceed evil thoughts, murders, adulteries, fornications, thefts, false witness, blasphemies:
>
> These are *the things* that defile a man: but to eat with unwashen hands defileth not a man. (Matthew 15:17-20)

The alacrity and the intelligence with which the Master here sprang to the defense of His disciples are notable. He was their leader, their protector, and their advocate. They could rely upon Him in any crisis or emergency. And the way He had faced down the powerful emissaries from Jerusalem gave them confidence in their discipleship. Yet, His gentle chiding of Peter suggested His expectation that the disciples were not free of responsibility and that His protection and advocacy must be accompanied by their diligence and awareness.

The incident stands as a metaphor for all disciples, in all places and in all circumstances, giving assurance the Master is near and will provide assistance and solace in all situations, as one is humble, faithful, and diligent.

CHAPTER SEVENTEEN

Three Significant Miracles

Daughter of a Greek Woman Is Healed

The Savior's life was now moving at a frenetic pace. The word of His miracles and His cogent discourse had rapidly spread abroad, creating a noisy clamor to see and to hear Him and to be healed by Him. He had sought some relief from this raucous routine following the feeding of the five thousand, but had been largely unsuccessful. Now, following the confrontation with the emissaries from Jerusalem and His discourse upon cleanliness, He was determined to find a place where, in privacy, He could obtain the respite He sorely needed and deserved. It was then He and His disciples traveled to the borders separating Palestine and Phoenicia. Here He "entered into a house, and would have no man know *it*" (Mark 7:24). He soon learned this hope was futile and that He "could not be hid," for here came a very loud and persistent Greek woman, presumably from the area near Tyre and Sidon, the largest cities in Phoenecia. This woman, considered by the Jews to be a heathen and a gentile, had heard of the Savior's celebrity and here pleaded with Him in behalf of her daughter: "Have mercy on me, O Lord, *thou* Son of David," she said; "my daughter is grievously vexed with a devil" (Matthew 15:22). The Savior totally ignored this urgent plea and said not a word to her. The disciples, apparently annoyed by the woman's urgent, noisy pleadings, came to the Savior requesting, "Send her away; for she crieth after us." His simple response was "I am not sent but unto the lost sheep of the House of Israel" (Matthew 15:23-24). While this dialogue between the Savior and His disciples was in progress, the determined woman had in some way gained entrance to the house. She then worshiped the Savior, presumably by prostrating herself before Him, and then said pleadingly, "Lord help me." The Savior's response to this humble, heartfelt request was shockingly blunt and seemingly out of character. Said He: "It is not meet to take the children's bread, and to cast it to dogs." (Matthew 15:25-26).

Many have sought to explain, to justify, or to condemn this forthright statement attributed to our Lord, although none of them seem persuasive. The Greek woman apparently took no offense at these words. This suggests that the cultural relationships between the Jews and the Greeks at the time were such as to rob the words of any demeaning intention on the part of the Savior. In this view, the interchange may be likened to a Latino calling an American a gringo. What is clear, however, is that the Greek woman, instead of being offended by these blunt words, used them as a foil to advance her argument. Responding to the analogy of the children's bread and the dogs, she said, "Truth, Lord: yet the dogs eat of the crumbs which fall from their master's table." Impressed by the persistence and the spunky attitude of the Greek woman, "Jesus answered and said unto her, O woman, great *is* thy faith: be it unto thee even as thou wilt. And her daughter was made whole from that very hour." (Matthew 15:27-28)

This incident is reminiscent of the healing of the nobleman's son, where the cure was effected by the mere words of the Savior while the recipient of the blessing was not present. Yet it is far different, for here for the first recorded time Jesus exercised His supernal powers in behalf of a gentile.

Moreover, the incident foreshadowed the time when the Savior would significantly expand the scope of those whom the apostles were authorized to teach and baptize. No longer would they be authorized to teach only those of the House of Israel. "Go ye therefore, and teach all nations," He told them after His resurrection, "baptizing them in the name of the Father, and of the Son, and of the Holy Ghost" (Matthew 28:19). The first recorded instance of that expanded authority being exercised was when Peter baptized the Roman Centurion, Cornelius (see Acts 10). This opened the door to aggressive proselytizing among the gentile nations, the Apostle Paul being in the forefront of this historic initiative.

Finally, the miracle of the insistent Greek woman stands as a testament of the genuine love Jesus Christ has for all people everywhere, regardless of their race, color, or creed. The only condition He imposes upon those who seek His beneficence is that they approach Him with sincerity, persistence, and absolute faith in the manner exhibited by the Greek woman.

A Deaf Man Is Healed

The place on the border of Phoenicia where the Savior had sought to relax in privacy was not far from the Roman resort Caesarea Philippi. This was the most northern point in Palestine that Jesus visited during His earthly ministry. It was near the base of Mount Hermon and the headwaters of the Jordan River. Angling in a southeasterly direction, Jesus and His party skirted the Sea of Galilee, bypassing Bethsaida, Capernaum, and Gergasa, ending up in the Ten Cities or Decapolis district. This was essentially "heathen territory," although it was embraced within the land of Israel. Located in this area were ancient monuments and statuary reflecting an earlier extensive worship of various Grecian divinities including Zeus, Astarte, Athene, Artemus,

Hercules, Dionysos, and Demeter. Wrote Edersheim: "It is important to keep in view that, although Jesus was now within the territory of ancient Israel, the district and all the surroundings were essentially heathen" (Book 3, Chapter 34, p. 504).

As had occurred in other places Jesus visited, when it was learned that He was present, large crowds gathered, seeking to hear Him speak or to be healed by Him. Among those who came to Him at this time, or who was brought to Him, was "one that was deaf, and had an impediment in his speech; and they beseech him to put his hand upon him" (Mark 7:32). The Savior took this man "aside from the multitude" and followed a procedure unlike any other recorded in the four gospels. First He "put his fingers into his ears." Then He spit and applied the saliva to the man's tongue. Then, looking up to heaven, He sighed and said "Ephphatha," which interpreted means "Be opened." Immediately "his ears were opened, and the string of his tongue was loosed, and he spake plain." (Mark 7:33-35)

The Savior then charged them not to speak of the incident,

> but the more he charged them, so much the more a great deal they published *it*;
> And were beyond measure astonished, saying, He hath done all things well: he maketh both the deaf to hear, and the dumb to speak." (Mark 7:36-37)

Except for the healing of the blind man at Bethsaida (Mark 8:23), this is the only recorded instance when the Savior directly applied saliva in the process of a healing. No explanation is given for this, or for the placing of His fingers in the ears or for the command "be opened." It is apparent these procedures were not essential to effect a healing, given the instances when healings were effected upon persons who were not even present. It has been suggested that the moral or intellectual strength of a person might determine, in part, the means the Lord employed in effecting a healing. In this view, the various physical maneuvers Jesus used in healing the deaf man, who presumably was one steeped in heathen beliefs in multiple, fictitious gods, might provide insight into the true and living God by relating his healing to the actions of God's emissary. These physical actions of the Savior were of such an unusual kind as not to be easily forgotten, and therefore readily recalled and reflected upon many years after the event.

The Savior's request that the one healed preserve confidentiality of the event is one He often made. As always, the consequences were the same, as they were in this instance. The one healed promptly violated the request of confidentiality, and the news of the healing spread rapidly, increasing the Savior's celebrity and swelling the size of the crowds that followed Him. To suggest that the Savior did not know what would happen following His admonition of confidentiality is to question His intelligence and supernal powers. Assuming He knew what would happen, and we surely must, why then did He make the request? Any answer is a pure speculation. Two possibilities are apparent: It was a test for the one who was healed; or it was a means of greatly broadening the scope of those who would hear the message and witness the convincing power of God. Absent today's mass communication capabilities, radio, television, and the internet, the word of mouth process utilized by the Savior was an efficient tool in the performance of His ministry. And that process was enhanced by spreading the word of the healing of the deaf man and others.

One other question remains; that is, why did the Savior go directly to the Ten Cities area immediately after leaving the area near Caesarea Philippi? There is no clear answer based upon the known facts. But what is known is intriguing. First, the Savior knew the Decapolis area was a hot bed of heathen culture. Why go there, since His mission was to the lost sheep of the House of Israel? He had emphasized that when He first told the disciples He had no intention of heeding the urgent cries of the Greek woman from Phoenecia. So as He approached the Sea of Galilee from the north, why did He not go to the populous cities on the west bank or revisit the population centers near Capernaum and Bethsaida? In these areas He would have had a better opportunity to fulfill His mission than among the Grecian-heathen residue in the Decapolis. Instead, He made almost a beeline for the Ten Cities. And there He performed a healing using novel physical maneuvers that would have been attractive to the heathen mind. Since the Savior knew that within a very short while He would remove the restriction that then prevented the disciples from teaching and baptizing gentiles, could this foray into a heathen dominated society, lying within the borders of Israel, be regarded as a bridge experience upon which the apostles could build when their mandate became international? It is logical. Whether it was factual remained to be seen.

Four Thousand Are Fed

The Savior and His disciples remained in the Ten Cities area for three days. During that time He healed many of their diseases and infirmities in addition to the deaf man already referred to. The multitude that witnessed or participated in these miraculous events came from the ten cities of the Decapolis, or from more distant communities. After three days, the food supplies of the multitude were exhausted, and the Savior was concerned that those who lived a long distance from the site of the gathering would be in peril were they to leave for home without food. He raised the issue with the disciples, who responded, "whence can a man satisfy these *men* with bread here in the wilderness?" (Mark 8:4) While the question seems to imply that the questioner did not recall the feeding of the five thousand in the wilderness, an alternate interpretation is that the questioner remembered well enough, but considered it impertinent to suggest that the miracle be repeated here. Learning there were seven loaves of bread and several small fishes among the multitude, the Savior directed that they be seated, and, taking the loaves of bread and the fishes, He blessed them in turn and directed that they be served to the people. This being done, and after all were filled, the remnants were gathered into seven baskets. The persons served were four thousand men, plus women and children. As was true with the feeding of the five thousand, many were more impressed by the volume of food provided than by the miracle that produced it.

CHAPTER EIGHTEEN

Jesus Speaks Again of Signs

Following the feeding of the four thousand, the Savior embarked on a ship that carried Him to the west coast of the Sea of Galilee. Mark identified the place of debarkation as the "parts of Dalmanutha" (Mark 8:10), while Matthew alluded to it as "the coasts of Magdala" (Matthew 15:39). This was a densely populated area where the villages literally encroached upon each other. This was the area where Mary Magdalene was born, who later would play a significant role in the Savior's life.

Soon after debarking, "The Pharisees also with the Sadducees came, and tempting desired him that he would shew them a sign from heaven" (Matthew 16:1). Mark's narrative does not mention the presence of Sadducees, which illustrates again that occasional differences in the gospel narratives may result from differences in the data available to the narrators. In responding to the request for a sign, Jesus referred to the process of predicting the weather according to the color of the sky and said, "O *ye* hypocrites, ye can discern the face of the sky; but can ye not *discern* the signs of the times" (Matthew 16:3). The Savior then uttered a scathing rebuke of His questioners, in the process alluding to a sign of His coming resurrection: "A wicked and adulterous generation seeketh after a sign," said he, "and there shall no sign be given unto it, but the sign of the prophet Jonas" (Matthew 16:4). Here the Savior alluded to the three days Jonas spent in the belly of a whale, which, by implication, referred to the three days between the Savior's death and His resurrection. Mark makes no reference to the prophet Jonas.

After leaving the west coasts of Galilee and while on the way to the area near Capernaum, the Savior said to His disciples: "Take heed and beware of the leaven of the Pharisees and of the Sadducees" (Matthew 16:6). In discussing this comment among themselves, the disciples concluded that the Master had made oblique reference to the fact that there was only one loaf of bread aboard ship, they having failed to replenish their stores before embarking. When Jesus perceived their concern about having no bread aboard ship, He reproved them: "O ye of little faith, why reason ye among yourselves, because ye have brought no bread?" (Matthew 16:8) He then rehearsed for them the feeding of the five thousand at Bethsaida Julias, when there were only five loaves, and the feeding of the four thousand at Decapolis, when there were only seven loaves, and of the large remnants that were not consumed. This recital brought embarrassing recognition to the disciples of the Master's meaning: "Then understood they how that he bade *them* not beware of the leaven of bread, but of the doctrine of the Pharisees and of the Sadducees" (Matthew 16:12). This incident reflects the ongoing effort of the Savior to teach the disciples to live by faith against the time when He would no longer be with them to answer their questions and to show them the way.

A Blind Man Is Healed

At Bethsaida, a blind man was brought to the Savior with the request "to touch him." The Savior took the man by the hand and led him out of town. There He touched his eyes with saliva, "and put his hands upon him, and asked him if he saw ought." The man responded, saying he saw "men as trees, walking." The Savior then placed his hands upon the man's eyes again, "and made him look up: and he was restored, and saw every man clearly." Jesus then instructed the man to go to his own home and to refrain from telling anyone about the healing. (Mark 8: 22-26)

The miracle is notable because of the physical maneuvers the Savior employed in effecting it. Moreover, it was the first time a healing by the Savior was effected in stages; and it was one of the few instances among the many healings performed by the Savior when the recipient of a blessing was required to perform some physical act as part of the healing process.

CHAPTER NINETEEN

Peter Testifies of the Christ

The Savior's earthly ministry was characterized by a remarkable mobility. He was constantly on the move. There was so much to be done and so little time in which to do it. After His thwarted efforts for a little relaxation near the Palestine-Phoenicia border, He had gone south, bypassing the northern and western ports of the Sea of Galilee to reach Decapolis where the four thousand were fed; thence He went to the west coast of the Sea of Galilee; thence to Capernaum. After healing the blind man at Capernaum, Jesus was prompted to return to northern Palestine. This time, His destination was Caesarea Philippi, the modern Banias. This was the capital of Philip's tetrarchy and the site of the ancient Greek city, Paneas, named after the Greek God, Pan, the God of pastures, flocks, and shepherds. When Herod's son Philip received the tetrarchy, he enlarged and beautified the ancient Paneas and called it Caesarea Philippi in honor of the Roman Emperor. This description of Caesarea Philippi, provided by Edersheim, sets the stage for the historic events that occurred there:

> The situation of the ancient Caesarea Philippi (1,147 feet above the sea) is, indeed, magnificent. Nestling amid three valleys on a terrace in the angle of Hermon, it is almost shut out from view by cliffs and woods. 'Everywhere there is a wild medley of cascades, mulberry trees, fig trees,

dashing torrents, festoons of vines, bubbling fountains, reeds and ruins' (*Tristam*, Land of Israel, p. 586) (Edersheim, Book 3, Chapter 37, p. 524).

These impressive surroundings, with comfortable accommodations and the seclusion and privacy they afforded, provided a unique opportunity for Jesus and His friends to review the status of the work and to plan for the future. So the Savior and His disciples settled down in Caesarea Philippi for six days, during which they met intermittently to confer and to pray. During one of these sessions, the Savior asked His disciples, "Whom do men say that I the Son of man am?" (Matthew 16:13) In answering they said,

> Some *say that thou art* John the Baptist: some, Elias; and others, Jeremias, or one of the prophets.
> He saith unto them, But whom say ye that I am?
> And Simon Peter answered and said, Thou art the Christ, the Son of the living God. (Matthew 16:14-16)

Mark and Luke, the other two narrators who recorded Peter's response, used the words, "Thou art the Christ"(Mark 8:29) and "The Christ of God" (Luke 9:20).

Before this incident, Peter had known the Savior was a great and powerful man, capable of performing extraordinary acts of healing and who taught with unusual power and perception. But there had been other gifted men who had exhibited unusual spiritual powers similar to those shown by Jesus. How then could Peter know with certainty that this man was indeed the promised Messiah?

The Savior provided an answer to this query: Said He,

Blessed art thou, Simon Bar-jona: for flesh and blood hath not revealed *it* unto thee, but my Father which is in heaven.

And I say also unto thee that thou art Peter, and upon this rock I will build my church; and the gates of hell shall not prevail against it.

And I will give unto thee the keys of the kingdom of heaven: and whatsoever thou shalt bind on earth shall be bound in heaven: and whatsoever thou shalt loose on earth shall be loosed in heaven. (Matthew 16:17-19)

Therefore, the only sure way one may know that Jesus is the Christ is by a revelation from God.

The Apostle Paul aptly described the church, here referred to, built or created by the Savior: "And he gave some, apostles; and some, prophets; and some, evangelists; and some, pastors and teachers." Paul then explained the purpose for which the church was created: "For the perfecting of the saints, for the work of the ministry, for the edifying of the body of Christ." He then declared how long this church would endure: "Till we all come in the unity of the faith, and of the knowledge of the son of God, unto a perfect man. (Ephesians 4:11-13)

The sure foundation upon which this church would be and was built was and is the revelation from the Almighty that Jesus Christ was and is the Promised One, the Holy Messiah upon whom the multitudes of the earth can rely with certainty and without fear or doubt. Moreover, the affairs of Christ's earthly church were to be administered by divinely called prophets, seers, and revelators who, successively, would hold "the keys of the kingdom of heaven," the apostle Peter being the first to occupy this supernal office.

Christ Teaches of His Death and Resurrection

During another session with His disciples at Caesarea Philippi, the Savior began to teach them about the momentous events which He would soon face in Jerusalem. "From that time forth began Jesus to show unto His disciples, how that he must go unto Jerusalem, and suffer many things of the elders and chief priests and scribes, and be killed, and be raised again the third day" (Matthew 16:21). Although the Savior had hinted of these dire events in the past, never before had they been expressed with such shocking particularity. Because the picture He painted of what was to transpire was so at variance with their own perceptions, the apostles were in a state of confused denial. Peter was the first to respond. Reflecting his customary bold and forthright manner, he began to "rebuke" the Savior, saying, "Be it far from thee, Lord: this shall not be unto thee" (Matthew 16:22). The response of the Savior to this outburst was prompt and withering: "he turned, and said unto Peter, Get thee behind me, Satan: thou art an offence unto me: for thou savourest not the things that be of God, but those that be of men" (Matthew 16:23). The gravity of this rebuke seems even more significant, given the fact that these words were identical with those used by the Savior in denouncing Satan himself following the forty day fast. The Savior has provided His restored Church with the criteria by which errant members may be censured for improper conduct: "Reproving betimes with sharpness, when moved upon by the Holy Ghost; and then showing forth afterward an increase of love toward him whom thou hast reproved, lest he esteem thee to be his enemy" (D&C 121:43).

The Savior provided this test of discipleship for His followers: "If any *man* will come after me, let him deny himself, and take up his cross, and follow me" (Matthew 16:24). The denial of self, which the discipleship of Christ requires, becomes a mandate of service to others, according to His word and Godly example. The analogy of taking up one's cross implies a willing assumption of the duties discipleship of Christ requires, as well as duties inherent in one's personal experience.

Contrasting the blessings that inure to the faithful disciple with the status of an unbeliever, the Savior uttered this oft-quoted truism:

> Whosoever will save his life shall lose it: and whosoever will lose his life for my sake shall find it.
> For what is a man profited, if he shall gain the whole world, and lose his own soul? Or what shall a man give in exchange for his soul? (Matthew 16:25-26)

Finally, the Savior observed that when He returns with His angels in the glory of His father, every man will be rewarded "according to his works." Jesus concluded, saying there were some standing there who would not die "till they see the Son of man coming in his kingdom." (Matthew 16:27-28)

CHAPTER TWENTY

The Mount of Transfiguration

A week following the significant events at Caesarea Philippi when the disciples learned of the dire events which would transpire at Jerusalem, Jesus took Peter, James, and John and repaired to a high mountain to pray in privacy. The holy record is silent as to the matters that occupied them during the previous week. We can assume with confidence the time was not devoted to the frivolous activities that drew many people to this well-known resort, but was spent in earnest discussions and prayer about the work. Neither is the mountain identified by name in the scriptures. Because of its close proximity to Caesarea Philippi, it is assumed the mountain was part of the mountain range of which Mount Hermon is the most prominent.

It was not an easy climb, so when the four reached the summit, Peter, James, and John sat down to rest and recuperate. While in a state of pleasant drowsiness, they were suddenly jarred fully awake by a sight so spectacular and awesome as to defy description. Alluding to the Savior, it was reported, "the fashion of his countenance was altered, and his raiment *was* white *and* glistening" (Luke 9:29). Mark described the scene in more graphic terms, saying, "he was transfigured before [us] and his raiment became shining, exceeding white as snow; so as no fuller on earth can white them" (Mark 9:2-3). Matthew added this to the scene, which drew their attention in a focused manner: "his face did shine as the sun, and his raiment was white as the light" (Matthew

17:2). The impact of this brilliant, unearthly scene was increased profoundly when there suddenly appeared with the Savior two heavenly beings identified as Moses and Elias. It is noted that the term Elias appears in the New Testament as the Greek transliteration of the Hebrew name Elijah. It was reported that these heavenly beings "appeared in glory, and spake of his decease which he should accomplish at Jerusalem" (Luke 9:31). It is easy to imagine the stressful impact of this conversation upon Peter, reminding him of his inappropriate rebuke of the Savior when He broached this subject at Caesarea Philippi.

The three apostles were astonished at what they had just witnessed. Seeing the glory that enveloped the Savior and the two heavenly visitors placed them in a wholly unstructured situation. This was something new and unexpected. They were frightened and felt ill at ease and unsure of themselves. Yet the circumstances seemed to demand some response from them, some recognition of the novelty and significance of the event. It was then Peter said: "Master, it is good for us to be here: And let us make three tabernacles; one for thee, and one for Moses, and one for Elias: not knowing what he said." Even as Peter spoke, "there came a cloud, and overshadowed them: and they feared as they entered into the cloud." Then a voice spoke from the cloud saying, "This is my beloved Son: hear him." (Luke 9:33-35)

In his version of the incident, Matthew quoted the voice as saying: "This is my beloved Son, in whom I am well pleased; hear ye him" (Matthew 17:5), while in his account of the incident, Mark said the Savior "charged them that they should tell no man what things they had seen, till the Son of man were risen from the dead" (Mark 9:9). The words about rising from the dead were strange and unfamiliar to the apostles, since they had little comprehension about the resurrection. Indeed, their understanding about it was not complete until after the Savior was resurrected and appeared to them saying, "handle me, and see; for a spirit hath not flesh and bones, as ye see me have" (Luke 24:39).

The three apostles understood the scriptures to mean that Elijah would appear before the great and dreadful day of the Lord. Since they had seen the Lord transfigured before them, they were puzzled. And so as they descended from the mount with the Savior, they asked Him, "Why then say the scribes that Elias [or Elijah] must first come?" Jesus answered saying, "Elias [or Elijah] truly shall first come and restore all things. But I say unto you, That Elias is come already, and they knew him not." Later the apostles "understood that he spake unto them of John the Baptist." (Matthew 17:10-13)

From this it is apparent that the word Elias is used both as a name and an office. Thus John the Baptist acted in "the spirit and power of Elias" in his role as the forerunner of the Savior. This role was predicted for him when Gabriel visited Zacharias before John was born (see Luke 1:17).

The appearance of Moses and Elias on the Mount of Transfiguration is fraught with historical significance. The law given by Moses had been practiced by the Israelites over the centuries. The Savior had proclaimed that He came to fulfill the law, not to destroy it. In the process of fulfillment, the Savior's message of love, faith, repentance, and redemption would become the main focus of priestly teaching instead of the enforcement of the numerous laws of diet and hygiene with which the Law of Moses had become encumbered. Meanwhile, the laws of personal relationships enumerated in the Ten Commandments would remain as the standard of personal and public morality.

The transition from the Law of Moses to the law of Christ was monumental in its impact. The conversation Jesus had with Moses on the Mount of Transfiguration could be regarded as the tipping point that marked the historic transition from the Mosaic Law to the law of Jesus Christ. In the discussion on the Mount about the awesome events Jesus would soon face in Jerusalem, it is unknown whether the historic transition here referenced came into the conversation. Given its significance, it would not be surprising if it did.

Anciently Elijah was known for his extraordinary spiritual powers, as when during the reign of King Ahab, he sealed the heavens so there was no rain for three and a half years (1 Kings 17:1). This resulted in a disastrous drought. As all Israel suffered because of the drought, they began to repent and to call upon the Lord for relief, following which Elijah unsealed the heavens and the blessed rain came again. This sealing and unsealing of the physical heavens was a precursor of the sealing powers Elijah would exercise later in the spiritual realm. This other, and infinitely more significant power was foreshadowed on September 21, 1823, as Joseph Smith prayed to the Lord for guidance. It was then Joseph Smith was told through the Angel Moroni who appeared to him, that the priesthood would be revealed to him,

> by the hand of Elijah the prophet, before the coming of the great and dreadful day of the Lord.
> And he will plant in the hearts of the children the promises made to the fathers, and the hearts of the children shall turn to their fathers.
> If it were not so, the whole earth would be utterly wasted at his coming. (D&C 2:1-3)

This promise of Moroni to Joseph Smith was fulfilled on April 3, 1836, when Elijah appeared to him and Oliver Cowdery in the Kirtland Temple. At that time there was conferred upon them the keys "To turn the hearts of the fathers to the children, and the children to the fathers" (D&C 110:15). With this conferral was the inherent power to seal forever the familial relationships between living persons and between the living and the dead.

It is historically significant that both Moses and Elijah, who appeared on the Mount of Transfiguration, were translated beings who never tasted of mortal death. Some unexplained change was wrought upon them, by which they retained their physical identity, but were received into heaven in that state. This made it possible for them to appear on the Mount of Transfiguration and, presumably, to confer upon Peter, James, and John the keys and authority they possessed. Without this change in their physical status, they could not have conferred the keys of priesthood authority they possessed by the laying on of hands (see D&C 129; *Encyclopedia of Mormonism*, Vol. 2, p. 450).

Descent Into the Maelstrom

As Jesus left the Mount of Transfiguration and headed south, there lay ahead the dire, culminating events of His earthly ministry. These had been subjects of serious discussion, both at Caesarea Philippi and on the Mount. He knew exactly what was to happen to Him. He knew about the stressful confrontations with the Jewish leaders, the trial before the Roman officials, the betrayal of Judas Iscariot, and about His arrest and imprisonment. He knew about the agonies of Gethsemane and Golgotha and about that crucial moment at the end when He would be left alone, bereft, for the moment, of the comforting, sustaining influence of His Father. Logic suggests the idea that the physical part of His being, the inheritance from His mother Mary, may have invested these thoughts with a sense of foreboding, perhaps even of fear. Could He hold up under the crushing burden and agony entailed in His death? Since the option was His, why not rescind His commitment, give up and avoid all the pain and suffering? Speculations such as this are intriguing to the human mind. However, they ignore the divine and controlling part of His being. This divine part imbued Him with the sure knowledge that He could do this and that it was within His power to lay down His life willingly to serve the ends of justice and mercy for all mankind. Can there be any doubt that these portentous thoughts came to the Savior's mind intermittently as the time of His final hours in mortality drew near?

CHAPTER TWENTY-ONE

Ministering Along the Way

A Demoniac Is Healed

When Jesus descended from the Mount with the three apostles the day following the transfiguration, He found a "great multitude," among which were many disciples, followers, and certain scribes. "And straightway all the people, when they beheld him, were greatly amazed, and running to *him* saluted him." It soon became apparent that there had been a lively contention among the multitude, and, suspecting the source of it, "he asked the scribes, What question ye with them?" (Mark 9:14-16)

Before the scribes could answer, a voice spoke from the crowd saying,

> Master, I have brought unto thee my son, which hath a dumb spirit; and wheresoever he taketh him, he teareth him: and he foameth, and gnasheth with his teeth, and pineth away: and I spoke to thy disciples that they should cast him out; and they could not. (Mark 9:17-18)

Learning this, Jesus manifested a combined sense of impatience and annoyance, saying to His disciples, "O faithless generation, how long shall I be with you? how long shall I suffer you? bring him unto me." When the son was brought into the presence of the Savior, the evil spirit in the boy tore him, and "he fell on the ground, and wallowed foaming." Seeing this pitiful display, Jesus asked how long the boy had been so afflicted and was told, "Of a child." Then the father elaborated on his son's malady, saying: "And ofttimes it hath cast him into the fire, and into the waters, to destroy him." Then speaking with a voice of doubtful urgency, the father added, "but if thou canst do anything, have compassion on us, and help us." Because of the father's dubious response, the Savior then challenged him saying, "If thou canst believe, all things *are* possible to him that believeth." With this ray of hope shining through the dark cloud of misery which had overshadowed both him and his son, the father in tears cried out in faith, yet with a plea for stronger faith saying, "Lord, I believe; help thou mine unbelief." Jesus then rebuked the foul spirit, ordering him to come out of the boy, "and enter no more into him, And *the spirit* cried, and rent him sore, and came out of him: and he was as one dead. . . . But Jesus took him by the hand, and lifted him up; and he arose." (Mark 9:19-27)

When the Savior was alone with the disciples following the miracle, they asked him, "Why could not we cast him out?" His answer, "This kind can come forth by nothing, but by prayer and fasting," seems to soften the criticism He offered when first arriving on the scene. What He learned later about the background of the victim made it plain this was an unusual case, quite unlike anything He had encountered before. (Mark 9:28-29)

Several factors illustrate why this healing stands out above the others. Here the Savior questioned the father about the son's condition, and this led to a further elaboration by the father. Here, unlike other cases of healing, the Master not only ordered the evil spirit to depart, but never to return. Finally, by way of illustrating the especially vindictive and virulent nature of this evil spirit, it attacked the son even after it had been ordered to leave, as if to add an exclamation point to the end of his tenure of the boy's body.

The Miracle of the Tribute Money

Following the healing of the demoniac, the Master and His disciples returned to Galilee. The purpose here was not to undertake another teaching effort but it merely was a stop on the way to the winding up scenes in Jerusalem. It is apparent from the holy record that these dreadful events, which were discussed at both Caesarea Philippi and on the Mount, were very much on the Savior's mind.

> And while they abode in Galilee, Jesus said unto them, The Son of man shall be betrayed into the hands of men:
> And they shall kill him, and the third day He shall be raised again. And they were exceeding sorry. (Matthew 17:22-23)

This sense of sorrow and foreboding lay like a dead weight upon the spirits of the disciples. But they were reluctant to seek consolation by discussing it among themselves or by obtaining clarification or further information from the Master.

Later at Capernaum an unusual event occurred when the official charged with collecting the tribute money came to Peter and asked, "Doth not your master pay tribute?" (Matthew 17:24)

Based upon the mandate found in Exodus 30:13, every male in Israel twenty years of age and older was expected annually to contribute to the Temple Treasury one-half shekel or two-attic drachma. Since Matthew was a tax collector before his call to the Twelve, it is interesting that he was the only one of the four gospel narrators to include this story in his manuscript. It is interesting too that this official came to Peter instead of going directly to the Savior. Doing so implied recognition that Peter bore a special relationship to Jesus unlike that of any other disciple. It also implied sensitivity toward approaching Jesus personally about the tribute money, since priests and rabbis generally claimed immunity from paying the tribute

In responding to the collector as to whether his master paid tribute money, Peter answered, "Yes." Apparently Jesus overheard this conversation, so when Peter entered the house, the Savior accosted him saying: "What thinkest thou, Simon? of whom do the kings of the earth take custom or tribute? of their own children, or of strangers?" Answering the Lord, Peter said, "Of strangers," to which the Savior responded, "Then are the children free."(Matthew 17:25-26)

Here Jesus spoke by analogy, likening himself to the kings of the earth. But, of course, He was much more than an earthly king. He was the Messiah, the Son of God, the creator of the heavens and the earth. Peter, speaking in behalf of the Twelve, had acknowledged this at Caesarea Philippi, saying, "Thou art the Christ the Son of the living God." By acknowledging this, Peter knew that the temple and all its accouterments, ordinances, and workers, including the collector of the tribute, were subordinate to Jesus Christ, the Messiah. The artful analogy the Savior used would have brought all these things to the understanding of Peter, along with, it is assumed, a sense of regret and embarrassment for his presumption in speaking for the Savior without authority.

In this state of things, there remained the issue of what to do about the collector of tribute who had been told by Peter that his master paid tribute. Because of His preeminent status, Jesus could have ignored the matter or could have asserted His sovereignty, either of which would have embroiled Him in needless controversy, thereby diverting Him from His course. The Savior solved the dilemma in this diplomatic manner, saying to Peter:

> Notwithstanding, lest we should offend them, go thou to the sea, and cast an hook, and take up the fish that

first cometh up; and when thou hast opened his mouth, thou shalt find a piece of money: that take and give unto them for me and thee. (Matthew 17:27)

The complexity of this miracle is astonishing. Consider the odds of Peter catching a fish on his first try which has a coin in its gullet. Consider also the odds that this coin is of sufficient value to pay the tribute money for both the Master and Peter. And consider the odds that the fish with the coin in its gullet swims by at the very moment Peter casts his line. This is not to mention the happenstance that such a coin was cast into the water in some unexplained way and that this particular fish grabbed and swallowed it. To the human mind, the imponderables involved in this series of isolated events, which culminated in Peter finding the coin as predicted by the Savior, is far beyond human comprehension. But to the mind possessed of godly powers and perceptions such as those with which Jesus was endowed, piercing through this maze of imponderables was elementary to Him. After all, He created the earth and the amazing panoply of living and inanimate beings and objects within it. He knew everything about these in the minutest detail. Thus the solution to the dilemma of the collector of the tribute was a matter of routine to Him.

Because of the dual nature of His being, Jesus was different from all other men. It was a difference that could not be bridged. He was careful to preserve that difference in the minds of His associates out of respect for the Almighty and to the sacred role He would play as the Savior and Redeemer of mankind. He occasionally emphasized that difference by word, as when He told Peter to give the coin He would find in the gullet of the fish to the collector of the tribute "for me and thee" (Matthew 17:27), deliberately declining to use the plural "for us." This made it patently clear that while Jesus loved and cherished His disciples, there was a gulf that separated them which could never be bridged. This reality was expressed on other occasions, as when He referred to "my Father, and your Father" and "my God, and your God" instead of our Father and our God (John 20:17).

The miracle of the tribute money could be viewed as another episode in the process of training Peter for his ultimate role as the earthly head of the Church and as Christ's mouthpiece on earth. In those roles, Peter would act as an agent, not as a principal. It would be incumbent upon him to make certain his words and actions, uttered and performed in these roles, represented the mind and will of the Lord, consistent with the teachings of His earthly ministry, and according to the manifestations of the Holy Ghost. Acting in those sacred roles, Peter could not freelance and express his own views and desires as he had done in responding to the collector of the tribute. Because of his innate impulsiveness and self-confidence, reflected, for instance, in his rebuke of the Savior at Caesarea Philippi, Peter had to learn to be disciplined and absolutely submissive to the mind and will of the Lord. In this pursuit, the example of the Savior's relationship to His Heavenly Father was compelling. From the time of His selection in the preexistence to be the Savior of all mankind, the hallmark of the Master's relationship with the Father had been that of total and undeviating obedience to the mind and will of the Father. Often during His earthly life and ministry, Jesus had affirmed that His sole purpose upon the earth was to execute the mind and will of the Father. The great challenge and opportunity for Peter was to endeavor to replicate in his association with the Savior the kind of relationship that existed between the Father and the Son. It was a daunting task, fraught with difficulties and challenges, as when, for instance, Peter later denied he knew the Savior on three occasions. The humiliation and agony he later suffered and the genuine repentance which followed were elements of the transformation Peter underwent in his efforts to become qualified to be the head of Christ's earthly Church and His mouthpiece on earth. Peter's experience in connection with the miracle of the tribute money can be logically viewed as another element in that process.

A Sermon on Meekness and Humility

As the Savior and His disciples walked toward Capernaum, He heard them disputing along the way. Arriving at their destination, He said to them: "What was it that ye disputed among yourselves by the way?" (Mark 9:33) They were embarrassed to answer because they had been arguing as to whom would be the greatest in Christ's kingdom. It is obvious that at this stage, the disciples had a confused idea as to the nature and purpose of this kingdom once it became operable. Their apparent idea was that Christ's kingdom would be similar to the political-military organization created by King David. Thus in their view there would be officers of different rank in the army, the diplomatic corps, and the administrative sector. They could envision themselves occupying various offices of distinction within this imagined structure, and it was about this they had been arguing with each other. Seeking to bring understanding to His misguided disciples, Jesus sat down "and called the twelve, and saith unto them, If any man desires to be first, *the same* shall be last of all, and servant of all" (Mark 9:35). Then to add significant meaning to His words, Jesus took a child in His arms and said:

> Verily I say unto you, Except ye be converted, and become as little children, ye shall not enter into the kingdom of heaven.

> Whosoever therefore shall humble himself as this little child, the same is greatest in the kingdom of heaven.
>
> And whoso shall receive one such little child in my name receiveth me. (Matthew 18:3-5)

The disciples could not have failed to see the vast difference between their proud, self-important concept of greatness and the Savior's concept of greatness as reflected in this humble, dependent, and submissive child. In the kingdom of God, therefore, the subjects of the King must reflect this kind of character and attitude toward Him, else they are not fit subjects of the kingdom.

In the sense it is used here, the term "little child" does not imply that the subjects of the kingdom of God are to be childish and irresponsible. It means rather that they must embody in their conduct and character the qualities of dependence, submissiveness, and teachableness seen in the little child. The Apostle Paul captured this distinction in his first epistle to the Corinthian saints. Wrote he: "When I was a child, I spake as a child, I understood as a child, I thought as a child: but when I became a man, I put away childish things" (1 Corinthians 13:11).

As He occasionally did, the Savior then pivoted in His discourse and discontinued speaking of the conduct and character of the little child in His arms as a model for those who hoped to dwell in His kingdom and referred to him instead as a victim. Said He, "But whoso shall offend one of these little ones which believe in me, it were better for him that a millstone were hanged about his neck, and *that* he was drowned in the depth of the sea" (Matthew 18:6). The Savior then elaborated about the offenses that had victimized the little child: "Woe unto the world because of offences! For it must needs be that offences come; but woe to that man by whom the offence cometh" (Matthew 18:7). Then followed counsel for the offender in this marvelously layered discourse:

> Wherefore if thy hand or thy foot offend thee, cut them off, and *cast* them from thee: it is better for thee to enter into life halt or maimed, rather than having two hands or two feet to be cast into everlasting fire.
>
> And if thine eye offend thee, pluck it out, and cast *it* from thee: it is better for thee to enter into life with one eye, rather than having two eyes to be cast into hell fire. (Matthew 18:8-9)

The message to the offender is clear: whatever the cost, whether loss of treasure, reputation, or social standing, cast off or repent of offenses committed, thereby avoiding the direful penalties which await the unrepentant offender.

Here the Savior pivoted once more, referring again to the little child He held in His arms: "Take heed that ye despise not one of these little ones; for I say unto you, That in heaven their angels do always behold the face of my Father which is in heaven" (Matthew 18:10). The use of the word "their" raises again the interesting question whether specific angels are assigned to guard and protect specific individuals on earth.

After this, the Savior pivoted still again to say that while He had been sent to save all that were lost, yet He rejoiced especially over the recovery of the one who had strayed from the ninety and nine. He concluded this remarkable discourse with this: "Even so it is not the will of your Father which is in heaven, that one of these little ones should perish" (Matthew 18:14).

Discourse on Resolving Disputes: Forgiveness

While the disciples were yet together following the multi-layered sermon on humility and meekness, the Savior broached the subject of resolving disputes between brethren. One wonders whether this was prompted by the disputation between the brethren as to who would be the greatest in the kingdom. He began the discussion saying, "Moreover if thy brother shall trespass against thee, go and tell him his fault between thee and him alone: if he shall hear thee, thou hast gained thy brother" (Matthew 18:15). This method of settling disputes and clearing the air is simple and effective as between those of good will and intention. If followed routinely, it would be the means of eliminating much of the stress and animosity that afflict mankind. However, the complexities of human nature and of personal issues involved in a given situation may result in a stalemate. In that event, "one or two more" (Matthew 18:16) should be brought into the discussion for further deliberation and, hopefully, for a resolution. Any matter in dispute should be brought before the church only if an accord cannot be reached by this private process. The Lord endorsed the efficacy and the importance of this process in these words:

> if two of you shall agree on earth as touching anything that they shall ask, it will be done for them of my Father which is in heaven.
>
> For when two or three are gathered together in my name, there am I in the midst of them." (Matthew 18:19-20)

However, the Lord made it plain that if a dispute could not be settled either by personal consultation or by church decree, "if he neglect to hear the church, let him be unto thee as an heathen man and a publican" (Matthew 18:17).

During the discussion of these matters, the Lord uttered a statement of profound importance as to the scope and the efficacy of apostolic authority. Said He, "Verily I say unto you, whatsoever ye shall bind on earth shall be bound in heaven: and whatsoever ye shall loose on earth shall be loosed in heaven" (Matthew 18:18). Never before had the Savior undertaken to define with such precision the scope of apostolic authority. Here was power and influence that extended beyond the earth into heaven. This would have been a stark awakening for the brethren, who, a few hours before, had been arguing about who would be the greatest in what they conceived to be a military-political kingdom similar to that of King David. It would take time for them to adjust their thinking to this new reality.

The conversation about disputes and their resolution prompted Peter to ask, "Lord, how oft shall my brother sin against me, and I forgive him? till seven times? (Matthew 18:21) The answer may have startled Peter, for the Savior said: "I say not unto thee, Until seven times: but, Until seventy times seven." (Matthew 18:22) In this circumstance, it is doubtful Peter would have thought the principle of forgiveness would be rendered meaningless after seventy times seven. This being so, it is likely the Savior's answer brought home to him that forgiveness is an eternal principle, applicable at all times and in all places for those who hope to dwell forever in the presence of the Almighty.

Parable of the Unforgiving Servant

This is a fictitious story about the forgiveness or waiver of monetary indebtedness. Thus it is unlike the forgiveness for personal infractions or misbehavior previously referred to by Peter. This also is a fictitious story about the greed and arrogance of an influential man whose sovereign forgave him of a huge debt and who then, in a selfish fashion, failed to forgive the paltry debt owed him by another.

The influential status of the first man is inferred from the size of his debt, estimated by Edersheim to have been "two and a quarter millions sterling" (Book 4, Chapter 19, p. 679). On the other hand, the amount owed this influential man was in the range of thirty to fifty dollars.

The scene opens with the king holding court, assessing the amounts owed him by his principal subjects. "And when he had begun to reckon, one was brought unto him, which owed him ten thousand talents." When this influential man was unable to pay, the sovereign, whose kingdom apparently was founded upon slavery, "commanded him to be sold, and his wife, and children, and all that he had, and payment to be made." At this the servant fell down and worshiped at his master's feet, saying, "Lord, have patience with me, and I will pay thee all." Moved with compassion by this emotional plea, the Lord "loosed him, and forgave him the debt." Notwithstanding the liberality of his lord, who went beyond the servant's request for patience and forgave the debt, this servant soon accosted a fellow servant, who owed him an hundred pence, and "laid hands on him, and took *him* by the throat, saying, Pay me that thou owest." The fellow servant pleaded for patience, using the identical language the servant had used in pleading with the lord. Callously ignoring this heartfelt plea, the servant "cast him into prison, till he should pay the debt." Other servants, witnessing this travesty, reported it to the lord, who summoned the offending servant, saying to him: "O thou wicked servant, I forgave thee all that debt, because thou desiredst me: Shouldest not thou also have had compassion on thy fellow servant, even as I had pity on thee?" Being angry with the wicked servant, the lord "delivered him to the tormentors, till he should pay that was due unto him." Then addressing His disciples, and likening their situation to the wicked servant who had incurred monetary debt, Jesus said: "So likewise shall my heavenly Father do also unto you, if ye from your hearts forgive not every one his brother their trespasses." (Matthew 18:24-35)

Being acquainted with the Savior's adroit way of impliedly teaching eternal principles through parables, Peter and his brethren could have inferred from this parable an affirmation of the principle that much is expected of him who receives much. Moreover, the indebtedness of the wicked servant to his lord could have reminded them of the indebtedness mortals owe to God for violation of His commandments, an indebtedness mortals cannot satisfy without divine assistance. The apostles would learn more about this process as their understanding of the atonement became more complete.

The Demands of Dedicated Service

As Jesus "steadfastly set his face to go to Jerusalem," He paused near a village in Samaria. Proposing to spend the night there, He sent messengers ahead to make the arrangements. When word came that the Samaritans would not receive the party, James and John were annoyed to the point of anger saying, "Lord, wilt thou that we command fire to come down from heaven, and consume them, even as Elias did?" This brought an instant rebuke from the Savior who said to them, "Ye know not what manner of spirit ye are of. For the Son of man is not come to destroy men's lives, but to save *them*. And they went to another village." (Luke 9:51-56)

Along the way, Jesus encountered three men whose circumstances suggest some of the demands of dedicated service. The first one said to Him, "Lord, I will follow thee whithersoever thou goest." Responding to the man, while providing insight into the nature of the service He had volunteered, Jesus said: "Foxes have holes, and birds of the air *have* nests; but the Son of man hath not where to lay *his* head." The second man was invited by the Savior to join Him, saying "Follow me." The man balked at the invitation responding, "Lord, suffer me first to go and bury my father," to which Jesus answered: "Let the dead bury their dead: but go thou and preach the kingdom of God." The third man, who also seems to have been invited to join Him, said, "Lord, I will follow thee; but let me first go bid them farewell, which are at home at my house." The Savior's answer was not only a summation of His response in all these episodes, but also provided a criterion for all who might wish or aspire to be dedicated disciples of Jesus Christ: "No man, having put his hand to the plough, and looking back, is fit for the kingdom of God." (Luke 9:57-62)

The Seventy Are Called and Sent Forth

After the Savior first undertook His ministry and had been preaching in the villages and synagogues of Palestine, He was moved with compassion toward the large multitude that followed Him, who "fainted, and were scattered abroad, as sheep having no shepherd." Observing this pitiful condition, He had said to His disciples: "The harvest truly *is* plenteous, but the labourers *are* few; Pray ye therefore the Lord of the harvest, that he will send forth labourers into his harvest." (Matthew (9:36-38)

Soon after this urgent plea for assistance in teaching and nurturing the multitude, Jesus called and instructed the Twelve and sent them forth (see Matthew 10:1).

Soon after the incidents that illustrated the elements of dedicated service, the Savior felt the need to call other workers, in addition to the Twelve, to labor in the vineyard. Using language almost identical to that which preceded the call of the Twelve, He said, "The harvest truly *is* great, but the labourers *are* few: pray ye therefore the Lord of the harvest, that he would send forth labourers into his harvest." (Luke 10:2) It was then "the Lord appointed other seventy also, and sent them two and two before his face into every city and place, whither he himself would come." (Luke 10:1)

It is significant that the Savior did not send forth the Twelve again, but elected to keep them close by Him. It is inferred that the reasons for this were for sociality and for protection. At that time, He was moving into Judea, having passed through Samaria, and was then in a dangerous place since the scribes and the Pharisees had made it plain they intended to kill Him. Therefore, the presence of twelve young, powerful men about Him would have provided some protection against Him being killed before His mission had been completed. Another assumed reason for keeping the Twelve near at hand was to give them further instruction that would help prepare them to shoulder the responsibilities of the kingdom once the Savior had departed. Two recent incidents, Peter's rebuke of the Savior at Caesarea Philippi and James and John's inquiry whether fire should be called down on the Samaritan innkeeper, suggest the apostles yet had much to learn about the Savior and His kingdom.

The process by which the Seventy were chosen is not explained in the scriptures. The assumption is that the calls were made on the basis of personal acquaintance between the Savior and the Seventy, or on the recommendations of members of the Twelve, or upon revelation given to Jesus at the time of the calls.

As the Savior sent the Seventy on their way, He said: "Go your ways: behold, I send you forth as lambs among wolves. Carry neither purse, nor scrip, nor shoes: and salute no man by the way" (Luke 10:3-4). Once having reached the area of their assignment, they were to select a house that would be their headquarters, sharing without complaint the food of the householders. They were not to go "from house to house" (Luke 10:7). Once having become established in a permanent place, they were to "heal the sick that are therein, and say unto them, The kingdom of God is come nigh unto you" (Luke 10:9). The record is silent as to what the Seventy were to teach the people about the kingdom of God. Since Christ's earthly kingdom was in a formative stage at the time, it is assumed that they taught about the calls of the Twelve and the Seventy and about the things Jesus had proclaimed in the synagogues, the streets, and the countryside of Palestine.

Jesus told the Seventy that if they were rejected by a city to move on to another. He then prescribed a procedure they were to follow on exiting such a city as a sign of rebuke and condemnation:

> go your ways out into the streets of the same, and say,
>
> Even the very dust of your city, which cleaveth on us, we do wipe off against you: notwithstanding be ye sure of this, that the kingdom of God has come nigh unto you:
>
> But I say unto you, that it shall be more tolerable in that day for Sodom, than for that city. (Luke 10:10-12)

The Savior singled out several cities for special condemnation: "Woe unto thee, Chorazin! woe unto thee, Bethsaida! for if the mighty works had been done in Tyre and Sidon, which have been done in you, they had a great while ago repented, sitting in sackcloth and ashes" (Luke 10:12-13). The Savior declared it would be "more tolerable" in the final judgment for the evil cities of Tyre and Sidon than for the cities that rejected the Seventy. He had a final word of condemnation for Capernaum, the city "exalted to heaven," which he said would be "thrust down to hell." Finally, the Savior emphasized the status and the authority of the Seventy by saying that whosoever received them, received Him. He added that whosoever despised the Seventy despised Him too, but more significantly despised "him that sent me." (Luke 10:14-16)

The Seventy Return and Report

The joy and the excitement of the Seventy upon their return is evident from this: "And the seventy returned again with joy, saying, Lord, even the devils are subject unto us through your name" (Luke 10:17). The reference to devils evoked from Jesus a comment about an incident in the preexistence, which lay at the root of the presence of devils upon the earth. Said he, "I beheld Satan as lightning fall from heaven." This reminiscence, in turn, prompted the Savior to confer upon the seventy power over "the enemy," which would have included power over Satan himself and over Satan's followers. These are the Savior's words which accompanied this investiture of power: "Behold, I give unto you power to tread on serpents and scorpions, and over all the power of the enemy: and nothing by any means hurt you." The Savior cautioned the seventy not to rejoice in this significant investiture of power but rather to rejoice, "because your names are written in heaven." (Luke 10:18-20)

The supernal joy experienced by the Seventy on this occasion was replicated in the supreme happiness the Savior felt. "I thank thee, O Father, Lord of heaven and earth," he said, "that thou hast hid these things from the wise and prudent, and hast revealed them unto babes" (Luke 10:21). The use of the word "babes" to describe the seventy obviously was not intended as a pejorative, but as a means of distinguishing them, in a positive way, from the proud, self-righteous priestly class whose vaunted learning had served only to turn them away from the truth. Continuing with His prayer of gratitude, the Savior uttered a profound statement explaining the means by which knowledge of the Father is obtained: "No man knoweth who the Son is, but the Father, and who the Father is, but the Son, and *he* to whom the Son will reveal him" (Luke 10:22). Then turning to the disciples, the Savior said to them privately:

> Blessed *are* the eyes which see the things that ye see;
> For I tell you, that many prophets and kings have desired to see those things which ye see, and have not seen

them; and to hear these things which ye hear, and have not heard *them.* (Luke 10:23-24)

CHAPTER TWENTY-TWO

Jesus Ministers Again in Judea

Feast of Tabernacles

Jewish life was marked by a long procession of feast days, some of which commemorated special events in Jewish history, as, for instance, the feast of the Passover. Other feasts that were celebrated with regularity were the feast of unleavened bread, the feast of Pentecost, the feast of harvest, the feast of Purim, the feast of Esther, the Feast of Dedication, and the Feast of Lights. In addition to these annual feasts were the weekly Sabbaths commemorating God's rest from creation. Of all these feasts, the "most holy and most eminent," according to Josephus, was the Feast of Tabernacles (Antiquities 8.4.1). This feast initially was dictated by the Lord, through Moses, saying, "Speak unto the children of Israel, saying, The fifteenth day of this seventh month *shall be* the feast of tabernacles *for* seven days unto the Lord" (Leviticus 23:34). Over time, an eighth day was added to the feast so that it extended over a week and two Sabbaths. A significant aspect of this feast was "the strange leafy booths in which they lived and joyed, keeping their harvest-thanksgiving; and praying and longing for the better harvest of a renewed world" (Edersheim, Book 2, Chapter 9, p. 159). These booths, which were constructed of the branches of trees, were "erected everywhere, in court and on housetop, in street and square, for the lodgment and entertainment of that vast multitude; leafy dwellings everywhere, to remind of the wilderness-journey, and now of the goodly land" (Edersheim, Book 4, Chapter 6, p. 577). Only the Roman complex Antonio was free of these leafy booths during the feast.

It is interesting that of the four gospel narrators, only John recorded the incident of the appearance of Jesus at the Feast of Tabernacles. According to John, while the Savior was yet in Galilee, "his brethren" came to Him and urged Him to attend the Feast of Tabernacles. Doing this, they argued, would greatly expand the scope of His notoriety and increase the audience who would hear His message. The presumption of this suggestion, taken with John's statement, "For neither did his brethren believe in him" (John 7:5), suggest these so-called brethren had serious deficiencies in both tact and understanding. Jesus brushed off these men, saying: "Go ye up unto this feast. I go not up yet unto this feast: for my time is not yet full come" (John 7:8). Sometime after the others had departed for Jerusalem, "then went he also up unto the feast, not openly, but as it were in secret" (John 7:10). Once the Master arrived at the feast, He found there was much disputation about Him, "for some said, He is a good man: others said, Nay; but he deceiveth the people." But none of these spoke openly about him, "for fear of the Jews." (John 7:12-13)

About the middle of the feast, Jesus went up into the temple and began to teach. There is no record of what He said on this occasion. But the impact of His words is clearly evident for the Jews marveled at His discourse saying, "How knoweth this man letters, having never learned?" (John 7:15) It was a repetition of what occurred when Jesus entered the temple as a young boy and was found by His parents discoursing with the learned rabbis. There was no logical way to explain how this man, raised as a laborer, spoke with the language and the depth of understanding of the most learned among them. The Savior was quick to deflect any suggestion of His personal abilities or achievements, saying: "My doctrine is not mine, but his that sent me," adding, "If any man will do his will, he shall know of the doctrine, whether it be of God, or *whether* I speak of myself" (John 7:16-17). Jesus then differentiated between Himself and those who egotistically speak of themselves, saying, "he that seeketh his glory that sent him, the same is true, and no unrighteousness is in him" (John 7:18).

Among the throng who surrounded the Savior in the temple were those who believed Him, and others who were merely intrigued by His message. But there were still others who had bought into the beliefs of the scribes and Pharisees and wanted to kill Him. It was to this last group the Master directed the question, "Why go ye about to kill me?" (John 7:19) There were two main reasons why this last group sought His death: because He had performed a healing on the Sabbath, and because of His supposed blasphemy. This last charge dated back to His statement in the synagogue at Nazareth when He said that Isaiah's prophecy about the Christ was fulfilled in Him. As to the complaint of His having performed a healing on the Sabbath, Jesus undertook to demonstrate the fallacy of this complaint. Said He, "If a man on the Sabbath day receive circumcision, that the law of Moses should not be broken; are ye angry at me, because I have made a man every whit whole on the sabbath day?" (John 7:23) His accusers, having no answer for this convincing response, quickly changed the subject to speculate why the authorities allowed this man to speak out so boldly in the temple. "Do the rulers know indeed that this is the very Christ?" (John 7:26) Then reasoning among themselves, they observed that when Christ would come, "no man knoweth whence he is" (John 7:27), but they knew where Jesus came from—Nazareth. This evoked a powerful response from the Savior who said,

Ye both know me, and ye know whence I am: and I am not come of myself, but he that sent me is true, whom ye know not. But I know him: for I am from him, and he hath sent me." (John 7:28-29)

Some among the multitude who considered these words to be blasphemous "sought to take him: but no man laid hands on him, because his hour was not yet come" (John 7:30).

When the Pharisees and chief priests heard of the murmuring among the multitude against Jesus, they sent officers to take Him. When accosted by these officers, Jesus told them He would soon return "to him that sent me," and that, "Ye shall seek me, and shall not find *me*: and where I am, *thither* ye cannot come" (John 7:33-34). These words touched off conversation among the Jews as to what Jesus meant, speculating He might have referred to a ministry to those dispersed among the gentiles.

On the last day, the great day of the feast, Jesus stood and cried saying, "If any man thirst, let him come unto me and drink." He declared that from those who did this, believing in Him, would "flow rivers of living water" (John 7:37-38). Hearing these words, some said, "This is the Christ." But others said, "Shall Christ come out of Galilee?" (John 7:41), a statement that reflected ignorance of the Savior's birth in a manger in Bethlehem. And so there was a division among the people because of Him; "and some of them would have taken him; but no man laid hands on him" (John 7:44).

When the officers who were sent to arrest Jesus reported to the Pharisees and chief priests, they were asked, "Why have ye not brought him?" They answered, "Never man spake like this man." Perhaps surprised by this response, they hastened to accuse the officers of being deceived and to affirm that the learned leaders did not believe Jesus. At this, Nicodemus, a member of the Sanhedrin who had come to Jesus by night, spoke up to say that under Jewish law, no man is to be judged until he has been heard. The Jewish leaders immediately sought to discredit Nicodemus by asking whether he, too, was of Galilee and then disparaged his scholarship, saying "Search, and look: for out of Galilee ariseth no prophet." (John 7:45-52)

The Woman Taken in Adultery

Soon after the Feast of Tabernacles ended, the Savior was found early in the morning, seated in the temple with a throng gathered about Him. As He taught them, discussing and answering their questions, the scribes and Pharisees saw a woman before Him, saying, "Master, this woman was taken in adultery; in the very act. Now Moses in the law commanded us, that such should be stoned: but what sayest thou?" (John 8:4-5) Their purpose was to lead Him into statements that would support the case of blasphemy they were building against Him or that would injure Him in the eyes of His followers. Acting as if He didn't hear the question, The Master stooped down and wrote with His finger on the ground. "So when they continued asking him, he lifted up himself, and said unto them, He that is without sin among you, let him first cast a stone at her" (John 8:7). So saying, the Savior again stooped down and wrote on the ground with His finger. Convicted by their conscience, those who heard left one by one until the Savior was left alone, with the woman standing in the midst. When Jesus looked about and saw no one but the woman present, He said to her, "Woman, where are those thine accusers? hath no man condemned thee?" When she answered, "No man, Lord," He responded, "Neither do I condemn thee: go, and sin no more" (John 8:10-11).

It is easy to see in this episode a tipping point between the rigid Law of Moses and the Savior's law of mercy and forgiveness. Because the Savior completed His work in the Garden of

Gethsemane and on the cross at Calvary and burst the bonds of death at the garden tomb, the tender mercy shown to this lonely woman as a universal gift is available to men and women everywhere, from the fall of Adam forward, conditioned upon their faith and repentance and upon the Savior's cautionary word to the woman, that they sin no more.

The Light of the World

The Savior often alluded to nearby physical objects as a point of reference to illustrate the subject of His discourse. He used this teaching device again a short while after the Feast of Tabernacles ended as He sat teaching in the court of the treasury. Nearby were great lamps, which had been set up as part of the celebration and had not yet been removed. In that setting, the Master commenced His discourse, saying, "I am the light of the world: he that followeth me shall not walk in darkness, but shall have the light of life" (John 8:12). The Pharisees who were present challenged this statement because the Law of Moses required two witnesses to establish a fact.

"Thou bearest record of thyself," they declared, therefore, "thy record is not true" (John 8:13). In answer Jesus said, "I am one that bear witness of myself, and the Father that sent me beareth witness of me" (John 8:18). The Savior then brushed off the impudent question, "Where is thy father," saying "Ye neither know me, nor my Father: if ye had known me, ye would have known my Father also" (John 8:19). Notwithstanding these bold statements made in the temple, linking himself with the Father, which would undoubtedly have been regarded by them as blasphemous, yet "no man laid hands on him; for his hour was not yet come" (John 8:20). Continuing His discourse, Jesus said: "I go my way, and ye shall seek me, and shall die in your sins: whither I go, ye cannot come" (John 8:21). These enigmatic words caused some consternation among the Jews, who said, "Will He kill himself? because He sayeth, Whither I go, ye cannot come?" (John 8:22) The Savior's response, far from making His meaning clear, only seemed to add to their mystification. Said He:

> Ye are from beneath; I am from above: ye are of this world; I am not of this world.
> I said therefore unto you, that ye shall die in your sins: for if ye believe not that I am *he*, ye shall die in your sins." (John 8:23-24)

Unable to make sense of His words, the Jews spoke out in frustration: "Who art thou?" Answering, Jesus said,

> Even *the same* that I said unto you from the beginning.
> I have many things to say and to judge of you: but He that sent me is true; and I speak to the world those things which I have heard of him. (John 8:25-26)

Speaking parenthetically, John observed that the Jews did not understand that Jesus spoke of His Father. Sensing there was little comprehension as to the meaning of His words among the Jews generally, He concluded, saying: "When ye have lifted up the Son of man, then shall ye know that I am *he*, and *that* I do nothing of myself; but as my father hath taught me, I speak these things" (John 8:28). The record reports that as He spoke these words, "many believed on him." As to these, He concluded by saying: "If ye continue in my word, *then* are ye my disciples indeed; And ye shall know the truth, and the truth shall make you free" (John 8:30-32).

The Two Great Commandments

Once as the Savior taught the multitude, a certain lawyer "stood up, and tempted him, saying, Master what shall I do to inherit eternal life?" (Luke 10:25) Saint Luke's use of the word "tempted" implies a devious intention by the lawyer to lead the Savior into a comment or a definition that could be twisted by further questioning into something detrimental to Him. The lawyer's plan was thwarted when Jesus asked him, "What is written in the law?" (Luke 10:26) Thus, instead of getting an extemporaneous statement or definition from the Savior that could become distorted through skillful questioning, the lawyer was forced to quote or to read this statement from the law, with which he was well acquainted: "Thou shalt love the Lord thy God with all thy heart, and with all thy soul, and with all thy strength, and with all thy mind; and thy neighbor as thyself" (Luke 10:27). When the lawyer had finished speaking, the Master said, "Thou hast answered right: this do, and thou shalt live" (Luke 10:28). Much to the lawyer's discomfiture, this essentially ended the conversation. His question had been answered with his own words quoted from the law, which was part of his professional expertise. Moreover, the lawyer had been challenged to put these words to use by observing them. Unwilling to be silenced in this embarrassing way and in an attempt to justify himself, the lawyer then asked: "And who is my neighbour?" (Luke 10:29)

Parable of the Good Samaritan

In answer to this question, Jesus related a story about a man who traveled from Jerusalem to Jericho, where he was attacked by thieves who stripped off his clothing, wounded him severely, and left him half dead. First a priest then a Levite passed by the wounded man without offering to help him. Then came along a Samaritan who bound up the man's wounds, pouring in oil and wine, and then conveyed him on his own animal to an inn, where the man was cared for and accommodated at the Samaritan's expense. The next morning before he departed, the Samaritan gave the innkeeper two pence, saying, "Take care of him; and whatsoever thou spendest more, when I come again, I will repay thee." Then addressing the lawyer, Jesus asked, "Which now of these three, thinkest thou, was neighbor unto him that fell among the thieves? And he said, He that shewed mercy on him. Then said Jesus unto him, Go, and do thou likewise" (Luke 10:35-37).

In asking the question, "Who is my neighbor?" the lawyer knew full well that to a Jew, none but Jews were considered to be neighbors. Only to those of their tribe were they obligated by the law to show the kind of love and concern they owed to the Lord. In this context, the idea that a Jew would or could love a Samaritan as himself was beyond belief, given the contempt and opprobrium in which the Samaritans were held. That the Samaritans were well aware of this attitude toward them by the Jews was reflected in the surprise and disbelief of the Samaritan woman at Jacob's well when the Savior asked her for a drink of water.

The Savior's parable of the Good Samaritan can be viewed as an episode in the process of tearing down destructive stereotypes among the tribes of Israel, while emphasizing His message of mercy and love. The noble character of the Samaritan, shown in his concern and liberality toward the wounded victim, who presumably was a Jew from Jerusalem, is exemplary and worthy of emulation by all, regardless of tribal affiliation. And while the priest and the Levite are shown in a bad light, there is no hint that their conduct was considered to be representative of their entire tribe. And the frank declaration of the lawyer that the conduct of the Samaritan was superior to that of his tribesmen, the Levite, and the priest, is significant as signaling a new emphasis on the importance of personal conduct over the negative influences of tribal traditions.

Jesus Visits Martha and Mary

Leaving Jericho, which appears to have been the site of the Parable of the Good Samaritan, Jesus and several of His followers traveled along the so-called Red Path or Bloody Way which led to Bethany, a village located some two miles from Jerusalem, just over the hill from the Garden of Gethsemane. This highway had earned its gruesome name because of the numerous killings that had been committed there at the hands of highway thugs and robbers. So frequently had violent murders been committed on this deadly strip that the Romans once had a military garrison stationed there to protect travelers.

In Bethany, Jesus was accommodated in the home of sisters Martha and Mary, who shared the home with their brother Lazarus, who appears not to have been home at the time. Luke is the only one of the four New Testament narrators who reported this incident. It is assumed, therefore, that his knowledge of it came from either Martha or Mary.

Martha apparently was the older of the two sisters, given this: "a certain woman named Martha received him into her house" (Luke 10:38). The geniality of the circumstances suggests that Jesus had been a guest in this home on previous occasions. As the scene opens, Mary is seen sitting at the feet of Jesus listening to His discourse on the word, while Martha is busy preparing the meal. "But Martha was cumbered about much serving, and came to him, and said, Lord, dost thou not care that my sister hath left me to serve alone? bid her therefore that she help me" (Luke 10:40). In answer, Jesus uttered these words which have been quoted incessantly over the years: "Martha, Martha, thou art careful and troubled about many things. But one thing is needful: and Mary hath chosen that good part, which shall not be taken away from her" (Luke 10:41-42).

This story underscores the reality that children of the same parents often reflect different qualities of personality and character. It is plain that Martha, whether by necessity or choice, was fully committed to the performance of menial household tasks. Mary, on the other hand, was more inclined toward spiritual and intellectual things. It is possible that this propensity in Mary was encouraged by Martha's incessant work. Mary's sensitive, spiritual nature is shown by the fact she sat at Jesus' feet "and heard his word." When Martha appeared to ask for help in the kitchen, she accosted Jesus with the accusatory statement, "dost thou not care" that she was serving alone.

This evoked the Savior's coaxing, gentle statement, "Martha, Martha, thou art careful and troubled about many things." Then to place the conversation in the proper perspective, He said that of these "many things" only one was needful, or absolutely necessary, and that was "the word" which He had been sharing with Mary. The Savior then mildly reproved Martha, saying that "good part," that is hearing Him expound the word, would not be taken from Mary.

Anyone who reads into this narrative a denigration of menial work does so in ignorance or disregard of the fact that for thirty years of His life, Jesus performed menial tasks at the direction of Joseph and Mary. Jesus was an advocate of honest toil and labor and expected that each one of the flock would perform his allotted share. But His discussion with Martha made it clear that "the word" was the one absolutely needful thing in the lives of His followers.

Jesus Teaches His Disciples to Pray

While in the area near Bethany, Jesus was observed praying. "When he ceased, one of his disciples said unto him, Lord, teach us to pray, as John also taught his disciples" (Luke 11:1). In response, Jesus uttered the following, which is known as The Lord's Prayer:

> Our Father which art in heaven, Hallowed be thy name: Thy kingdom come. Thy will be done, as in heaven, so in earth.
> Give us day by day our daily bread.
> And forgive us our sins; for we also forgive every one that is indebted to us. And lead us not into temptation; but deliver us from evil. (Luke 11:2-4)

Earlier, in His sermon on the mount, Jesus offered essentially the same prayer couched in different terminology (see Matthew 6:9-13). The language of Matthew's version is more familiar to the reader and is more often quoted than the version in Luke. Both versions of the prayer contain the nebulous statement "lead us not into temptation." To use that language in imploring the Lord for blessings implies a devious quality in the Lord, for it suggests that He might be amenable to leading us into temptation. Joseph Smith's translation of Luke 11:4 reads, "and let us not be led into temptation," which clarifies the nebulous language. The same change was made by Joseph Smith in his translation of Matthew 6:13.

The use of the wording, "lead us not into temptation," in the two versions of the Lord's Prayer found in Luke and Matthew clearly reflect errors in translation of the King James Version of the Bible. And the Prophet Joseph Smith's translation of those verses, correcting the errors, reinforces the credibility of the Church's eighth Article of Faith.

The process by which the King James translation of the Bible was effected reflects how errors of translation like these occurred. Fifty-four noted scholars were brought together to produce the King James translation. These scholars were divided into six groups of nine each and various portions of the holy scriptures were assigned to each of these groups for analysis and composition. This division of responsibility made their monumental task manageable. Available to the scholars for their work were all of the records, translations, retranslations, memoranda, and scholarly treatises in various languages pertaining to the holy scriptures that had been accumulated over the centuries. In light of the magnitude of the task, it is easy to see how errors of the kind alluded to here could have occurred. That errors did occur as in these cases does not detract from the overall impact, value, and reliability of the Bible as an accurate account of God's dealings with His earthly children over the generations of time.

Persistence in Prayer

Having provided the form and the content of a prayer in response to the request, the Savior proceeded to describe the elements of personal effort and intensity that must attend an efficacious prayer. He did this by telling the story of a man who went to the home of a friend at midnight, asking for loaves of bread. The householder said, "I cannot rise and give thee," because he and his family were already in bed and unwilling to respond. The Savior then described a tactic which would overcome the householder's reluctance: "I say unto you, Though he will not rise and give him, because he is his friend, yet because of his importunity he will rise and give him as many as he needeth" (Luke 11:8). In other words, if the man refused to take no for an answer and remained at the door knocking and asking for bread, the householder would respond merely to preserve the peace of his household.

The parable of the importunate neighbor prompted the Master to elaborate on the principal of prayer and on the consequences of heartfelt prayer. Said He,

> Ask, and it shall be given you; seek and ye shall find; knock, and it shall be opened unto you.
> For every one that asketh receiveth; and he that seeketh findeth; and to him that knocketh it shall be opened. (Luke 11:9-10)

The Savior then drew an analogy between men who give gifts to their children and God who bestows gifts upon His children on earth. He said,

> If a son shall ask bread of any of you that is a father will he give him a stone? Or if he ask a fish, will he for a fish give him a serpent?
> Or if he shall ask an egg will he offer him a scorpion? (Luke 11:11-12)

In light of this litany of examples of men bestowing gifts upon their children, Jesus asked the question: "If ye then, being evil, know how to give good gifts unto your children: how much more shall *your* heavenly Father give the Holy Spirit to them that ask him?" (Luke 11:13) It is notable Jesus did not describe a litany of gifts men might ask of the Father, only the gift of the Holy Spirit. This suggests the amplitude of that gift, once it is received.

Jesus Casteth Out a Dumb Devil

While still in the area near Bethany, the Savior cast a dumb devil out of a man. When this occurred, the dumb devil began to speak, which caused a sense of wonder among the onlookers and raised questions about the significance of what they had just witnessed. It was then one of them spoke up to say, "He casteth out devils through Beelzebub the chief of the devils" (Luke 11:15). But Jesus,

> knowing their thoughts, said unto them, Every kingdom divided against itself is brought to desolation; and a house *divided* against a house falleth.
> If Satan also be divided against himself, how shall his kingdom stand? because ye say that I cast out devils through Beelzebub. (Luke 11:17-18)

How neatly the Savior demonstrated the fallacy of the idea that He cast out devils by the power of Satan. If the power to occupy a host body is countered by the power to evict the occupant, a stalemate occurs, rendering impotent satanic power and influence over the host body.

Then, referring to the evil dumb spirit He cast out of the man, the Master said:

> When the unclean spirit is gone out of a man, he walketh through dry places, seeking rest; and finding none, he saith, I will return to my house whence I came out.
> And when he cometh, he findeth *it* swept and garnished.
> Then goeth he, and taketh *to him* seven other spirits more wicked than himself; and they enter in, and dwell there: and the last *state* of that man is worse than the first. (Luke 11:24-26)

These scriptures reaffirm that evil spirits, emissaries, or tools of Satan, exist upon the earth in varying degrees of wickedness. They also reaffirm that multiple evil spirits can inhabit a single body. These evil spirits are possessed of intelligence and reasoning powers and have feelings and desires, among which is the desire to inhabit human bodies. That the dumb spirit had been evicted from the man by the power of Christ was no apparent impediment to his return, along with the other evil spirits. However, that the man's condition was then worse than before does not mean this cannot be reversed, either through another intervention of heavenly power, or through the acquisition of spiritual strength by the man sufficient to withstand the influence of the evil spirits.

Jesus Speaks Again of Cleanliness

The Savior was invited to dine with a Pharisee. Whether by accident or design, Jesus neglected to wash His hands before sitting down for the meal. To the Jews, this was considered to be a grievous infraction of their intrusive laws of cleanliness. Jesus was well aware of these laws, which poses the question whether He acted deliberately in order to provide a teaching moment. The reaction of the host was prompt as he "marvelled that he had not first washed before dinner" (Luke 11:38). The Savior was equally prompt in responding to this rude comment, hardly the kind one would expect from a host to his dinner guest:

> Now do ye Pharisees make clean the outside of the cup and the platter; but your inward part is full of ravening and wickedness.
> Ye fools, did not he that made that which is without make that which is within also?" (Luke 11:39-40)

Here the Savior laid bare the blindness that had afflicted the Jews for centuries, a blindness that focused only upon the overt, physical aspects of life while ignoring the covert spiritual aspects of it. He then chastised them for their stingy habits in offering alms and paying tithes while ignoring the weightier matters of "judgment and the love of God" (Luke 11:42). Jesus also berated them for vanity in seeking the upper seats in the synagogue and glorying in respectful greetings in the market place.

The Savior was well aware that this broad indictment of the Pharisees would not change their practices or alter their intention to kill him. Nor did this Pharisee host believe breaking bread with Jesus would change their relationship. Why then did he invite Him to dinner? Presumably he hoped to elicit comments from Jesus that would strengthen the case the Pharisees were building against Him. And why did the Savior accept the invitation to dinner? He certainly had a reason for doing so, or He would not have gone. Whatever the reason that prompted Jesus to accept the invitation to dine, one consequence of the event was to place on the record the tragic scope of the blindness of the Jews, which the rigid observance of their oppressive rules of cleanliness had helped to produce. And this had relevance to the ultimate fulfillment of the Law of Moses.

Jesus Denounces the Lawyers

Following the Savior's denunciation of the Pharisees, a lawyer asked a question he may have regretted later. Said he, "Master, thus saying thou reproachest us also" (Luke 11:45). "Woe unto you also, *ye* lawyers!" Jesus answered, "for ye lade men with burdens grievous to be borne, and ye yourselves touch not the burdens with one of your fingers" (Luke 11:46). Jesus then denounced the lawyers for building sepulchres for the prophets whom their fathers had killed. He said the blood of the prophets, which was shed from the foundation of the world, would be required of this generation. "From the blood of Abel unto the blood of Zacharias . . . verily I say unto you, It shall be required of this generation" (Luke 11:51). Jesus also accused the lawyers of lacking knowledge and of hindering others from acquiring it. As He continued His denunciation of the lawyers, the scribes and Pharisees urged Him on, "Laying wait for him, and seeking to catch something out of his mouth, that they might accuse him" (Luke 11:54). After the Savior's verbal scourging of the lawyers, the one who had asked the leading question may well have reflected with regret upon his violation of a cardinal rule of lawyers everywhere: "Never ask a question unless sure of the answer."

Parable of the Foolish Rich Man

Following the chastisement of the Pharisees and the lawyers, Jesus was found teaching an "innumerable multitude" of people, so large that "they trode one upon another." He began by warning against "the leaven of the Pharisees, which is hypocrisy" (Luke 12:1). He also warned against attempts to cover one's sins,

> For there is nothing covered, that shall not be revealed. . . .
> Therefore whatever ye have spoken in darkness shall be heard in the light; and that which ye have spoken in the ear in closets shall be proclaimed upon the housetop. (Luke 12:2-3)

He admonished them to fear no man, but to "Fear him, which after he hath killed hath power to cast into hell; yea, I say unto you, Fear him" (Luke 12:5), an apparent reference to Satan. The Master also declared that whosoever confessed Him before men, He would confess before the angels of God; and whosoever denied Him before men "shall be denied before the angels of God" (Luke 12:9).

He announced that whosoever spoke a word against Him would be forgiven, but he that blasphemed against the Holy Ghost would not be forgiven. Illustrating the ineffable power of the Holy Ghost, He told them to take no thought about their defense when brought before synagogues or magistrates, "For the Holy Ghost shall teach you in the same hour what ye ought to say." At this juncture, one spoke from the audience asking Jesus to instruct his brother to share an inheritance with him. A sense of impatience with the request can easily be inferred from the Lord's answer; "Man, who made me a judge or a divider over you?" The Savior also warned against covetousness, saying, "A man's life consisteth not in the abundance of the things which he possesseth" (Luke 12:10-15).

Jesus then taught by means of a parable. The scene was set at the estate of a certain rich man whose fields produced plentifully, so much so that his barns were unable to hold the yield from his crops. He solved the problem of crop surplusage by razing the old barns and building new and larger ones. Afterward, when the large new barns had been built and were full, the rich man exulted over his good fortune: "I will say to my soul, Soul, thou hast much goods laid up for many years; take thine ease, eat, drink, *and* be merry" (Luke 12:19). The Lord's trenchant response to the rich man's greed and selfishness was sobering: "*Thou* fool, this night thy soul shall be required of thee: then whose shall those things be, which thou hast provided? So *is* he that layeth up treasure for himself, and is not rich toward God"(Luke 12:20-21). Here was plainly taught the transient nature of earthly wealth and the foolishness of relying upon it while ignoring the eternal riches which obedience to God's laws and commandments will yield.

Addressing the disciples among the multitude, the Lord taught them what their focus should be: "Therefore I say unto you, Take no thought for your life, what ye shall eat; neither for the body, what ye shall put on. The life is more than meat, and the body *is more* than raiment" (Luke 12:22-23). Then by analogy, the Lord taught the disciples a profound lesson in faith. Said He, "Consider the ravens: for they neither sow nor reap; which neither have storehouse nor barn; and God feedeth them: how much more are ye better than the fowls?" (Luke 12:24) The essence of this message was "do not worry" about physical things, but have faith they will be provided by the Lord. To drive this point home He added, "Which of you with taking thought [or worrying] can add to his stature one cubit? If ye then be not able to do that thing which is least, why take ye thought for the rest?" (Luke 12:25-26) But the Master was not through speaking about this supernal subject. Using still another analogy, He said:

> Consider the lilies how they grow: they toil not, they spin not; and yet I say unto you, that Solomon in all his glory was not arrayed like one of these. If then God so clothe the grass, which is today in the field, and to morrow is cast into the oven; how much more will he clothe you, O ye of little faith? (Luke 12:27-28)

Shifting from the subject of raiment, the Savior spoke of food and mental focus: "And seek not ye what ye shall eat or what ye shall drink, neither be ye of doubtful mind" (Luke 12:29). The Savior said the nations of the earth sought after these temporal things—shelter, food and clothing—but the disciples were not to be concerned about them, because "your father knoweth that ye have need of these things," which would be provided for them through the exercise of their faith. So, instead of seeking after temporal things, the disciples were admonished to seek "the kingdom of God," with the promise that "all these things shall be added unto you." (Luke 12:30-31)

Jesus also taught the disciples not to be fearful, assuring them it was the Father's good pleasure to give them the kingdom. They were told to sell all they had and to give the proceeds as alms to the poor, while providing themselves "with bags which wax not old, a treasure in the heavens that faileth not. . . . For where your treasure is, there will your heart be also (Luke 12:33-34).

By way of emphasis, the Savior related the parable of the faithful servant who waited patiently for his lord and was prepared to receive him when he returned. Applying the parable to the disciples, Jesus said, "Be ye therefore ready also: for the Son of man cometh at an hour when ye think not" (Luke 12:40). Peter then spoke up to ask: "Lord, speaketh thou this parable to us, or even to all?" (Luke 12:41) At first Jesus did not differentiate between the disciples and the multitude. He merely said the reward of faithful waiting would be to be made "ruler over his household" and to receive "his portion of meat in due season" (Luke 12:42). The Master then added; "Blessed *is* that servant, whom his lord when he cometh shall find so doing. Of a truth I say unto you, that he will make him ruler over all he hath" (Luke 12:43-44). The Savior differentiated between the penalties for disobedience incurred by those who knew the Lord's will and those who did not. As to the former, He said they would be beaten with many stripes while the latter would be beaten with few stripes. "For unto whomsoever much is given, of him shall be much required," while less is expected of those who receive less (see Luke 12:45-48).

Jesus Heals a Man Blind From Birth

As Jesus walked by, He saw a blind man who had been born sightless. This blind man was well known in the neighborhood and was often seen begging. The disciples asked the Savior, "Master, who did sin, this man, or his parents, that he was born blind?" (John 9:2) The question implied a belief by the disciples of a preexistent life and that either the parents or the son, or both, were guilty of misconduct there, which accounted for the son's blindness. Jesus answered the question saying, "Neither hath this man sinned, nor his parents: but that the works of God should be made manifest in him" (John 9:3).

So saying, Jesus "spat on the ground, and made clay of the spittle, and he anointed the eyes of the blind man with the clay." He then told the blind man to go wash in the pool of Siloam, which he did, "and came seeing." The neighbors disputed among themselves whether the man they now saw having good vision was, indeed, the man they had known as the blind beggar. Some said it was he, others said it only resembled him, while the blind man said, "I am *he*." When the astonished neighbors asked how this miracle had occurred, he explained what Jesus had done and said, "and I went and washed, and I received sight." When he was asked the whereabouts of the man who had performed the healing, he said, "I know not." He was then taken to the Pharisees, who asked him how he had received his sight. In answer, "He said unto them, He put clay upon mine eyes, and I washed, and do see." Because the miracle was performed on the Sabbath, some of the Pharisees said, "This man is not of God, because he keepeth not the sabbath day. Others said, How can a man that is a sinner do such miracles?" Continuing with their clumsy examination, the Pharisees asked the man what he thought of the one who had given him sight. His answer further embarrassed them: "He is a prophet." Changing their strategy, the Pharisees turned to the man's parents in an attempt to show that he was not really blind. As if to demonstrate their prosecutorial ineptitude, they asked: "Is this your son, who ye say was born blind? how then doth he now see?" (John 9:6-19)

Their answer was a startling rebuke of the Pharisees and so bold and explicit as to open them to a charge of disrespect. Said they,

> We know that this is our son, and that he was born blind:
> But by what means he now seeth, we know not; or who hath opened his eyes, we know not: he is of age; ask him: he shall speak for himself. (John 9:20-21)

John suggests the parents spoke in such a bold way as a means of completely separating themselves from anything their son might say or do, thereby insulating them from any penalties imposed by the synagogue.

Returning their attention to the man who was blind, and presumably being anxious to deflect attention from the Savior as the source and cause of the miracle, the Pharisees said to him, "Give God the praise: we know that this man is a sinner." The man's answer gave them little comfort for he said, "Whether he be a sinner *or no*, I know not. One thing I know, that, whereas I was blind, now I see." What the Pharisees lacked in prosecutorial skills, they more than compensated for in their persistence for they now came back with a question they had asked before: "What did he to thee? how opened he thine eyes?" The question not only was repetitious, it was really quite surprising for it in essence admitted Jesus opened the blind man's eyes; they merely wanted to know how He did it. The man's answer was both impudent and disrespectful. Said he, "I have told you already and ye did not hear: wherefore would ye hear *it* again? will ye also be his disciples?" (John 9:24-27)

The Pharisees were enraged at the suggestion they might become disciples of Jesus and lashed back at the man, rebuking him and saying: "Thou art his disciple; but we are Moses' disciples. We know that God spake unto Moses: *as for* this *fellow*, we know not from whence he is" (John 9:28-29). The man responded to this comment in language and with a depth of understanding one would hardly expect of a beggar, blind from his birth. Said he,

> Why herein is a marvellous thing, that ye know not from whence he is, and *yet* he has opened mine eyes.
> Now we know that God heareth not sinners: but if any man be a worshipper of God, and doeth his will, him he heareth.
> Since the world began was it not heard that any man opened the eyes of one that was born blind.
> If this man were not of God, he could do nothing. (John 9:30-33)

Unmoved by this man's eloquence and angered by his words, they denounced him, saying, "Thou wast altogether born in sins, and dost thou teach us?" (John 9:34) With that, the Pharisees cast him out, a penalty that in the restored Church is analogous to excommunication.

Later the Savior came to the man, asking, "Dost thou believe on the Son of God?" When the man asked the questioner's identity, he was told, "Thou hast both seen him, and it is he that talketh with thee." The man then said, "Lord I believe. And he worshipped him." (John 9:35-38)

Later the Savior was heard to say, "For judgment I am come into this world, that they which see not might see; and that they which see might be made blind" (John 9:39).

Some of the Pharisees who heard these words said to Him in prideful mockery, "Are we blind also?" Answering, the Savior said: "If ye were blind, ye should have no sin: but now ye say, We see; therefore your sin remaineth" (John 9:41). In other words, were the Pharisees humble and obedient like the blind man who was given sight, they would be without sin. However their sins would remain as long as they rejected the Savior and persisted in their spiritual blindness.

Parable of the Good Shepherd

Of the four gospel narrators in the New Testament, only John recorded the story of the beggar who was blind at birth. And only John recorded the parable of the good shepherd. These stories reflect again how the gospel narrators composed their records based upon the information available to them. These two stories recorded by John also illustrate the precision and attention to detail that characterizes all of his writings.

He began the parable of the good shepherd by emphasizing that Christ has prescribed a specific process by which one may enter the kingdom of God. Wrote he: "Verily, verily, I say unto you, He that entereth not by the door into the sheepfold, but climbeth up some other way, the same is a thief and a robber" (John 10:1). By way of contrast, He said those who enter by way of the door are led by the shepherd of the sheep, who "hear his voice: and he calleth his own sheep by name, and leadeth them out. And when he putteth forth his own sheep, he goeth before them, and the sheep follow him: for they know his voice" (John 10:2-4). Also by contrast, He said the sheep would not heed the voice of a stranger nor follow him but would flee from him. When it appeared they did not understand this parable, the Master began again, saying that He was the door to the sheepfold and that those who came before Him were "thieves and robbers" and that the sheep "did not hear them." However, those who enter the sheepfold by the door "shall be saved, and shall go in and out and find pasture." (John 10:8-9) The Master contrasted the consequences of following the thief or himself: "The thief cometh not, but for to steal, and to kill, and to destroy: I am come that they might have life, and that they might have *it* more abundantly" (John 10:10). Dwelling further on contrasts, Jesus contrasted His life role with that of a hireling:

> The good shepherd giveth his life for the sheep.
> But he that is an hireling . . . whose own the sheep are not, seeth the wolf coming, and leaveth the sheep, and fleeth: and the wolf catcheth them, and scattereth the sheep.
> The hireling fleeth, because he is a hireling and careth not for the sheep. (John 10:11-13)

There followed the Savior's declaration of himself as the good shepherd: "I am the good shepherd, and know my *sheep*, and am known of mine. As the father knoweth me, even so know I the Father: and I lay down my life for the sheep" (John 10:14,15). Herein is portrayed the intimate relationship between the Savior and His followers, or His sheep, and between the Son and the Father. Moreover, the Master's sacrificial role in behalf of His sheep is revealed and it is emphasized that His life was given up voluntarily and was not taken from Him. This suggests that in His voluntary, sacrificial death and His resurrection, He had overcome all.

There followed this statement which is wholly unrelated to His death: "And other sheep I have, which are not of this fold: them also I must bring, and they shall hear my voice; and there shall be one fold, *and* one shepherd" (John 10:16). This would have been a startling revelation to Christ's followers in Palestine, who had observed that He did not minister beyond its boundaries. Moreover they would have been intensely interested to know the identity and the whereabouts of this other fold that would be visited by the Savior. This mystery was solved later when Jesus Christ appeared to the inhabitants of the American continent, telling them, among other things:

> And verily I say unto you, that ye are they of whom I said: Other sheep I have which are not of this fold; them also I must bring, and they shall hear my voice; and there shall be one fold, and one shepherd. (3 Nephi 15:21)

John then returned to the subject of Christ's death:

> Therefore doth my Father love me, because I lay down my life, that I might take it again.
> No man taketh it from me, but I lay it down of myself. I have power to lay it down, and I have power to take it again. This commandment I have received of my Father. (John 10:17-18)

As we shall see, the fulfillment of this commandment was attended by the most trying and bloody scene of the Savior's life, ending with the terrifying moment when the Father withdrew His presence, leaving the Christ to fulfill His life's mission, alone.

Discourse During the Feast of Dedication

During the winter, after uttering the parable of the good shepherd, Jesus was found on the porch of Solomon in the Temple of Herod. Soon a crowd of Jews gathered about Him, asking, "How long dost thou make us to doubt? If thou be the Christ, tell us plainly" (John 10:24). Jesus answered saying He had responded already to their question, and they did not believe Him, adding, "the works that I do in my Father's name, they bear witness of me" (John 10:25). He said they did not believe Him because they were not of "His sheep" who heard and followed His voice and to whom He had given eternal life. He concluded saying, "My Father, which gave *them* me, is greater than all; and no *man* is able to pluck *them* out of my Father's hand. I and *my* Father are one" (John 10:29-30). These last words enraged the Jews, who took up stones as if to attack Him. Jesus withstood them, calling attention to the many good works He had performed, which were from the Father, and asking: "for which of those works do ye stone me?" The Jews answered, saying "For a good work we stone thee not; but for blasphemy; and because that thou, being a man, makest thyself God" (John 10:32-33).

Jesus countered saying, "Is it not written in your law, I said, Ye are Gods?" (John 10:34; see Psalms 82:6). This being so, how could they charge Him with blasphemy? And though they might not believe Him, they should "believe the works: that ye may know, and believe, that the Father *is* in me, and I in him" (John 10:38). At this they sought to take Him, but He escaped "and went away again beyond Jordan into the place where John at first baptized; and there he abode" (John 10:40).

CHAPTER TWENTY-THREE

Jesus Ministers in Perea

A Crippled Woman Is Healed on the Sabbath

As Jesus taught on the Sabbath, in a synagogue in Perea near the place where John first baptized, there was present a woman who, for eighteen years, had been "bowed together, and could in no wise lift up *herself*" (Luke 13:11). Moved with compassion toward the woman, Jesus said to her, "Woman, thou art loosed from thine infirmity. And he laid *his* hands on her: and immediately she was made straight, and glorified God" (Luke 13:12-13). Wholly ignoring the miracle that had just occurred, the ruler of the synagogue denounced the Savior because the healing had been performed on the Sabbath. Then addressing the congregation He said, "There are six days in which men ought to work: in them therefore come and be healed and not on the sabbath day" (Luke 13:14). The Savior responded with understandable vehemence, addressing the ruler as "Thou hypocrite." He said there was not a person present who, on the Sabbath, would fail to remove his ox or his ass from the stall and lead it to water. This being so, He added, "And ought not this woman, being a daughter of Abraham, whom Satan hath bound, lo, these eighteen years, be loosed from this bond on the sabbath day?" (Luke 13:16) After these words were spoken, the Savior's adversaries were ashamed, "and all the people rejoiced for all the glorious things that were done by him" (Luke 13:17).

Two important things stand out in this incident. First, there were two distinct steps in the healing process. The Savior told the woman she was "loosed" from her infirmity, but it was not until He laid hands on her that she was "made straight." We saw in the healing of the nobleman's son, who was in Capernaum at the time, that the words alone of the Savior, uttered in Cana, were sufficient to effect a healing. There is no explanation why in this instance the words, "thou art loosed," seem not to have been sufficient to bring about a healing. Perhaps there was something in the woman's background, or level of comprehension, which made it important, or desirable, that the healing be accomplished in two stages.

Note too, the woman's infirmity apparently was not caused by physical disabilities, but by Satanic influences which had bound her "lo these eighteen years." Her healing by the combination of the Savior's words and actions affirm the broad scope and efficacy of the Savior's power to heal His children from either physical disabilities or satanic influences.

Parable of the Mustard Seed

On the occasion of the healing of the crippled woman on the Sabbath, the Savior posed the question: "Unto what is the kingdom of God like? and whereunto shall I resemble it?" (Luke 13:18; compare Matthew 13:31 and Mark 4:30) Answering His own question, the Savior said the kingdom of God was like a mustard seed, which a man planted in his garden, which grew into "a great tree; and the fowls of the air lodged in the branches of it" (Luke 13:19). This imagery of the kingdom of God, growing from a very small seed into a mighty tree, would have been startling to the Jews, who believed the kingdom of God would be ushered in with great pomp and pageantry, led by a mighty military leader in the image of King David. The idea of a kingdom coming into being through slow, incremental growth, obtaining its nutrients imperceptibly over time from the environment in which it was planted, was entirely alien to Jewish thought and expectations. This startling idea that Jesus presented to the Jews had elements similar to the principle of faith He had been speaking about often. It is not surprising then that He used the imagery of the mustard seed in chiding the people for their lack of faith (see Matthew 17:20).

Parable of the Leaven

On the occasion that the Savior related the parable of the mustard seed, He immediately followed it with the parable of the leaven. "Whereunto shall I liken the kingdom of God? It is like leaven, which a woman took and hid in three measures of meal, till the whole was leavened" (Luke 13:20-21). It is notable the Savior placed these two short parables side by side. While the results in both instances were the same, namely, that by small means great and notable things are accomplished, yet, the processes for attainment are vastly different. As to the mustard seed, the process of growth began as the seed was nourished by external influences, initially deriving nutrients from water and the surrounding soil and later from air, sunshine, and cultivation. On the other hand, the growth of the leaven came about through the internal effect of the yeast upon the meal, causing it to rise and, ultimately, to be formed into loaves of bread. In terms of the quantity of its production, that of the mustard seed is more profound, due to the process of regeneration it undergoes through pollination in the open atmosphere. But in terms of longevity, there is little distinction between the two processes, since repeated "starts" of the leaven can continue the process of bread making indefinitely. From an eternal perspective, the two parables teach of the profundity and the endless reach of the kingdom of God in the lives of His children.

Who Will Be Saved?

As Jesus taught in the cities and villages of Perea, one said to Him: "Lord, are there few that be saved?" (Luke 13:23) Answering, the Savior said: "Strive to enter in at the strait gate: for many, I say unto you, will seek to enter in, and shall not be able" (Luke 13:24). By way of affirmance, Jesus related this parable: A householder who, after the house had been secured, refused entry to those outside who pleaded urgently to be allowed to enter. When the outsiders boasted that they had taken food with the householder and had heard him teach in their streets, He answered, "I tell you, I know you not whence ye are; depart from me, all *ye* workers of iniquity" (Luke 13:27). The effect upon the outsiders of this blunt rejection was heart-rending: "There shall be weeping and gnashing of teeth, when ye shall see Abraham, and Isaac, and Jacob, and all the prophets, in the kingdom of God, and you *yourselves* thrust out"(Luke 13:28). The parable ended with an account of those who would come from all points of the compass to "sit down in the kingdom of God. And behold, there are last which shall be first, and there are first which shall be last" (Luke 13:29-30). The implication here that there are gradations in the kingdom of God accords with D&C 131:1.

Certain Pharisees Warn Jesus About Herod Antipas

On the same day the parable of the forthright householder was uttered, there came to Jesus certain Pharisees, saying:

Get thee out, and depart hence: for Herod will kill thee.

> And he said unto them, Go ye, and tell that fox, Behold, I cast out devils, and I do cures to day and to morrow, and the third *day* I shall be perfected.
>
> Nevertheless I must walk to day, and to morrow, and the *day* following: for it cannot be that a prophet perish out of Jerusalem. (Luke 13:31-33)

This scripture presents a striking anomaly, for here we find Pharisees speaking benignly and protectively of the Savior. This is a radical departure from the norm, as the Pharisees are almost always portrayed as being the evil, conniving enemies of Jesus, intently focused upon bringing about His death. Why then in this instance do we find Pharisees whose object was to warn and to protect the Savior against death at the hands of Herod Antipas? The answer seems to rest upon the reality there were some among the Pharisees who secretly believed in Jesus, or were men of such integrity they could not accept the morbid view of most Pharisees that Jesus must be killed. We have already seen how Nicodemus, a Pharisee and ruler of the Jews, came to Jesus by night saying to Him, "Rabbi, we know that thou art a teacher come from God" (John 3:2). We know too of Gamaliel, Paul's teacher, a man skilled in the law and held in honor by all the people (see Acts 5:34), whose integrity would not have allowed him to accede to the bloody demands of the vocal majority of Pharisees. And doubtless there were other Pharisees, who kept their views hidden, of the kind who came to warn Jesus about Herod Antipas in Perea.

The Savior was well aware of the perfidious nature of Herod Antipas, suggested by His use of the word "fox" in alluding to him. At the time of this comment, Jesus was not far from the prison in which John the Baptist was beheaded on the order of Herod Antipas. The order was given in fulfillment of a pledge he had made to Salome whose artful dancing had pleased him. The frivolous, brutal, and unsteady character of the king, which this incident reveals, was reason enough for the Pharisees to warn Jesus about him and to justify the use by the Savior of the term "fox" to describe him.

It is significant that in responding to the warning of the Pharisees about Herod Antipas, Jesus implied that He would be resurrected, that is "perfected," on the third day.

And His comment that it could not be that "a prophet perish out of Jerusalem" seemed to portend that His ministry in Perea was near the end and that the final journey back to Jerusalem was about to begin.

Man With Dropsy Healed on the Sabbath: Two Related Parables

Jesus entered the home of one of the chief Pharisees on the Sabbath day to eat bread. Present also were other Pharisees and certain lawyers who, according to their usual practice, carefully "watched him" (Luke 14:1). Their hope, of course, was to find something in His words or actions that would support the case they were building against Him. In this setting, there appeared before the Master a man with dropsy who had come seeking a blessing. Before acting upon the request, Jesus "spake unto the lawyers and Pharisees, saying, Is it lawful to heal on the sabbath day?" (Luke 14:3) Hearing no response to His question, the Savior proceeded to heal the man and send him on his way. He then challenged the Pharisees and lawyers, asking which one of them having an ox or an ass that had fallen into the pit would fail to pull him out on the Sabbath day. Again there was stony silence, as "they could not answer him" (Luke 14:6). This was not the first time Jesus had silenced the Pharisees and lawyers with a simple statement and question that demonstrated their hypocrisy.

Being aware of the tendency of Pharisees and lawyers to aggrandize themselves, and seeking to alter their behavior for the better, the Savior related this parable: When bidden to a wedding feast, the guest should not sit down in the highest room lest the host come and say, "Give this man place; and thou begin with shame to take the lowest room" (Luke 14:9). Instead, when one is bidden to a wedding feast, he should sit down in the lowest room so that when he that invited him comes, he shall say, "Friend, go up higher. . . . For whosoever exalteth himself shall be abased; and he that humbleth himself shall be exalted" (Luke 14:10-11). The Savior then turned to the Pharisee who had invited Him, counseling that when he prepared a dinner or a supper that he not invite his friends, nor his brethren, nor his rich neighbors, through whom he would be compensated by reciprocal invitations to dinner. Instead he should invite "the poor, the maimed, the lame, the blind." Then said the Master, "thou shalt be blessed; for they cannot recompense thee: for thou shalt be recompensed at the resurrection of the just" (Luke 14:13-14). This thought would have resonated with the Pharisees since, unlike the Sadducees, they believed in a resurrection and in the principle that in the resurrection a person will be rewarded for good deeds performed on earth. Here also is a message for all true believers, that their main focus in life should be that of service to others, especially service to those who lack the ability or the resources to repay. By this means and process, the true believer lays up treasures in heaven, where moth and rust do not corrupt nor do thieves break through and steal (see Matthew 6:19-20).

On this same occasion there was a man present who spoke out saying, "Blessed *is* he that shall eat bread in the kingdom of God" (Luke 14:15). In response, the Savior related this second parable: A certain man prepared a great feast and sent his servant to invite the special guests. All declined to come, giving various reasons. One said he had a piece of property which needed tending; another explained he had purchased cattle which required his attention; and still another declined because he had recently been married and could not leave his bride. When the servant reported these things, his master was angry and instructed him to go into the streets and lanes of the city to invite the poor, the lame, and the blind to attend the feast. When it was found there were still empty chairs at the banquet table, the servant was instructed to go out to the highways and the hedges to "compel" them to come to the feast "that my house may be filled." Then the host of the banquet declared: "For I say unto you, That none of those men which were bidden shall taste of my supper" (Luke 14:23-24).

Likening the Savior to the host of the banquet, this parable has sobering implications for all believers. The excuses given for not attending the banquet were obviously contrived, insincere, and rude. The host of the banquet was a man of influence and reputation in the community who was angered by the cavalier way in which those on the special guest list responded to the invitation extended by the host's servant. It is risky and perilous to snub such a one. And likening the believers to those on the special guest list, it is risky and perilous to snub and disrespect the Lord, for He has made it plain that "God will not be mocked."

Qualifications of a Disciple

Being in the presence of a great multitude, Jesus turned to them and said: "If any *man* come to me, and hate not his father, and mother, and wife, and children, and brethren, and sisters, yea, and his own life also, he cannot be my disciple" (Luke 14:26). This language implies that no member of a disciple's family, or any aspect of his own life can take precedence over the disciple's allegiance and commitment to the Savior. Hence, the first qualification of a disciple of Jesus Christ is recognition of His preeminence and perfection and of the subservient, imperfect status of the disciple and his absolute intention and willingness to accomplish the will of the Savior in all things.

Continuing with His discourse, Jesus said: "And whosoever doth not bear his cross, and come after me, cannot be my disciple" (Luke 14:27). Everyone has personal burdens and responsibilities whether of a physical, mental, or spiritual nature. Anyone who wishes or aspires to become a disciple of the Lord Jesus Christ must be prepared to bear their individual burdens as well as the burdens discipleship might entail. The ability or the capacity to bear these combined burdens of care and responsibility thus becomes another qualification for discipleship.

The Savior counseled that an aspirant for discipleship should count the cost of that life before embarking on it. He cited two examples: First, the builder of a tower should first sit down "and counteth the cost, whether he have *sufficient* to finish it" (Luke 14:28). Failure to do this might result in his becoming an object of ridicule by onlookers who, seeing the tower only partly finished, might say, "This man began to build, and was not able to finish" (Luke 14:30). The second example was of like import. Here a king failed to provide in advance for the needs of his army and was forced to sue for peace in the midst of battle. The Master concluded His discourse on discipleship saying, "So likewise, whosoever he be of you that forsaketh not all that he hath, he cannot be my disciple" (Luke 14:33).

CHAPTER TWENTY-FOUR

A Series of Parables and Discourses

Parable of the Lost Sheep

Once Jesus was surrounded by a group of Publicans and sinners who had gathered to hear His discourse. Nearby were Pharisees and scribes who murmured, saying: "This man receiveth sinners, and eateth with them" (Luke 15:2). Overhearing their criticism, Jesus responded with a parable. Which one of you, He asked, having a hundred sheep would not leave ninety-nine of them and go into the wilderness in search of the one which had become lost? He was speaking to men who understood the gentle and kind relationship between a shepherd and the sheep in his flock, each one having a name and each one being cherished and loved, even as a member of his family. This being true, the remainder of the Savior's parable would have resonated with them. He said,

> when he hath found *it* [the lost sheep], he layeth it on his shoulders, rejoicing.
> And when he cometh home, he calleth together *his* friends and neighbors, saying unto them, Rejoice with me; for I have found my sheep which was lost. (Luke 15:5-6)

Instead of leaving His hearers to interpret the parable as He sometimes did, the Savior provided the interpretation: "I say unto you, that likewise joy shall be in heaven over one sinner that repenteth, more than over ninety and nine just persons, which need no repentance" (Luke 15:7). The parable obviously does not mean that those in heaven do not love and respect the just among us. It is only that one who has been lost and then is found, or who has sinned and has then repented, is an object of special joy among all.

This parable is also found in Matthew 18:12-14. The two versions are essentially the same, except the version in Matthew does not portray the tender picture of the shepherd placing the lost sheep on his shoulders, nor does it refer to sinners, but comments that none "of these little ones should perish" (Matthew 18:14).

Parable of the Ten Pieces of Silver

The Savior uttered this parable on the same occasion that He uttered the parable of the lost sheep. The message of the two parables is essentially the same.

Here is a woman with ten pieces of silver. When one of them became lost, she lit a candle and swept the house diligently until she found the lost coin. When the lost coin was found, she called "*her* friends and *her* neighbours together, saying, Rejoice with me; for I have found the piece which I had lost" (Luke 15:9). Then, as with the parable of the lost sheep, the Savior provided the interpretation of the parable. Said He, "Likewise, I say unto you, there is joy in the presence of the angels of God over one sinner that repenteth" (Luke 15:10). It is noted here that the joy in heaven over the repentant sinner is not said to exceed the joy felt over those who need no repentance.

Parable of the Prodigal Son

This is the third of a trilogy of parables that dealt with something which had been lost. The Savior taught these during the same discourse. The first of the three parables told of a lost sheep, the second discussed a lost coin, and this third parable tells of a son who was lost to a life of sin and degradation and was found.

This son was the younger of two brothers whose father was a man of wealth and reputation. Unlike his brother, who was a hard worker and dependable, the younger son was frivolous and fun loving. Becoming weary of the drudgery and constant demands of farm life, the younger son went to his father saying, "Father, give me the portion of the goods that falleth *to me*." When the father complied, the younger son "gathered all together, and took his journey into a far country, and there wasted the substance with riotous living" (Luke 15:12-13). The combination of his profligate spending and a famine in the land brought the prodigal son into poverty. The only employment he could find was as a swineherd tending pigs in the field. In appraising his degraded and humiliating condition, the prodigal son thought to himself: "How many hired servants of my father's have bread enough and to spare, and I perish with hunger!" This reflection prompted him to decide, "I will arise and go to my father, and will say unto him, Father, I have sinned against heaven, and before thee, And am no more worthy to be called thy son: make me as one of thy hired servants" (Luke 15:18-19). With these thoughts in mind, the prodigal son returned to his father's house. And when he was some distance away, the father came running to him with joy and embraced and kissed him. After the prodigal son admitted he had sinned against heaven and was no longer worthy to be considered a son, the father ordered his servants to put the best robe on him and to place a ring on his finger. He then ordered that the fatted calf be killed for a feast, saying, "let us eat, and be merry: For this my son was dead, and is alive again; he was lost, and is found. And they began to be merry" (Luke 15:23-24).

As this celebration was in progress, the older son, who had been toiling in the field, returned to the house. Hearing the music and dancing, he asked one of the servants what was going on. When told his younger brother had returned and that the father had killed the fatted calf and was celebrating, "he was angry and would not go in" (Luke 15:28). When the father came out to inquire why the older brother would not come into the house, he told his father:

> Lo, these many years do I serve thee, neither transgressed I at any time thy commandment: and yet thou never gavest me a kid, that I might make merry with my friends:
> But as soon as this thy son was come, which had devoured thy living with harlots, thou hast killed for him the fatted calf. (Luke 15:29-30)

In an effort to explain himself and to placate the son, the father said:

> Son, thou art ever with me, and all that I have is thine.
> It was meet that we should make merry, and be glad: for this thy brother was dead, and is alive again; and was lost, and is found." (Luke 15:31-32)

The obvious thrust of the parable was to emphasize the process of repentance through which the prodigal son passed, which resulted in his return to the good graces of his father whom he had disrespected and disgraced. When he was reduced to the humiliation of feeding swine, he realized how far he had fallen and that his decline was assignable to his own misconduct. In returning to his home, he had no intent or expectation of being reinstated in his status as a son, but merely wished to be considered a servant. What happened resulted from the joy of the father, not from any devious intent of the prodigal son.

Aside from the core narrative of the parable, the story of a son who was lost but then was found, the parable has meaningful significance relative to its impact on the older brother and on the father. What are we to think of the anger of the older son, his childish refusal to enter the house, and his sense of being a victim of the father's partiality toward the younger son? Despite these flaws, there is much here to engender sympathy for the older son. He was obedient, hardworking, and reliable—the opposite of his brother. It is true he stood to inherit his father's wealth, but that lay in the uncertain future. The reality of the present was a life of toil and subservience with little or no recognition being shown him by the father. The final indignity was to come home after a hard day in the field to find music and dancing in honor of his profligate brother who wore the noble robe and displayed the princely ring on his finger.

As for the father, while acknowledging the undoubted love he had for both sons, how he must have struggled with finding a way to deal with each son's unique temperament. For instance, when the younger son came to request his share of the patrimony, a request which of itself was outlandish, he knew of this son's frivolous and unreliable nature, but still proceeded to grant the request. Then, when the prodigal son returned, he determined to bestow the royal robe and the princely ring upon him, kill the fatted calf, and begin the celebration with music and dancing, all with knowledge that the older son was still toiling in the field. He thereby relinquished the opportunity to confer with the older son and bring him into the process, which might have mitigated the angst that the older son suffered.

Parable of the Unjust Steward

On the same occasion that the Savior related the parable of the prodigal son, He also related the parable of the unjust steward. This steward, who managed the temporal affairs of a wealthy man, was discharged because "he had wasted his goods" (Luke 16:1). Faced with a loss of income, the steward appraised his future. Concluding he was incapable of doing physical work and was ashamed to beg, he decided on a strategy: "I am resolved what to do, that, when I am put out of the stewardship, they [the master's debtors] may receive me into their house" (Luke 16:4). Exercising the extensive legal authority he had to bind his master, likened to one who holds a power of attorney, he negotiated with the debtors to reduce the amounts owed to his master. While this inured to the detriment of the master, it enriched the debtors while creating in them a correlative sense of obligation toward the steward. While the steward may have enjoyed a temporary benefit from his dishonesty, he suffered an eternal detriment as this statement of the Savior suggests: "If therefore ye have not been faithful in the unrighteous mammon [i.e. dishonest riches], who will commit to your trust the true *riches*?" (Luke 16:11)

The Savior concluded the parable saying: "No servant can serve two masters: for either he will hate the one, and love the other; or else he will hold to the one, and despise the other. Ye cannot serve God and mammon" (Luke 16:13). Mammon as used here denotes earthly riches or wealth. Obviously riches or wealth are not evil per se. It is the love of riches, so intense as to alienate one from God, which is to be censured.

The following words in the parable require comment: "the lord commended the unjust steward, because he had done wisely" (Luke 16:8). It seems apparent the Lord was not complimenting the unjust steward because he had wasted his master's wealth, but because he had acted wisely to create a good place for himself in the future. So also the disciple of Christ is wise to keep the commandments as a means of assuring him a good place or situation in the future.

A Discourse on Covetousness

As Jesus delivered the parable of the unjust steward, "the Pharisees also, who were covetous, heard all these things: and they derided him" (Luke 16:14). Being covetous, these Pharisees were inordinately greedy for the riches of others. This being so, they likely scoffed at the denigration of unrighteous mammon and were put off by the allusion to "the true riches." As usual, Jesus was prompt and direct in His response to their criticism. Said He to the Pharisees, "Ye are they who justify yourselves before men; but God knoweth your hearts: for that which is highly esteemed among men is abomination in the sight of God" (Luke 16:15). Having thus accused the Pharisees of hypocrisy, the Savior noted that while the kingdom of God had superseded the law, there were enduring aspects of the law, in support of which He said: "Whosoever putteth away his wife, and marrieth another, committeth adultery: and whosoever marrieth her that is put away from *her* husband committeth adultery" (Luke 16:18). Thus, God's condemnation of adultery in the Law of Moses continues to apply, notwithstanding that the kingdom of God has superseded the law.

Parable of the Rich Man and Lazarus the Beggar

On the occasion that Jesus uttered the discourse on covetousness, He also related the parable of the rich man and Lazarus the beggar. This rich man lived sumptuously every day, dressed in royal purple and fine linen. He was oblivious of Lazarus the beggar, who lay at the gate of his lavish estate begging for crumbs from his table. Lazarus was not only hungry and poverty stricken, but his emaciated body was full of sores, which dogs gathered around to lick. "And it came to pass, that the beggar died, and was carried by the angels into Abraham's bosom" (Luke 16:22). The rich man then died, was buried and sent to hell. Living in torment, the rich man, with Abraham afar off and Lazarus in his bosom, "cried and said, Father Abraham, have mercy on me, and send Lazarus, that he may dip the tip of his finger in water, and cool my tongue; for I am tormented in this flame" (Luke 16:23-24). Father Abraham declined this request, reminding the rich man that during life he enjoyed good things while Lazarus enjoyed evil things, "but now he is comforted, and thou art tormented" (Luke 16:25). Father Abraham went on to say that beside all this there was a great gulf separating them that would not allow contact between them. In these circumstances, the rich man asked that Lazarus be sent to his father's house to warn his five brothers against the peril of ending up in the place of torment as he had done. Father Abraham's answer to this request was brief and to the point. Said he, "They have Moses and the prophets; let them hear them" (Luke 16:29). The rich man countered, "Nay, father Abraham: but if one went unto them from the dead, they will repent" (Luke 16:30). The answer that followed ended the conversation: "If they hear not Moses and the prophets, neither will they be persuaded, though one rose from the dead" (Luke 16:31).

This is the first parable in which the Savior's fictitious characters included persons among both the living and the dead. It would have had special meaning for the Pharisees present, who believed in the resurrection and in the rewards or detriments resulting from a person's conduct on earth. Also this parable foreshadowed the Pharisees' refusal to acknowledge the reality of

Christ's resurrection. In other words, the Pharisees would not believe even though Christ had risen from the dead.

Discourse on Offenses, Repentance, Forgiveness

As He taught the disciples, Jesus observed, "It is impossible but that offences will come," but He warned that the prevalence of offenses does not give license to commit them, saying, "but woe *unto him* through whom they come!" (Luke 17:1) The Master said there was one class of offenses that was more censurable than all the others. He defined this class of offenses and the consequences of committing them in this way: "It were better for him that a millstone were hanged about his neck, and he cast into the sea, than that he should offend one of these little ones" (Luke 17:2). The thing that makes offenses against little children so egregious is their innocence, their trusting natures, and their confidence in and reliance upon adults.

As to the forgiveness of offenses, the Savior said, "Take heed to yourselves: If thy brother trespass against thee, rebuke him; and if he repent, forgive him" (Luke 17:3). Having made the principle clear, the Savior gave emphatic support to it in these words: "And if he trespass against thee seven times in a day, and seven times in a day turn again to thee, saying I repent; thou shalt forgive him" (Luke 17:4).

Lazarus Is Raised

The raising of Lazarus from the dead is the third time in scriptural history when Jesus Christ performed this miracle. This instance, however, is more notable than the others because when Jesus arrived at Bethany where Lazarus had lived with his sisters Martha and Mary, the brother had been dead for four days. In the two other instances of a raising from the dead—the son of the widow of Nain and the daughter of Jairus—the deceased had been dead for a much shorter period.

When the Savior first received word from his sisters that Lazarus was sick, He said, "This sickness is not unto death, but for the glory of God, that the Son of God might be glorified thereby" (John 11:4). When there was uncertainty among the disciples about the condition of Lazarus because of the Savior's statement that he was not sick unto death, "said Jesus unto them plainly, Lazarus is dead" (John 11:14).

On learning of the death of Lazarus, many friends of the family came from Jerusalem, a short fourteen furlongs away (roughly two miles) to offer their condolences to the sisters. These, added to the friends in Bethany, comprised a large group of mourners who were present when Jesus arrived. Learning of His approach, Martha went alone to meet Jesus outside the city. Her greeting was more of a reproach, for she said to Him, "Lord, if thou hadst been here, my brother had not died." But then, perhaps sensing her remarks were inappropriate, she added; "But I know, that even now, whatsoever thou wilt ask of God, God will give *it* thee" (John 11:21-22). In response, Jesus said simply, "Thy brother shall rise again" (John 11:23). Martha answered, saying she knew Lazarus would rise in the resurrection, to which Jesus uttered one of the most complete and incisive statements ever about the resurrection. He said, "I am the resurrection, and the life: he that believeth in me, though he were dead, yet shall he live: And whosoever liveth and believeth in me shall never die. Believeth thou this?" In answer Martha said, "Yea, Lord: I believe that thou art the Christ, the Son of God, which should come unto the world" (John 11:25-27).

Having said this, Martha returned to the family home in town to tell Mary that the Savior wished to see her. Mary left hastily, causing some of the mourners to observe, "She goeth unto the grave to weep there." Instead she went outside town to meet Jesus. And seeing Him, "she fell down at his feet, saying unto him, Lord, if thou hadst been here, my brother had not died" (John 11:31-32) This accusatory statement and the weeping of Mary and of those who had followed her troubled the Savior and caused Him to groan in the spirit.

Asking where Lazarus had been laid, they said, "come and see." At this Jesus wept, causing the Jews to observe, "Behold how he loved him!" (John 11:34-36) Others were heard to ask why Jesus, who had caused the blind to see, could not have prevented Lazarus from dying. This caused the Savior to groan once again and, arriving at the grave, which was a cave, asked that the stone that lay upon it be removed. But Martha protested, saying, "Lord by this time he stinketh: for he has been *dead* four days" (John 11:39). He answered, "Said I not unto thee, that, if thou wouldst believe, thou should see the glory of God?" (John 11:40) As the stone was removed, the Master said, "Father, I thank thee that thou hast heard me, and I knew that thou hearest me always; but because of the people which stand by I said *it* [what I did], that they may believe thou hast sent me" (John 11:41-42). Jesus then spoke with a loud, commanding voice saying, "Lazarus, come forth." To the astonishment of all, "he that was dead came forth, bound hand and foot with grave clothes: and his face was bound about with a napkin" (John 11:43-44). There were many who witnessed this extraordinary event, or who heard about it through credible witnesses, who then believed that Jesus was the promised Messiah.

The news of what had occurred at Bethany was conveyed immediately to the Jewish leaders in Jerusalem. The Pharisees promptly convened a meeting of the council to discuss the implications of what had happened. They concluded "If we let him thus alone, all *men* will believe on him: and the Romans shall come and take away both our place and nation" (John 11:48). So from that day, under the leadership of Caiaphas, who was the high priest that year, "they took counsel together for to put him to death" (John 11:53). Because of this decision of the Jewish leaders, "Jesus therefore walked no more openly among the Jews; but went thence unto a country near to the wilderness, into a city called Ephraim, and there continued with his disciples" (John 11:54).

Meanwhile, since the celebration of the feast was near at hand, many Jews began assembling in Jerusalem. Because of the notoriety caused by the raising of Lazarus and the Master's other miracles, there was much speculation about Him in Jerusalem. "What think ye," they asked each other "that he will not come to the feast?" (John 11:56) At the same time, the chief priests and the Pharisees "had given a commandment, that, if any man knew where he were, he should shew *it*, that they might take him" (John 11:57). These events portended great danger for Jesus and foreshadowed the conspiracy and betrayal that would result in His earthly death and glorious resurrection.

CHAPTER TWENTY-FIVE

The Savior's Final Journey to Jerusalem

Following the Sanhedrin's edict of death and the publication of the directive that any knowledge of the Master's whereabouts be made known to them, Jesus "walked no more openly among the Jews." At that time He went to "a country near to the wilderness, into a city called Ephraim, and there continued with his disciples" (John 11:54). The exact location of this city is unknown. It is generally thought to be the locality elsewhere called Ephrain or Ephron, situated a little less than twenty miles northerly from Jerusalem. However, Edersheim opines that "the text seems to require a place in Peraea and close to Galilee" (Edersheim, Book 4, Chapter 21, p. 700, footnote 45). Whatever its location, it is clear that Jesus and His disciples retired to this place for some period of time, counseling together in seclusion and privacy. While in this place, Jesus undertook to instruct His disciples about some of the dire circumstances He would face in Jerusalem. Among other things, He said:

> Behold, we go up to Jerusalem, and all things that are written by the prophets concerning the Son of man shall be accomplished.
> For he shall be delivered unto the Gentiles, and shall be mocked, and spitefully entreated, and spitted on:
> And they shall scourge *him*, and put him to death: and the third day he shall rise again. (Luke 18:31-33)

It is incredulous that the disciples "understood none of these things: and this saying was hid from them, neither knew they the things which were spoken" (Luke 18:34).

This was the last of a series of similar statements made to His disciples by the Savior in an effort to prepare them for the time He would no longer be present on the earth to instruct and to guide them. These efforts appear to have been in vain. As we shall see at the time of the Savior's crucifixion and resurrection, the disciples were oblivious as to what had happened and the consequences to them in terms of their personal responsibility and obligation to the obscure and struggling church that the Master had organized.

The route Jesus followed in this last journey toward Jerusalem was erratic and serpentine. As was true of all journeys He undertook, this one was marked by special experiences and spiritual ministrations and by various parables and instructions uttered along the way.

Healing of the Ten Lepers

While passing through Galilee and Samaria, Jesus and His disciples entered a certain village, where "there met him ten men that were lepers, which stood afar off: And they lifted up *their* voices, and said, Jesus, Master, have mercy on us" (Luke 17:12-13). When the Savior saw these men, He said to them:

> Go shew yourselves unto the priests. And it came to pass, that, as they went, they were cleansed.
> And one of them, when he saw that he was healed, turned back, and with a loud voice glorified God,
> And fell down on *his* face at his feet, giving him thanks: and he was a Samaritan. (Luke 17:14-16)

Jesus answering said,

> Were there not ten cleansed? but where *are* the nine?
>
> There are not found that returned to give glory to God, save this stranger,
>
> And he said unto him, Arise, go thy way: thy faith hath made thee whole. (Luke 17:17-19)

These remarkable healings were affected at a distance, like the son of the nobleman, without any touching and without the utterance of any words of healing. The incident brings into focus the virtue of gratitude, reflected in the conduct of the Samaritan. Also, standing in contrast to the gratitude of the Samaritan is the ingratitude of the nine lepers who hurried away after their healings to find their priests, as Jesus had directed. Under Jewish law only a priest could authorize a healed leper to return to his family and to Jewish society generally. Perhaps some element of understanding can be accorded to these nine men who failed to show gratitude for their healings. Undoubtedly they had been separated from their families and friends for years, an opprobrium to their fellowmen being required to call out "unclean" to anyone seen approaching. And the terrible disease they lived with every day was painful and terrifying.

This dramatic episode also demonstrates that the practice of a virtue has its own reward, in this instance, the reward that inured to the benefit of the Samaritan because he was grateful, in learning from the Savior why he had been healed. It was because of his faith. Isolated as he had been because of his disease, this stranger presumably had never had the opportunity to learn the principles of the gospel of Jesus Christ. Now that he had witnessed the effect of this foundational principle, faith, upon the curing of his physical body, there was now laid out a pathway before him that could lead him to the salvation and exaltation of his eternal soul.

Discourse on the Kingdom of God

Then came the Pharisees, demanding to know when the kingdom of God should come. Jesus answered saying, "The kingdom of God cometh not with observation: Neither shall they say, Lo here! Or, lo there! for, behold, the kingdom of God is within you" (Luke 17:20-21).

(*Note:* Many translations read "among" instead of "within" because the pronoun "you" is plural here in Greek; see note for Luke 17:21. Thus it accords with both reason and authority that the Master taught that the kingdom of God was among them, not within them.)

He then turned to the disciples and taught them that He must "suffer many things, and be rejected of this generation" (Luke 17:25). He explained that the circumstances surrounding His second coming would be like it was in the days of Noah and Lot when doubters were planting, selling, and marrying until the day they were drowned, in the case of Noah, or were consumed by fire and brimstone, in the case of Lot. After the Master had described the scenes of death and desolation which would precede His second coming, the disciples asked, "Where Lord?" seemingly wishing to know the place of safety. His enigmatic answer was, "Wheresoever the body *is*, thither will the eagles be gathered" (Luke 17:37), implying that their safety lay amidst a gathering of the Saints.

Parable of the Importunate Widow

Unlike most other parables, this one announced its purpose at the outset: "And he spake a parable unto them *to this end*, that men ought always to pray and not to faint" (Luke 18:1).

There was in a city a judge "which feared not God, neither regarded man. And there was a widow in that city; and she came unto him, saying, Avenge me of mine adversary"(Luke 18:2-3). For a while the judge refused to consider the widow's appeal and sided with her adversary. Over time, however, the judge changed his mind and decided to grant the widow's appeal. The frivolous reason given for this change illustrates perfectly the corrupt character of the judge, who said of himself, "this widow troubleth me, I will avenge her, lest by her continual coming she weary me" (Luke 18:5). There apparently was no consideration given to the merits of the controversy between the widow and her adversary, but only a consideration of what effect the decision would have upon the judge. At this point, the Lord entered the conversation, saying: "Hear what the unjust judge saith" (Luke 18:6). The judge answered thus: "And shall not God avenge his own elect, which cry day and night unto him, though he bear long with them? I tell you that he will avenge them speedily" (Luke 18:7-8). Having thus spoken, He raised this crucial question: "Nevertheless when the Son of man cometh, shall he find faith on the earth?" (Luke 18:8) The question is crucial because the fulfillment of God's promises is conditioned upon faith.

Parable of the Pharisee and the Publican

On the same occasion that the Savior spoke of the importunate widow, He uttered a parable to certain persons "which trusted in themselves that they were righteous, and despised others" (Luke 18:9). While the moral of the parable is applicable to all, it appears to have been directed chiefly to those of the pharisaical class who considered themselves to be of a superior status and who looked with disdain and condescension upon all others.

The story involved two men who went up into the temple to pray, "the one a Pharisee and the other a publican" (Luke 18:10). The Pharisee "stood and prayed thus within himself, God, I thank thee, that I am not as other men *are*, extortioners, unjust, adulterers, or even as this publican" (Luke 18:11). Having thus distinguished himself and his class in the best pharisaical manner, he proceeded to enumerate some of the things that endowed him with such distinction: "I fast twice in the week, I give tithes of all that I possess" (Luke 18:12). In contrast to this prideful, self-congratulatory recital, the publican, "standing afar off, would not lift up so much as *his* eyes unto heaven, but smote upon his breast, saying, God be merciful to me a sinner" (Luke 18:13). The Savior, having laid this factual foundation, uttered His memorable statement about pride and humility and their consequences. Said He: "I tell you, this man went down to his house justified *rather* than the other: for every one that exalteth himself shall be abased; and he that humbleth himself shall be exalted" (Luke 18:14).

As already indicated, here are enumerated timeless principles of moral behavior applicable to everyone at any time in any place. Despite the earlier statement that the parable seems to have been aimed at the pharisaical community of the day, we must wonder whether the Savior had in mind a mild, indirect caution to some of His most intimate associates who on occasion had shown a tendency toward self-seeking or self-promotion.

A Discussion About Marriage and Divorce

Jesus now "departed from Galilee, and came into the coasts of Judaea beyond Jordan" (Matthew 19:1). The words "beyond Jordan" imply that the Master's route on this His last journey to Jerusalem had taken Him into Perea. "And great multitudes followed him; and he healed them" (Matthew 19:2). As usual, there was a group of Pharisees among the multitude, ever watchful for any statement or implication of the Savior that would bolster their case against Him and provide so-called justification for carrying out the decree of death the Sanhedrin had ordered following the raising of Lazarus.

In that setting, "The Pharisees also came unto him, tempting him, and saying unto him, Is it lawful for a man to put away his wife for every cause?" (Matthew 19:3) It should be remembered that it was in Perea where John the Baptist encountered serious difficulty with Herod Antipas because John had been outspoken in his criticism of Herod Antipas for having married Herodias, his brother's wife. And, of course, it was this incident that resulted in John's beheading in the Macheus prison in Perea. It was against this background that the Savior undertook to answer the Pharisees' question about divorce. Said He,

> Have ye not read, that he which made *them* at the beginning made them male and female,
> And said, For this cause shall a man leave father and mother, and shall cleave to his wife: and they twain shall be one flesh?
> Wherefore they are no more twain, but one flesh. What therefore God hath joined together, let not man put asunder. (Matthew 19:4-6)

This caused the Pharisees to question, "Why did Moses then command to give a writing of divorcement, and to put her away?" (Matthew 19:7) He responded that this was because of the hardness of men's hearts, "but from the beginning it was not so" (Matthew 19:8). The Master then described some of the grave consequences that derived from the deviation of the Mosaic Law as to men putting away their wives. Said He, "Whosoever shall put away his wife, except *it be* for fornication, and shall marry another, committeth adultery: and whoso marrieth her which is put away doth commit adultery" (Matthew 19:9).

On learning about these grave consequences, some of the disciples, seemingly astonished by them, said to the Savior, "If the case of the man be so with *his* wife, it is not good to marry" (Matthew 19:10). The Master passed over this observation with an implied acknowledgment that marriages were a good and necessary element of a stable society, while at the same time He acknowledged that there were a few men who avoided marriage, either because of the inability to fulfill the requirements of marriage or because of a desire to live a celibate life so as to be able to serve God more fully.

This incident underscores the Master's supreme concern for the dignity and the status of women. In the original pattern of marital relations, the woman was deemed to be a partner who enjoyed an equal status in the eyes of God. With the Mosaic deviation, which allowed men to put their wives away, the women were reduced to an inferior, subservient status with no way to preserve or enforce the noble status God had intended for them.

Jesus Blesses Little Children

In ministering to the multitudes that followed Jesus, His focus was almost exclusively upon the adults. It was they who had the size and the strength to make their way through the jostling crowd to a point near enough to make their pleading heard. So over the months of His public ministry, He had heard those urgent pleas at gatherings held all over Palestine where He performed countless miracles, causing the blind to see, the deaf to hear, the dumb to speak, the lame to walk, and the diseased to be made clean. It was a rare exception for the very young, lively children to be the object of His blessings. Such an exception occurred in Perea as the Savior made His way toward Jerusalem for the last time. The report of this incident will be found in Matthew 19:13-15, Mark 10:13-16, and Luke 18:15-17.

The three narratives are essentially the same, although the little ones are referred to as "infants" in Luke's account. This present narrative is based upon Mark's account. It is interesting that this story immediately follows the discussion about marriage and divorce.

It is apparent that the little children, or infants, were accompanied by their mothers as they approached the Master. Mark writes, "they brought young children to him, that he should touch them" (Mark 10:13). But the disciples who carefully protected the Savior's time and public exposure, "rebuked" those who brought the children. Jesus, who observed this, "was much displeased, and said unto them, Suffer the little children to come unto me, and forbid them not: for of such is the kingdom of God" (Mark 10:14). Then in a tender demonstration of His love and concern for little children, the Master took each one of them in His arms, one by one, and blessed them. As we shall see, this tender scene was repeated with little children in the New World when Jesus appeared on the American continent following His resurrection.

We see in this touching incident not only an example of the Savior's love and concern for children, but we also see a classic lesson for those who aspire to be disciples of the Lord Jesus Christ in the kingdom of God. This lesson was especially cogent and direct for the disciples who witnessed it. These were men who had been reared in Jewish homes, who from childhood had been taught that the Messiah would be a great political and military leader who would occupy the throne of King David and would restore it to the position of political and military power it had once occupied. But the gospel Jesus taught and the humble, submissive life He lived was wholly at variance with what they had been taught and believed from their youth as to the character of the promised Messiah. It was the disconnect of their preconceptions about the Messiah's character and persona and the reality of His being that caused His followers to misunderstand what He told them.

Thus the lesson the Savior taught to His disciples, and indeed to all mankind through His blessing the little children, was that their character and conduct as it relates to the kingdom of God must be like that of a little child—submissive, gentle, and kind—not officious, demanding, and brusque, as political and military discourse can be and often is.

The Rich Young Ruler

A rich young ruler approached the Savior, asking, "Good Master, what shall I do to inherit eternal life?" (Luke 18:18) The Savior responded in a somewhat uncharacteristic, light-hearted manner, saying, "Why callest thou me good? none *is* good save one, *that is*, God" (Luke 18:19). Then in a more serious vein, the Master said: "Thou knowest the commandments, Do not commit adultery, Do not kill, Do not steal, Do not bear false witness, Honour thy father and thy mother" (Luke 18:20). When the young ruler said he had kept all these things from his youth up, Jesus said, "Yet lackest thou one thing: sell all that thou hast, and distribute unto the poor, and thou shalt have treasure in heaven: and come, follow me" (Luke 18:22). Hearing this, the young ruler was sorrowful, for he was very wealthy. Observing his reaction, the Savior said: "How hardly shall they that have riches enter into the kingdom of God!" By way of emphasis, the Master cited the well-known proverb, "For it is easier for a camel to go through a needle's eye, than for a rich man to enter into the kingdom of God" (Luke 18:24-25).

On hearing these things and observing the rich young ruler withdrawing in sadness, the disciples were sorrowful also, asking, "Who then can be saved?" (Luke 18:26) Jesus reminded them that all things are possible to God, implying they should recall the amazing miracles that had occurred because of the faith exhibited by those who had been healed. Peter then observed that the disciples had left all their personal possessions and employments behind in order to follow and to serve the Savior. In response, Jesus described some of the supernal blessings, earthly and spiritual, which await those who sacrifice for the kingdom of God. Said He:

> Verily I say unto you, There is no man that hath left house, or parents, or brethren, or wife, or children, for the kingdom of God's sake,
> Who shall not receive manifold more in the present time, and in the world to come life everlasting. (Luke 18:29-30)

The obvious lesson taught by this incident is that the ultimate blessings of God cannot be obtained as long as one prizes earthly riches and attainments above them. Nothing can supersede the blessings and emoluments of the Almighty. The ultimate lack of this rich young man was that he was unwilling to lay aside, or to forfeit, his riches in order to obtain eternal life. He wanted both, and when it was made to appear that this was impossible, he left in sadness, clinging to the riches he could not do without.

At the same time, it is clear from the incident that the doors to heaven are not barred to a rich man, only if he loves his riches more than eternal life. Yet, the allurements of wealth, ease, and earthly renown are so enticing and pleasurable that it is almost impossible to renounce them in favor of the far off and dimly defined blessing of eternal life.

The wisdom and justice of God do not warrant us in concluding that the only process by which a rich man may attain eternal life is to sell all he has and give the proceeds to the poor and to undertake a life of itinerant proselyting. That was the option offered to the rich young ruler, based upon the Savior's appraisal of his status and character. The wide differences in the character, personality, and proclivities of individuals suggest that this process may not be universal, but may vary with the circumstances of the individual case and the needs of the kingdom at the time.

Parable of the Laborers in the Vineyard

The Savior once likened the kingdom of heaven unto "a man *that is* an householder, which went out early in the morning to hire labourers into his vineyard" (Matthew 20:1). There he hired a group of laborers, agreeing to pay them a penny a day, and sent them into his vineyard. Later, at the third, sixth, and ninth hours, he hired additional laborers for his vineyard without an agreement as to their compensation, saying only "whatsoever is right I will give you" (Matthew 20:4).

At the eleventh hour, the householder went again to the labor pool "and found others standing idle, and saith unto them, Why stand ye here all the day idle?" (Matthew 20:6) They answered that no one had hired them. They were then told to go into the vineyard and that "whatsoever is right, *that* shall ye receive" (Matthew 20:7). At the end of the day the householder instructed the steward to pay the laborers, "beginning from the last unto the first" (Matthew 20:8). When the laborers who had agreed to work for a penny saw that the other laborers received the same amount, they murmured saying: "These last have wrought *but* one hour, and thou hast made them equal unto us, which have borne the burden and the heat of the day" (Matthew 20:12). The householder responded, saying:

> Friend, I do thee no wrong: didst thou not agree with me for a penny?
> Take *that* thine *is* and go thy way: I will give unto this last, even as unto thee.
> Is it not lawful for me to do what I will with mine own? (Matthew 20:13-15)

The householder then ended the conversation, saying, "So the last shall be first, and the first last: for many be called, but few chosen" (Matthew 20:16). As to the meaning of the statement "the last shall be first," a modern apostle has provided important insight. Wrote he:

> By implication we may understand that not all the last, though some of them, may be counted among the first. Of the many called or permitted to labor in the vineyard of the Lord, few may so excel as to be chosen for exaltation above their fellows. Even the call and ordination to the Holy Apostleship is no guarantee of eventual exaltation in the celestial kingdom. Iscariot was so called and placed among the first; now, verily he is far below the last in the kingdom of God. (J.E. Talmage, *Jesus the Christ*, p. 482)

It remained for Joseph Smith, the prophet of the Restoration, to define those who are chosen. Wrote he,

> Behold, there are many called, but few are chosen. And why are they not chosen?
> Because their hearts are set so much upon the things of this world, and aspire to the honors of men, that they do not learn this one lesson—

That the rights of the priesthood are inseparably connected with the powers of heaven, and that the powers of heaven cannot be controlled nor handled only upon the principles of righteousness. (D&C 121: 34-36)

Likening the householder to the Lord, the vineyard to the kingdom, and the laborers to workers in the kingdom, this parable has significant meaning and implications. At the outset, the first laborers were under contract to work for a certain period at a fixed compensation. When, at the end of the day, they murmured because those laborers who were hired later received the same compensation, they had no legal or moral basis for complaint. Their murmuring was a direct and insulting criticism of the Lord, implying that He was unjust and partial. Their conduct revealed a gross misunderstanding of their relationship to the Lord and of the appropriate way of raising a question about their compensation. Nevertheless, the Lord, who is just and reasonable, made it plain that He rules in His kingdom and is justified in the manner in which He conducts its operations.

The laborers who were hired in the third, sixth and ninth hours and at the end of the day worked under an arrangement by which the householder alone was to determine their compensation, if any. These laborers obviously knew of his reputation for honesty and were willing to take a chance on earning something, which was preferable to remaining idle.

The laborers hired at the eleventh hour were in a category different from all the others. These had hardly had a chance to perform any work at all when the steward called all the laborers together to pay them. Yet they received the same salary as the others, compensation that, almost in its entirety, came to them because of the merciful grace of the Lord, not for anything they had done. The principle of grace illustrated here lies at the heart of the Savior's atoning sacrifice since this is the essential element of our salvation and exaltation, after all we can do.

Jesus Again Describes the Final Dire Events

On several occasions Jesus described for His disciples the dire events that would accompany His death and resurrection. Because nothing resembling this had occurred in the history of the world, He wanted them to understand and to be prepared when it actually happened. So shortly after relating the parable of the laborers, on His solemn, final journey to Jerusalem, this occurred:

> And Jesus going up to Jerusalem took the twelve disciples apart in the way, and said unto them,
> Behold, we go up to Jerusalem; and the Son of man shall be betrayed unto the chief priests and unto the scribes, and they shall condemn him to death,
> And shall deliver him unto the Gentiles to mock, and to scourge, and to crucify *him*: and the third day he shall arise again. (Matthew 20:17-19)

It is difficult to think of a more precise and succinct description of what the Savior was to experience in Jerusalem than this one. Yet, in Luke's account of the incident, we find this: "and they understood none of these things: and this saying was hid from them, neither knew they the things which were spoken" (Luke 18:34).

It is an easy thing for those of us sitting comfortably hundreds of years after the event reading these things and knowing of the outcome, to wonder why these intelligent men failed to understand what was told them and which had been repeated to them several times. The circumstances merely underscore the depth and the durability of the misconceptions they had about the true nature and purposes of the Messiah, misconceptions that were drilled into their minds from infancy onward that the Messiah would be a mighty military and political figure. They simply could not perceive the reality that the Messiah, instead of being the kind of person they had learned about from infancy, would be a humble, compassionate, non-militaristic person like Jesus of Nazareth.

Preferences Sought for James and John

While Jesus was near Jericho on His last journey toward Jerusalem, Salome, the wife of Zebedee, and her two sons, James and John, came to Him. Salome was the sister of Mary, the Savior's mother. Thus Salome was the Master's aunt and the sons were His first cousins. It may have been this close family relationship which emboldened Salome to make this astonishing request of the Savior; "Grant that these my two sons may sit, the one on thy right hand, and the other on the left, in thy kingdom" (Matthew 20:21). Perhaps startled by this extraordinary request, Jesus said, "Ye know not what ye ask." Then addressing the two sons, He asked whether they were prepared to endure the crushing burdens and responsibilities He faced. When they answered, "We are able" (Matthew 20:22), He said to them:

> Ye shall drink indeed of my cup, and be baptized with the baptism that I am baptized with: but to sit on my right hand, and on my left, is not mine to give, but *it shall be given to them* for whom it is prepared of my Father. (Matthew 20:23)

When the other apostles heard of this incident, "they were moved with indignation against the two brethren" (Mark 20:24).

While bridging the division in the Twelve that the incident had created, Jesus undertook to teach all of them about humility and service to others. Said He:

> Ye know that the princes of the Gentiles exercise dominium over them, and they that are great exercise authority upon them.
> But it shall not be so among you: but whosoever shall be great among you, let him be your minister;
> And whosoever shall be chief among you, let him be your servant. (Matthew 20:25-27)

Then to make the lesson crystal clear to them, Jesus added this by way of illustration: "Even as the Son of man came not to be ministered unto, but to minister, and to give his life a ransom for many" (Matthew 20:28).

Jesus Heals the Blind Near Jericho

Matthew, Mark, and Luke all recorded the Savior's healing of the blind at or near Jericho (Matthew 20:29-34); Mark 10:46-52; Luke 18:35-43). Matthew wrote that there were two blind men whom Jesus healed by touching their eyes. Both Mark and Luke recorded that one blind man was healed by the word of the Savior, who declared the healing had taken place because of the faith of the blind man. Mark gives a name to the blind man, "Bartimaeus, the son of Timaeus" (Mark 10: 46). All the narrators agree that when the blind man learned Jesus was passing by, he began to plead loudly and persistently to be healed. Others among the throng called out for the blind man to desist in his loud pleadings, but to no avail. He continued to call out, perhaps in even a louder voice.

All three narrators agree that once the healing had occurred, the one healed joined in following the Savior along the "bloody path" leading to Bethany. As has been noted already, this highway was given this gory name because of the numerous murders committed along its path by thugs and robbers. For a time a Roman Garrison was established there to protect the travelers.

This episode illustrates again that the gospel narrators relied upon information available to them in writing their narratives. Since Matthew was a member of the Twelve and presumably was an eyewitness of the event, his account may be more credible as to the number of the blind involved. Despite the differences in the number and names of the blind, the three accounts are in complete accord as to the main thrust of the story, that is, one who was blind was made to see because of the intervention and the holy, healing power and influence of the Lord Jesus Christ and because of the faith of the one healed.

Zacchaeus the Publican

The Holy Scriptures, by their very nature and reverential thrust, are almost wholly devoid of any comedic sense or quality. This is to be expected of a literary work dealing with weighty and eternal principles like obedience and sin, repentance, baptism, confirmation, justification, and sanctification. There is nothing amusing or laughable about any of these supernal subjects. But the story of Zacchaeus, the publican, brings us very close to the brink of playful humor.

Zacchaeus was not only a publican, but he was the chief publican of a class that, though much maligned by the Jews, was a class noted for its power and influence in the community. Moreover, Zacchaeus was very rich and, by the way, he was very short (Luke 19:2-3). And so, on the day Jesus passed through Jericho amidst the usual clamorous throng that accompanied Him, Zacchaeus wanted to get a good look at this man whose reputation and renown resounded throughout Palestine. It is easy then to envision this wealthy, short, and notable man running alongside the jostling crowd trying to get a good look at the Savior. But there were too many tall and aggressive people in front of him to allow this to happen. So, apparently knowing the route the Savior would follow, Zacchaeus ran ahead and climbed up a sycamore tree, so when He came in sight, Zacchaeus had a perfect view of the Savior. He was not there to call attention to himself or to create a scene; he just wanted to look at Jesus. When the Master came near the sycamore tree, He looked up, and, seeing the little man perched there, He said: "Zacchaeus, make haste, and come down; for to day I must abide at thy house" (Luke 19:5). Imagine the excitement of Zacchaeus as he scrambled down the sycamore tree and led the Savior to his home. There, sitting across the table from the Savior of the world, he could satisfy his yearning merely to look into His holy face.

During the course of the meal, Zacchaeus stood and said: "Behold, Lord, the half of my goods I give to the poor; and if I have taken any thing from any man by false accusation, I restore *him* four old" (Luke 19:8). Obviously pleased with this recital and with the spirit and attitude exhibited by His host, Jesus responded saying: "This day is salvation come to this house, forsomuch as he also is a son of Abraham. For the Son of man is come to seek and to save that which was lost" (Luke 19:9-10).

Here the Savior reaffirms that His ministry extends to everyone, regardless of their status in life. That this man was a member of a class bitterly denigrated by the Jews was irrelevant to Him. He looked upon him as a son of Father Abraham and therefore a Son of God, who was entitled to His ministrations.

When the Jews saw Jesus enter the house of Zacchaeus, the publican, "they all murmured, saying, That he was gone to be guest with a man that is a sinner" (Luke 19:7).

This characterization of Zacchaeus is at odds with everything we learn about him in this scripture. He showed humility in the extraordinary effort he made just to get a good look at the Savior. That he was rich and powerful was not a deterrent to his running alongside the throng in an effort to get a clearer view of the great man he obviously admired. Then he cast aside any pretense of official dignity and importance by scrambling up the sycamore tree so as to get a better look at the Savior, thereby presenting a scene that must have seemed ludicrous to the onlookers. Then his recital to the Savior about his liberal and ethical dealings portrayed him to be a man of probity and justice. All this, together with the complimentary remarks made by the Savior, are at variance with the label of "sinner" which the Jews attached to Zacchaeus, merely because he was a publican. In the eternal scheme of things, surely one will not be judged by the labels others attach to him, but by his own conduct.

Parable of the Ten Pounds

As Jesus ended the story about Zacchaeus, "he added and spake a parable, because he was nigh to Jerusalem, and because they thought that the kingdom of God should immediately appear" (Luke 19:11). The parable was about a certain nobleman, likened unto Jesus, who went into a "far country to receive for himself a kingdom, and to return" (Luke 19:12). Before departing, he called in ten of his servants and gave each of them a pound with the instruction they were to manage the money until he returned. Meanwhile, it was reported, "his citizens hated him, and sent a message after him saying, We will not have this *man* to reign over us" (Luke 19:14). When the nobleman had received his kingdom and had returned, he called the ten servants to him and asked for an accounting of the money he had given to them, and "how much every man had gained by trading" (Luke 19:15). The first reported he had gained ten pounds, as to which the nobleman said: "Well, thou good servant: because thou hast been faithful in a very little, have thou authority over ten cities" (Luke 19:17). When the second servant reported he had gained five pounds, he was rewarded with authority over five cities. The third servant reported he had done nothing with the money given him because he knew the nobleman was an austere man who "taketh up that thou layest not down, and reapest that thou did not sow" (Luke 19:21). The upshot of this was that the money given to the third servant was taken from him and given to the first servant. When an objection was raised about this outcome, the nobleman said: "That unto every one which hath shall be given; and from him that hath not, even that he hath shall be taken away from him" (Luke 19:26). Then followed this shocking language: "But those mine enemies, which would not that I should reign over them, bring hither, and slay *them* before me" (Luke 19:27). The following language, contained in a revelation received by the Prophet Joseph Smith on November 1, 1831, has essentially the same meaning and import as the above language quoted by Luke: "And the arm of the Lord shall be revealed; and the day cometh that they who will not hear the voice of the Lord . . . shall be cut off from among the people" (D&C 1:14). That the language in Luke seems harsh and brutal to our ears, while the language in the *Doctrine & Covenants* seems mild, illustrates how time and place and ambience can have a significant impact upon the readers' comprehension. The words in Luke were uttered at a time not long removed from the crucifixion of the Savior by the Jews and from Herod's order to kill the babies at or near Bethlehem. It was a radically different time and place. And the language of that day conveys a far different meaning to us.

Jesus Returns to Bethany

After relating the parable of the ten pounds, Jesus continued along the bloody path toward Bethany. He arrived there six days before the Passover, accompanied by the throng that usually followed Him. Jesus here found Lazarus, whom He had raised from the dead, and his sisters, Martha and Mary. The excitement over the raising of Lazarus had not subsided, and the arrival of Jesus, coupled with the influx of numerous visitors who had come from afar to purify themselves in the temple before the Passover, created an ambience suffused with electric anticipation.

Shortly after the Master's arrival in Bethany, "they made him a supper; and Martha served: but Lazarus was one of them that sat at the table with him" (John 12:2). Then as the meal progressed, Mary quietly took "a pound of ointment of spikenard, very costly, and anointed the feet of Jesus, and wiped His feet with her hair: and the house was filled with the odour of the ointment" (John 12:3). Judas Iscariot, who managed the funds for the Twelve, deplored what Mary had done, and said the ointment should have been sold for three hundred pence and the proceeds given to the poor. Later, in commenting on his criticism of Mary, John wrote of Judas Iscariot: "This he said, not that he cared for the poor; but because he was a thief, and had the bag" (John 12:6), meaning the fund he kept for the members of the Twelve. It is assumed this criticism of Judas Iscariot was made after his betrayal of the Savior. Of the conversation about what Mary had done in anointing His feet, Jesus said: "Let her alone: against the day of my burying hath she kept this. For the poor always ye have with you; but me ye have not always" (John 12:7-8).

CHAPTER TWENTY-SIX

Prelude to the Final Events

Jesus Enters Jerusalem on a Colt

The streets of Jerusalem were crowded with people who had come to celebrate the Passover. When word spread that Jesus was on His way to the city, they "Took branches of palm trees, and went forth to meet him, and cried, Hosanna: Blessed *is* the king of Israel that cometh in the name of the Lord" (John 12:13). Meanwhile, "Jesus, when he had found a young ass, sat thereon; as it is written, Fear not, daughter of Sion: behold, thy King cometh, sitting on an ass's colt" (John 12:14-15).

Here again we see the tendency of the gospel narrators to connect events in the Master's life with ancient prophetic utterances.

The spontaneous reaction of the people was alarming to the Jewish leaders. It was a repetition of what had happened earlier when news of the raising of Lazarus had spread with electric impact throughout the community. The decree of death they had pronounced upon Jesus at the time, which had prompted His departure to Ephraim, was still in effect; and the recent events had increased the danger to their status and had added significant impetus to their resolve to do away with Him. Jesus was well aware of their intentions and of the ultimate consequences to Him. However, this did not deter Him from moving forward toward the dire events that faced Him in Jerusalem. There would be no detour as had occurred following the raising of Lazarus when Jesus was impressed to go to Ephraim.

Cursing of the Barren Fig Tree

For several days, Jesus traveled from Bethany to Jerusalem and back to Bethany on the same day. It is assumed that He used the home of Lazarus, Martha, and Mary as His headquarters in Bethany. The distance between the two cities was only about two miles. The route of His daily walks would have taken Him through the Mount of Olives and through or near the town Bethphage, which literally means the house of figs. It was here the disciples found the donkey on which the Savior rode as He entered Jerusalem. One day as He walked through Bethphage, Jesus was hungry and approached a fig tree to obtain some figs. Finding the tree was barren of fruit, He said: "Let no fruit grow on thee henceforward for ever. And presently the fig tree withered away" (Matthew 21:19). When the disciples expressed amazement at this phenomenon, Jesus uttered one of His most striking statements about the power of faith. Said He:

> Verily I say unto you, If ye have faith, and doubt not, ye shall not only do this *which is done* to the fig tree, but also if ye shall say unto this mountain, Be thou removed, and be thou cast into the sea; it shall be done. (Matthew 21:21)

Then followed this profound statement about prayer and belief: "And all things, whatsoever ye shall ask in prayer, believing, ye shall receive" (Matthew 21:22).

At the time the Savior uttered these words, He knew His days on earth were severely limited. Thus, His actions and statements as to the barren fig tree may be viewed as a final effort on His part to show the disciples the power and influence they could exert upon any and all physical objects through their fervent exercise of faith, prayer and belief.

Jesus Cleanses the Temple

During one of His visits to Jerusalem, Jesus cleansed the temple. Matthew, Mark, and Luke all recorded this significant event (Matthew 21:12-16; Mark 11:15-18; Luke 19:45-48). All three accounts are essentially in accord with this description of what happened, which is contained in Matthew:

> And Jesus went into the temple of God, and cast out all those that sold and bought in the temple, and overthrew the tables of the money changers, and the seats of them that sold doves,
> And said unto them, It is written, My house shall be called the house of prayer; but ye have made it a den of thieves. (Matthew 21:12-13)

Matthew then recorded these additional things, which are not mentioned in Mark and Luke:

> And the blind and the lame came to him in the temple; and he healed them.
> And when the chief priests and scribes saw the wonderful things that he did, and the children crying in the temple, and saying, Hosanna to the Son of David; they were sore displeased. (Matthew 21:14-15)

Hearing and observing these remarkable things, the chief priests and scribes accosted the Savior, saying: "Hearest thou what these say?" in answer to which, Jesus said "Yea; have ye never read, Out of the mouth of babes and sucklings thou hast perfected praise?" (Matthew 21:16) So saying, Jesus left the temple and returned to Bethany.

Without doubt, this incident seriously impacted the anxieties of the Jewish leaders. The edict of death they had ordered against Jesus had in no way deterred Him in His evangelical activities. And these continued to increase the number and the fervor of His followers. Now His cleansing of the temple was a direct challenge to their authority, as it was a threat to the revenues some of them doubtless had realized from the trafficking that had gone on there. But they had to move very carefully in their efforts to do away with Jesus because of His growing popularity. And so the pressures were building toward the final climax.

The Jews Question the Authority of Jesus

On the day Jesus cleansed the temple, the Jewish leaders were caught off guard. There obviously was great upset in the building as Jesus overturned the tables where the moneychangers did their business. Added to this was the furor that would have attended the interruption of the activities of those who sold doves. Amidst these things were the healings the Master performed and the excited cries of Hosanna from the children who were present. While the Jewish leaders were obviously upset by these things, the only action they took was to ask Jesus if He had heard the children adoring Him with cries of Hosanna.

In considering these matters overnight, the leaders apparently decided it was necessary for them to assert their authority over the temple and to challenge Jesus about His conduct. So the day after the cleansing, "the chief priests and the elders of the people came unto him as he was teaching, and said, By what authority doest thou these things? and who gave thee this authority?" (Matthew 21:23) It seems apparent that the object of asking these questions was to elicit from the Savior a statement about God, or the Savior's relationship to God, which, in their view, would be blasphemous, thus adding to their case against Him.

In this scenario, the Jews would soon learn about the futility of crossing forensic swords with a man who was also the Son of God. Instead of answering their questions, Jesus said, "I also will ask you one thing, which if ye tell me, I in likewise will tell you by what authority I do these things. The baptism of John, whence was it? from heaven, or of men?" (Matthew 21:24-25) In pondering the Savior's question, the Jewish leaders concluded that if they were to say the baptism of John was from heaven, He would then ask why they did not believe Him; and if they said it was of men, they feared the reaction of the people, for all regarded John as a prophet. Caught up in a dilemma, the rulers answered, "We cannot tell." Jesus then responded, "Neither tell I you by what authority I do these things" (Matthew 21:27). How neatly the Master closed the mouths of His adversaries with one simple question.

Parable of the Two Sons

This parable was uttered immediately after the Jewish leaders declined to answer the Master's question whether the baptism of John was from heaven or of men. In the parable a certain man had two sons. To the first he said, "Son, go work to day in my vineyard" (Matthew 21:28). At first he flatly refused to do it, "but afterward he repented, and went" (Matthew 21:29). When the father asked the second son to work in his vineyard, "he answered and said, I *go*, sir: and went not" (Matthew 2130). When asked which of the two sons had done the will of the father, "They say unto him, The first" (Matthew 21:31). The Savior then interpreted the parable in these telling words:

> Verily I say unto you, That the publicans and the harlots go into the kingdom of God before you.
> For John came unto you in the way of righteousness, and ye believed him not . . . and ye, when ye had seen *it*, repented not afterward, that ye might believe him. (Matthew 21:31-32)

The parable illustrates the power and the proficiency of repentance in that even the harlots and the hated publicans who obey the principle will enter the kingdom of God ahead of the arrogant and unrepentant. The parable also illustrates that mere words are insufficient to qualify one to enter the kingdom of God.

Parable of the Wicked Husbandmen

At the time Jesus taught the parable of the two sons, He also uttered the parable of the wicked husbandmen. This parable is recorded in Matthew 21:33-46; Mark 12:1-12; and Luke 20:9-18. The following narrative is based upon the account found in Matthew, who apparently was present at the time the parable was uttered.

It should be borne in mind that this parable was given only three days before the crucifixion. It clearly contains a message that severely condemns the chief priests and Pharisees, as indicated by these closing words of the parable:

> And when the chief priests and Pharisees had heard his parables, they perceived that he spake of them.
> But when they sought to lay hands on him, they feared the multitude, because they took him for a prophet. (Matthew 21:45-46)

The main characters of the parable are a householder, likened unto God, and the wicked husbandmen, likened unto the chief priests and Pharisees. The story begins with the householder who "planted a vineyard, and hedged it round about, and digged a winepress in it, and built a tower, and let it out to husbandmen, and went into a far country" (Matthew 21:33). This was not an uncommon legal arrangement whereby a person of means would create a valuable project and turn it over to agents to manage under delegations of authority from the owner and to account later for his stewardship. In the parable, however, when the householder sent servants at harvest time to collect the fruit he was entitled to, "the husbandmen took his servants, and beat one, and killed another, and stoned another" (Matthew 21:35). Other servants sent by the householder for an accounting received similar treatment.

After this pattern of abuse of the householder's servants, "last of all he sent unto them his son, saying, They will reverence my son" (Matthew 21:37). Far from reverencing the son, the wicked husbandmen "said among themselves, This is the heir; come, let us kill him, and let us seize on his inheritance. And they caught him, and cast *him* out of the vineyard, and slew *him*" (Matthew 21:38-39). This outcome prompted a question of the penalty the Lord of the vineyard would impose upon those who had killed his son. Some opined he would "miserably destroy those wicked men" and let out the vineyard to others (Matthew 21:41). This comment brought the following response: "Jesus saith unto them, Did ye never read in the scriptures, The stone which the builders rejected, the same is become the head of the corner: this is the Lord's doing, and it is marvellous in our eyes?" (Matthew 21:42) Then followed the conclusion of the matter:

> Therefore say I unto you, The kingdom of God shall be taken from you, and given to a nation bringing forth the fruit thereof.

And whosoever shall fall on this stone shall be broken: but on whomsoever it shall fall, it will grind him to powder. (Matthew 21:43-44)

Previously in private conversations with His disciples, Jesus had predicted His death at the hands of the Jewish leaders. Here in the temple He announced this fact in public for the first time. In doing so He illustrated the blindness and ignorance of the Jewish leaders who had failed to recognize Him as the cornerstone of the kingdom of God. As already noted, when the Jewish leaders finally realized that the parable of the wicked husbandmen was about them, they sought to lay hands on him, but were wary of doing so because of His popularity among the people.

This parable laid the groundwork for the trials and related events that would follow, culminating in the physical death of the Son of God. But that would prove to be a Pyrrhic victory for His enemies.

Parable of the King's Son

Continuing with the series of parables the Savior uttered in the temple this day, He said, "The kingdom of heaven is like unto a certain king, which made a marriage for his son" (Matthew 22:2). This would have been an affair of great significance, staged in the palace of the sovereign and designed to honor his son who was the heir to the throne. When the costly arrangements had been completed and the invitation list carefully prepared, the king sent "his servants to call them that were bidden to the wedding: and they would not come" (Matthew 22:3). This was an egregious breach of royal etiquette since the invitation, delivered in this manner and for this purpose, was, in essence, a sovereign command. Ordinarily such a flagrant display of impudence and disrespect would have been met with an immediate and dire response from the sovereign. For some unexplained reason, this did not occur, and so, "Again, he sent forth other servants, saying, Tell them which are bidden, Behold, I have prepared my dinner: my oxen and *my* fatlings *are* killed, and all things *are* ready: come unto the marriage"(Matthew 2:4). The response to this second invitation to attend the marriage feast was even more insulting than the first, as the scriptures attest: "But they made light of *it*, and went their way, one to his farms, another to his merchandise: And the remnant took his servants, and entreated *them* spitefully, and slew *them*" (Matthew 22:5-6). For these acts of murder and rebellion, the sovereign in his wrath sent his armies and destroyed the murderers and burnt their city (Matthew 22:7). This may be a prophetic allusion to the sacking and burning of Jerusalem in 70 A.D.

The foregoing is the first part of this parable. Then proceeded the second part, as the sovereign, seeing the wedding feast was ready, said to his servants: "Go ye therefore unto the highways, and as many as ye shall find, bid to the marriage." The servants obeyed and gathered together as many as they found, "both bad and good: and the wedding was furnished with guests" (Matthew 22:9-10).

These guests, found on the highways, symbolize the peoples of the world who occupied the banquet hall after the people of Israel had twice declined the invitation to attend. This incident foreshadowed the final mandate the Savior gave to His disciples, to go unto all the world and preach the gospel.

When the motley assembly of guests was finally seated in the banquet room of the palace, "the king came in to see the guests, [and] he saw there a man which had not on a wedding garment" (Matthew 22:11). The king accosted this man asking why he was not properly attired. The man was "speechless" at this criticism, according to the words of the parable. At first glance the reader might think this man was perfectly justified in his reaction. After all, he had been picked up on the highway, dressed in his traveling clothes, and brought to the palace. To be censured now for not having a wedding garment on would seem to be just cause for being speechless. The disconnect may be explained by an assumption which is not stated in the parable. That assumption is that the king, wishing the marriage banquet to be perfect in every respect, provided wedding garments for all the guests. Granting this assumption, the man presumably had been derelict in some aspect of the process of obtaining and donning the wedding garment. For this dereliction the man suffered dire consequences, being bound hand and foot and cast into outer darkness where "there shall be weeping and gnashing of teeth" (Matthew 22:13). All this, combined, taught the essential message of the parable: "For many are called, but few *are* chosen" (Matthew 22:14). This suggests that after one has received a calling, much is expected of him before he achieves the status of a chosen one.

A Question About Tribute

Following the Savior's utterance of the parable of the king's son, the Pharisees "took counsel how they might entangle him in *his* talk" (Matthew 22:15). Out of this discussion came a plan to entice Him into saying something derogatory about the Romans, who ruled over Palestine. To this end they sent to Him an embassy comprised of some of their associates and certain Herodians. The strategy of this group was first to curry the favor of Jesus through feigned words of commendation and then to pose a question that, hopefully, would elicit a response which would place Him at odds with the Roman rulers. Here are the honeyed words they used to set the stage for the crucial question: "Master, we know that thou art true, and teachest the way of God in truth, neither carest thou for any *man*: for thou regardest not the person of men" (Matthew 22:16).

Then came the question: "Tell us therefore, What thinkest thou? Is it lawful to pay tribute unto Caesar, or not?" (Matthew 22:17) Jesus saw immediately through this juvenile attempt to entrap Him and said: "Why tempt ye me, *ye* hypocrites?" He then asked them to show Him the tribute money, and they brought Him a penny. He then asked, "Whose *is* this image and superscription?" And they answered, "Caesar's." Then He said unto them, "Render therefore unto Caesar the things which are Caesar's; and unto God the things that are God's." When they heard this, "they marvelled, and left him, and went their way" (Matthew 22:20-22). His answer was such that the Romans could not have taken offense since He had merely stated the legal relationship that existed between the Romans and the Jews. The utter failure of the Jews on this occasion to derive any benefit from this issue did not deter them from raising it again when Jesus was brought before Pilate (see Luke 23:2).

A Question About Marriage After the Resurrection

On the same day, certain Sadducees came to Him, recalling the Mosaic practice whereby a man could marry the widow of his deceased brother in order to raise up seed unto him. In view of this practice, they posed the hypothetical question of seven men who in succession married the same woman, but left no seed. Then the woman died. In these circumstances, they posed the question: "in the resurrection whose wife shall she be of the seven? for they all had her" (Matthew 22:28). This was a vain and frivolous question because the Sadducees did not believe in the resurrection. Therefore, the answer to the question, whatever it might be, would be irrelevant to them because of their disbelief. Despite this, the Savior undertook to answer the question, presumably out of a desire to clarify the understanding of those to whom the question had meaning.

In direct answer to the question, Jesus observed that the children of the world marry and are given in marriage, "But they which shall be accounted worthy to obtain that world, and the resurrection from the dead, neither marry, or are given in marriage" (Luke 20:35). From this it is apparent that the marital status of those in the afterlife "must be settled before that time [the resurrection], under the authority of the Holy Priesthood, which holds the power to seal in marriage for both time and eternity" (Talmage, p. 548).

In response to the question posed by the Sadducees, the Savior also undertook to illustrate the fallacy of their belief that there is no resurrection. He observed that even Moses acknowledged the dead are raised, when at the bush (Exodus 3:2-6), "he calleth the Lord the God of Abraham, and the God of Isaac, and the God of Jacob. For he is not a God of the dead, but of the living: for all live unto him" (Luke 20:37-38). This was a direct refutation of the false and untenable belief of the Sadducees that there is no resurrection. Within a matter of hours after this confrontation with the Sadducees, the falsity of their belief would be resoundingly demonstrated, as Jesus emerged from the tomb, alive.

Questions About the Great Commandment

After fielding questions about the tribute and marriage after the resurrection, the Savior was asked, "Master, which *is* the great commandment in the law?" (Matthew 22:36) Matthew attributes the question to a lawyer, while Mark attributes it to a scribe, who is reported as having asked, "Which is the first commandment of all?" (Mark 12:28) This suggests that the titles lawyer and scribe may be used interchangeably to describe one who was knowledgeable about the law and who was often found present tempting the Savior into saying something detrimental. The incident also illustrates again the different sources of information the gospel narrators relied upon in writing their summaries. In this instance, Matthew was present at the time, while Mark would have relied upon secondary sources.

Answering the question as to what was the great commandment in the law, Jesus said:

> Thou shalt love the Lord thy God with all thy heart, and with all thy soul, and with all thy mind.
> This is the first and great commandment.
> And the second *is* like unto it, Thou shalt love thy neighbor as thyself.
> On these two commandments hang all the law and the prophets. (Matthew 22:37-40)

The wording of the Savior's answer to the question as quoted here from Matthew is essentially the same as in Mark, except that Mark's version adds the words "with all thy strength" (Mark 12:30). In addition, Mark's version adds these words as coming from the mouth of the scribe:

> Well, Master, thou hast said the truth: for there is one God; and there is none other but he:
> And to love him with all the heart, and with all the understanding, and with all the soul, and with all the strength, and to love *his* neighbor as himself, is more than all whole burnt offerings and sacrifice. (Mark 12:32-33)

Obviously impressed by these words and by the man's attitude, Jesus said, "Thou art not far from the kingdom of God." Such was the impact of these words, "no man after that durst ask him any *question*" (Mark 12:34).

It must be remembered that Moses gave the first and great commandment to the children of Israel before they occupied the Promised Land (see Deuteronomy 6:5).

Jesus Asks Whose Son Christ Is

After He had answered several questions, the Savior himself became the questioner, asking, "How say they that Christ is David's son?" (Luke 20:41) To demonstrate the fallacy of the belief that Christ is the son of David, the Savior is quoted as saying, "David himself saith in the book of Psalms, The LORD said unto my Lord, Sit thou on my right hand, Till I make thine enemies thy footstool" (Luke 20:42-43). The Master then concluded, "David therefore calleth him Lord, how is he then his son?"(Luke 20:44)

This was a rare instance in which the Savior relied upon scripture to support His contentions. The scripture alluded to obviously was Psalms 110:1: "The LORD said unto my Lord, Sit thou at my right hand, until I make thine enemies thy footstool." It is amazing how, on the spur of the moment, as it were, the Savior could call forth from among the vast collection of Jewish scriptures the exact one that was needed at the time. Yet it is not so amazing in consideration of exactly who He was, the Son of God.

It is unclear why the Savior took this occasion to teach the Jewish leaders that the promised Messiah was not to be the son of David. Nor is it clear whether they grasped this truth when it was taught to them. And what was the impact of this teaching upon the disciples who were present? They still seemed to entertain some doubts about the true identity of Jesus, doubts that would seem to persist even after His resurrection and ascension. As already suggested, the source of these doubts seems apparent. They had been reared in orthodox Jewish homes where the teaching was clear and persistent that the Messiah would mount the throne of His ancestor, King David, and would restore Israel to a place of political and military prominence in the world. It was difficult for them to envision the kind, loving, and caring Jesus filling that preconceived role

Jesus Denounces the Scribes and Pharisees

Almost the entire twenty-third chapter of Matthew is devoted to the Savior's denunciation of the scribes and Pharisees. On the other hand, Mark and Luke each devote only three verses to this significant event (see Mark 12:38-40; Luke 20:45-47). It is noted too that neither Mark nor Luke includes the Pharisees in their condemnatory statements. This omission may be explained by the fact many Pharisees were also scribes, a professional class intimately conversant with Jewish law and procedure as interpreted by the Sanhedrin.

The more extensive treatment given to this incident by Matthew may be explained by the fact that he was present and that the Savior's remarks were addressed "to the multitude, and to his disciples" (Matthew 23:1). The scope and the depth of the Savior's accusations and criticisms of the Jewish leaders are reflective of the mounting pressures being exerted upon Him, which would culminate in His death.

The Savior recognized the lawful authority of those who "sit in Moses' seat" and admonished all that "whatsoever they bid you observe, *that* observe and do." He hastened to add, however, "but do not ye after their works: for they say, and do not" (Matthew 23:2-3). So at the outset it was to be understood that the Jewish leaders were hypocritical and not to be trusted. They said one thing and did another. Moreover, these leaders "bind heavy burdens and grievous to be borne, and lay *them* on men's shoulders; but they *themselves* will not move them with one of their fingers" (Matthew 23:4). All their works were a sham, which they performed "to be seen of men." And they "love the uppermost rooms at feasts, and the chief seats in the synagogue" (Matthew 23:5-6). The disciples were warned not to use the titles rabbi, or father, or master as the Jews were wont to do, "for one is your Master, *even* Christ; and all ye are brethren." And the greatest among the brethren "shall be your servant." Then followed the warning, "whosoever shall exalt himself shall be abased; and he that shall humble himself shall be exalted" (Matthew 23:8,11-12).

The Savior then denounced the scribes and Pharisees as being blind hypocrites, "which strain at a gnat, and swallow a camel" (Matthew 23:24), and likened them unto "whited sepulchres, which indeed appear beautiful outward, but are within full of dead *men's* bones, and of all uncleanness" (Matthew 23:27). After calling them serpents and a generation of vipers, the Savior concluded with this final denunciation:

> Wherefore, behold, I send unto you prophets, and wise men, and scribes: and *some* of them ye shall kill and crucify; and *some* of them shall ye scourge in your synagogues, and persecute *them* from city to city.
>
> That upon you may come all the righteous blood shed upon the earth, from the blood of righteous Abel unto the blood of Zacharias son of Barachias, whom ye slew between the temple and the altar.
>
> Verily I say unto you, All these things shall come upon this generation. (Matthew 23:34-36)

The holy record is silent about the Jewish leaders' reaction to this resounding condemnation, which was even more embarrassing and humiliating to them because it was delivered within the holy precincts of the temple, which was under their jurisdiction. While the record does not reveal the anger and rage these words aroused in the Jewish leaders, can there be any doubt they existed and that they helped to increase the murderous clamor which was building by the hour?

Jesus Laments Over Jerusalem

Immediately following His harsh and unrestrained words of condemnation of the Jewish leaders, the Savior's mood changed to one of reflective contemplation. Said He: "O Jerusalem, Jerusalem, *thou* that killest the prophets, and stonest them which are sent unto thee, how often I would have gathered thy children together, even as a hen gathereth her chickens under *her* wings, and ye would not"(Matthew 23:37). It is easy to read into this plaintive cry of what might have been, a regretful love for these His Jewish brethren who had strayed from the righteous ways of their common ancestors. But no amount of reflective reminiscence could alter the grim reality of what these wayward brethren had become through their prideful lives of greed, dishonesty, and vengeful murders. Of this the Savior lamented, "Behold, your house is left unto you desolate" (Matthew 23:38).

Notwithstanding this sense of desolation, the Savior foresaw a better time, expressed in these words: "For I say unto you, Ye shall not see me henceforth, till ye shall say, Blessed *is* he that cometh in the name of the Lord" (Matthew 23:39). These words were uttered not long before the day of Pentecost, when Jerusalem would witness a scene of unparalleled spiritual power, which occurred at the threshold of the apostles' ministry and was performed at the direction of and in the name of the Lord Jesus Christ.

The Widow's Mite

As Jesus sat near the treasury one day, He observed those who cast in their offerings, among whom were "many that were rich [who] cast in much" and a poor widow, who "threw in two mites, which make a farthing" (Mark 12:41-42). Wishing to use the incident to teach an important lesson, He called the attention of His disciples to it, saying, "Verily I say unto you, That this poor widow hath cast more in, than all they which have cast into the treasury" (Mark 12:43). He then explained why this was so: "For all *they* did cast in of their abundance; but she of her want did cast in all that she had, *even* all her living" (Mark 12:44).

The disciples, who would soon have the responsibility to direct the affairs of the Church and to judge the worthiness of its members, were thus made to understand that its members were not to be judged merely by the quantity of their offerings but by the quantity relative to their capacity to give. No better illustration of the wisdom and justice of this principle can be found than in the payment of tithing. There the tithe payer's worthiness is assessed, not by how much he has paid, but whether the amount paid represents at least ten percent of his annual increase. Thus all saints, whether rich or poor, occupy the same status and are judged by the same standards before the Lord.

Jesus Teaches Certain Greeks

Among the many who came to Jerusalem this year to celebrate the Passover were certain Greeks. These were converts to Judaism who had adopted the teachings, the customs, and the celebrations of the Jews as their own. Despite their wholehearted conversion to Judaism, these persons felt uncertain about their status, given the Savior's forthright statements that His ministry was only to the House of Israel. So when these Greeks wished to speak with Jesus during the Passover, they were reluctant to approach Him directly, and so asked Philip, whom they knew, to arrange an interview. Philip seemed uncertain about the matter and sought counsel from Andrew, his fellow apostle. Being in accord, the two of them asked Jesus to meet with the Greeks, and He willingly agreed.

The somewhat truncated account of the interview was reported only by John, who began with these words: "And Jesus answered them, saying, The hour is come, that the Son of man should be glorified" (John 12:23). When the Greeks understood that the Savior's glorification presupposed His physical death, they were shocked and surprised that Jesus was to die. By way of explanation, the Savior said: "Verily, verily, I say unto you, Except a corn of wheat fall into the ground and die, it abideth alone: but if it die, it bringeth forth much fruit" (John 12:24). This analogy of planting a seed of wheat to the Savior's death and subsequent resurrection is significant. If the seed is not planted, it remains alive, but alone and unproductive. If however it is planted in the ground, it disappears, or dies, in the process of germination, but in that process produces life abundantly. So it is with the Savior; His death is essential in the process of resurrection and glorification.

The Savior then taught the Greeks another important lesson in these words: "He that loveth life shall lose it; and he that hateth his life in this world shall keep it unto life eternal" (John 12:25). So he who is self-centered, thinking only of himself, lives, but it is a sterile, fruitless life. By way of contrast, he who loses himself, or his life, in service to God and others, reaps eternal life and its manifold blessings.

In the midst of these teachings, the Savior's soul was troubled, perhaps as He thought about His last hours, and He asked reflectively, "what shall I say? Father, save me from this hour." Then, answering His own question, He said, "but for this cause came I unto this hour" (John 12:27).

After the Savior said, "Father, glorify thy name," there came a voice from heaven, saying, "I have both glorified *it*, and will glorify *it* again" (John 12:28). Some who heard the voice said it sounded like thunder, while others said an angel had spoken. The Savior responded, saying: "The voice came not because of me, but for your sakes" (John 12:30). He then uttered these significant words about the final events: "now shall the prince of this world be cast out," an allusion to Lucifer, and "I, if I be lifted up from the earth, will draw all *men* unto me. This he said, signifying what death he should die" (John 12:31-33). When the Greeks were confused, since they understood Christ lived forever: "how sayest thou, The Son of man must be lifted up? who is this Son of man?" (John 12:34) Without attempting to answer this question, Jesus concluded by saying, "While ye have light, believe in the light, that ye may be the children of light" (John 12:36).

This episode may be seen as foreshadowing the expanded teaching mandate given the apostles who, at Christ's ascension, were admonished to preach the gospel to all the world, not merely to the Jews. This would help eradicate distinctions between Jew and Gentile and would underscore the reality that all are alike before God.

Timidity of the Jewish Leaders Who Believed

The teachings and the example of Jesus affected people of every class and caused many to follow Him openly. Yet many "believed on him; but because of the Pharisees they did not confess *him*, lest they should be put out of the synagogue: For they loved the praise of men more than the praise of God" (John 12:42-43). This mindset was exemplified earlier by Nicodemus, a member of the Sanhedrin, who came to Jesus by night lest anyone should see him, thereby jeopardizing his status in the community.

Jesus declared that He came as a light to the world, a beacon of hope to those who sat in darkness. Nor did He come to "judge the world, but to save the world" (John 12:47). While the Savior disclaimed having come into the world to judge mankind, He warned that, "the word that I have spoken, the same shall judge him in the last day" (John 12:48). The Savior then explained with clarity why His word was of such surpassing importance:

> For I have not spoken of myself; but the Father which sent me, he gave me a commandment, what I should say, and what I should speak.
> And I know that his commandment is life everlasting: whatsoever I speak therefore, even as the Father said unto me, so I speak. (John 12:49-50)

Here is revealed again the ruling principle of the Savior's life on earth, that of total and absolute obedience to the will of the Father. It was this quality which prompted His designation as the Savior of mankind in the heavenly councils. It is a quality all the disciples of Christ should seek to emulate.

The Olivet Discourse

Jesus departed from the temple for the last time in midafternoon of the third day of Passion Week. The April sun had bathed the opulent structure in golden hues, creating a dazzling scene, which evoked approving comments from the disciples. In response the Savior said, "See ye not all these things? verily I say unto you, There shall not be left here one stone upon another, that shall not be thrown down" (Matthew 24:2). There were no comments or questions about this shocking prediction as the Savior and His disciples made their way across Kidron Valley and up the Mount of Olives on their way to Bethany. The party paused midway on their climb up the mount, sitting among ancient, gnarled olive trees, with the magnificent temple in full view to the west. "And as He sat upon the Mount of Olives, the disciples came unto Him privately, saying, Tell us, when these things shall be? and what *shall be* the sign of thy coming, and of the end of the world?" (Matthew 24:3) In answer, Jesus first focused on the events that would precede the utter destruction of the temple and the city of Jerusalem by Titus in 70 A.D. The disciples were warned to, "Take heed that no man deceive you, For many shall come in my name, saying, I am Christ; and shall deceive many" (Matthew 24:4-5).

Continuing, the Savior said, "When ye therefore shall see the abomination of desolation spoken of by Daniel the prophet, stand in the holy place, (whoso readeth, let him understand:) (Matthew 24:15). The abomination of desolation "comprized [sic] the forcible cessation of temple rites, and the desecration of Israel's shrine by pagan conquerors" (Talmage, p. 571).

There then followed this litany of the terrible circumstances that would attend the destruction of the temple and Jerusalem:

> Then let them which be in Judea flee unto the mountains:
> Let him which is on the housetop not come down to take any thing out of his house.
> Neither let him which is in the field return back to take his clothes.
> And woe unto them that are with child, and to them that give suck in those days!
> But pray ye that your flight be not in the winter, neither on the sabbath day:

For then shall be great tribulation, such as was not since the beginning of the world to this time, no, nor ever shall be. (Matthew 24:16-21)

The Savior concluded by saying if those days were not shortened, "there should no flesh be saved," but that they would be shortened for the elects sake (Matthew 24:22).

History attests to the enormity and the degradation of the bloody events surrounding the destruction of Jerusalem. Farrar provided this summary of the details of the event recorded by Josephus:

> The men going about in the disguise of women with swords concealed beneath their gay robes; . . . the priests struck by darts from the upper court of the Temple, and falling slain by their own sacrifices; "the blood of all sorts of dead carcasses—priests, strangers, profane—standing in lakes in the holy courts;" the corpses themselves lying in piles and mounds on the very altar slopes; . . . and what had been the Temple of Jerusalem, the beautiful and holy House of God, was a heap of ghastly ruin, . . .
>
> In that awful siege it is believed that there perished 1,100,000 men, besides the 97,000 who were carried captive, and most of whom perished subsequently in the arena or the mine. (Farrar, Chapter LII, pp. 573-74)

All these things attest to the literal fulfillment of the prophecy about the destruction of the temple Jesus uttered as He left the beautiful structure for the last time.

Jesus then turned to the second question asked by the disciples, "What shall be the sign of thy coming, and of the end of the world?" In answering, the disciples were admonished to remain focused and unmoved:

> Then if any man shall say unto you, Lo, here *is* Christ, or there; believe *it* not.
>
> For there shall arise false Christs, and false prophets, and shall shew great signs and wonders; insomuch that, if *it were* possible they shall deceive the very elect. (Matthew 24:23-24)

Continuing with His warning, Jesus said to the disciples: "Wherefore if they shall say unto you, Behold, he is in the desert; go not forth; behold, *he is* in the secret chambers; believe *it* not" (Matthew 24:26).

Then the circumstances of His second coming were made plain: "For as the lightning cometh out of the east, and shineth even unto the west; so also shall the coming of the Son of man be" (Matthew 24:27). Also:

> Immediately after the tribulation of those days shall the sun be darkened, and the moon shall not give her light, and the stars shall fall from heaven, and the powers of the heavens shall be shaken.
>
> And then shall appear the sign of the Son of man in heaven: and then shall all the tribes of the earth mourn, and they shall see the Son of man coming in the clouds of heaven with power and great glory.
>
> And he shall send his angels with a great sound of a trumpet, and they shall gather together his elect from the four winds, from one end of heaven to the other. (Matthew 24:29-31)

The Savior then admonished the disciples to heed the parable of the fig tree. "When his branch is yet tender, and putteth forth leaves, ye know that summer *is* nigh: So likewise ye, when ye shall see all these things, know that it is near, *even* at the doors" (Matthew 24:32-33).

As to the timing of the happening of this event, Jesus said: "Verily I say unto you, this generation shall not pass, till all these things be fulfilled. Heaven and earth shall pass away, but my words shall not pass away" (Matthew 24:34-35).

Obviously the reference here is to the generation in existence at the time the events shall occur, not the generation in existence at the time the Savior uttered the words on the Mount of Olives.

As to the time of the happening of these events, it was made clear, "knoweth no *man*, no, not the angels of heaven, but my Father only" (Matthew 24:36). Despite the secrecy that veils the timing of this event, the Savior gave this hint: "But as the days of Noe [Noah] were, so shall also the coming of the Son of man be" (Matthew 24:37). In the days before the flood, "they were eating and drinking, marrying and giving in marriage, until the day that Noe entered into the ark" (Matthew 24:38). From this it is apparent that the inattention of those living at the time of the flood will be replicated among those alive at the coming of the Son of man. This led to the Savior's caution, "Watch therefore: for ye know not what hour your Lord doth come" (Matthew 24:42). The Savior promised this reward for the servant who waited patiently and expectantly for His return: "Verily I say unto you, That he shall make him ruler over all his goods" (Matthew 24:47).

Parable of the Ten Virgins

Shortly after delivering the Olivet discourse, Jesus likened the kingdom of heaven unto ten virgins, five of whom were wise and five foolish. The five wise virgins had provided oil for their lamps, while the five foolish had none. As the virgins slept at midnight, a cry was made, "Behold, the bridegroom cometh; go ye out to meet him" (Matthew 25:6). As the virgins rose to trim their lamps, "the foolish said unto the wise, Give us of your oil; for our lamps are gone out" (Matthew 25:8). The wise virgins refused to share their oil with the foolish ones for fear they would not have enough for themselves. Instead of sharing, they told them to purchase oil from them that sell. "And while they went to buy, the bridegroom came; and they that were ready went in with him to the marriage: and the door was shut" (Matthew 25:10). Then came the foolish virgins, asking that they be admitted to the marriage. The Lord answered that He did not know them. Then came the disheartening comment to those who are not vigilant and watchful: "Watch therefore, for ye know neither the day nor the hour wherein the Son of man cometh" (Matthew 25:13). The message of this parable provided added emphasis to the one delivered during the Olivet discourse, which admonished constant watchfulness and diligence looking toward the coming of the son of man.

Parable of the Talents

This parable immediately followed the parable of the ten virgins. Here the kingdom of heaven was likened to a wealthy man who, as he planned to travel into a far country, called his servants about him, "and delivered unto them his goods" (Matthew 25:14). To one servant he gave five talents, to another two, and to another one. And then: "to every man according to his several ability; and straightway took his journey" (Matthew 25:15). The servant who received the five talents traded with them and made five other talents; and the servant who received two talents made two others. "But he that had received one went and digged in the earth, and hid his lord's money" (Matthew 25:18). After a long time the lord returned and reckoned with his servants. When the first servant reported he had gained five other talents, the lord congratulated him, saying, "Well done, *thou* good and faithful servant: thou hast been faithful over a few things, I will make thee ruler over many things: enter thou into the joy of thy lord" (Matthew 25:21). When the second servant, who had received two talents, reported that he had gained two more, he received the identical accolade from the lord that the first had received. However, when the servant who had received one talent came for his reckoning, he insulted the lord, saying, "I knew thee that thou art an hard man, reaping where thou hast not sown, and gathering where thou has not strawed" (Matthew 25:24). Following this astonishing tirade, he explained what he had done with the one talent he had received: "And I was afraid, and went and hid thy talent in the earth: lo, *there* thou hast *that is* thine" (Matthew 25:24-25). This impudent comment evoked a forthright condemnation from the Lord:

> *Thou* wicked and slothful servant, thou knewest that I reap where I sowed not, and gather where I have not strawed.
> Thou oughtest therefore to have put my money to the exchangers, and *then* at my coming I should have received mine own with ursury. (Matthew 25:26-27)

The lord then directed that the one talent be taken from the wicked and slothful servant and given to the servant with ten talents. There followed this appraisal of the concepts of increase and abundance: "For unto every one that hath shall be given, and he shall have abundance: but from him that hath not shall be taken away even that which he hath" (Matthew 25:29). Then came the dire edict upon the head of the unprofitable servant: "And cast ye the unprofitable servant into outer darkness: there shall be weeping and gnashing of teeth" (Matthew 25:30).

This parable is a reminder to all that there are consequences, good and bad, to the way in which we respond to the blessings or the commandments of God.

The Final Judgment

The parable of the talents was followed by this pronouncement about the final judgment of the Lord:

> When the Son of man shall come in his glory, and all the holy angels with him, then shall he sit upon his throne of glory:
>
> And before him shall be gathered all nations: and he shall separate them one from another, as a shepherd divideth *his* sheep from the goats. (Matthew 25:31-32)

After the sheep have been set on the right hand and the goats on the left, "Then shall the King say unto them on his right hand, Come, ye blessed of my Father, inherit the kingdom prepared for you from the foundation of the world" (Matthew 25:34). Then followed a recital of the qualities of character expected of those on the Lord's right hand:

> For I was an hungred, and ye gave me meat: I was thirsty, and ye gave me drink; I was a stranger and ye took me in;
>
> Naked, and ye clothed me: I was sick, and ye visited me: I was in prison, and ye came unto me. (Matthew 25:35-36)

When the righteous inquired as to whom they had performed these acts of kindness, the king answered:

"Verily I say unto you, Inasmuch as ye have done *it* unto one of the least of these my brethren, ye have done *it* unto me" (Matthew 25:40).

The Savior, sitting in judgment, then had this to say to those on his left hand: "Depart from me, ye cursed, into everlasting fire, prepared for the devil and his angels" (Matthew

25:41). Then in some detail He explained the reasons for this judgment:

> For I was an hungred, and ye gave me no meat: I was thirsty, and ye gave me no drink:
>
> I was a stranger, and ye took me not in: naked, and ye clothed me not: sick, and in prison, and ye visited me not:
>
> Then shall they also answer him, saying, Lord, when saw we thee an hungred, or athirst, or a stranger, or naked, or sick, or in prison, and did not minister unto thee?
>
> Then shall he answer them, saying, Verily I say unto you, Inasmuch as ye did *it* not to one of the least of these, ye did *it* not to me.
>
> And these shall go away into everlasting punishment: but the righteous into life eternal. (Matthew 25:42-46)

Here is clearly marked the pathway leading to eternal life in the presence of God. It is a pathway of service to God's children, a pathway in which the individual reaches out to ease the burdens of those about him, to give succor to those in need or difficulty, to give encouragement to the sad and lonely, and to lift up the hands that hang down.

CHAPTER TWENTY-SEVEN

The Final Events

The Betrayal Foretold: A Plot to Take Him

Following the two parables, and the announcement of the final judgment, the Savior said to His disciples: "Ye know that after two days is *the feast of* the passover, and the Son of man is betrayed to be crucified" (Matthew 26:2). This signified that the winding up scenes were near at hand. As the drama became more intense, the chief priests, the scribes, and the elders of the people gathered in the palace of Caiaphas, the high priest, where they "consulted that they might take Jesus by subtilty, and kill him" (Matthew 26:4). But they decided it should not be on the feast day lest there be an uproar among the people.

Jesus is Anointed in Bethany

Both Matthew (26:6-13) and Mark (14:3-9) recorded the incident when Jesus dined at the home of Simon the Leper in Bethany. During the meal, an unnamed woman came with an alabaster box of very precious ointment and poured it on the Savior's head as He sat at meat. When the disciples saw this, they were indignant, saying, "To what purpose *is* this waste? For this ointment might have been sold for much, and given to the poor" (Matthew 26:8-9). The Savior remonstrated with the disciples for criticizing the woman because what she had done was a good thing, adding, "For in that she hath poured this ointment on my body, she did *it* for my burial" (Matthew 26:12). The Savior also observed: "For ye have the poor always with you; but me ye have not always" (Matthew 26:11). The Master had this to say about the significance of the event: "Verily I say unto you, Wheresoever this gospel shall be preached in the whole world, *there* shall also this, that this woman hath done, be told for a memorial of her" (Matthew 26:13).

Saint John made record of another dinner served in Bethany in honor of the Savior. The following entry suggests this dinner was held in the home of Lazarus and his sisters, Martha and Mary:

> There they made him a supper; and Martha served: but Lazarus was one of them that sat at the table with him.
> Then took Mary a pound of ointment of spikenard, very costly, and anointed the feet of Jesus, and wiped his feet with her hair: and the house was filled with the odour of the ointment. (John 12:2-3)

It was reported Judas Iscariot said: "Why was not this ointment sold for three hundred pence, and given to the poor? This he said, not that he cared for the poor; but because he was a thief, and had the bag" (John 12:5-6). Of the criticism of Mary's action, Jesus said, "Let her alone: against the day of my burying hath she kept this. For the poor always ye have with you; but me ye have not always" (John 12:7-8). Of the large crowd which had gathered outside the banquet house it was said, "They came not for Jesus' sake only, but that they might see Lazarus" (John 12:9), who had gained much attention because of his raising. This popularity caused the Jews to consider putting Lazarus to death also.

Because of the similarity of the two stories, some have sought, without success, to identify Mary with the sinful woman who anointed the Savior's feet with oil and wiped them with her hair at the house of Simon the Pharisee (see Luke 7).

Judas Arranges the Betrayal

Soon after the supper with Simon the Leper, "Then entered Satan into Judas surnamed Iscariot, being of the number of the twelve. And he went his way, and communed with the chief priests and captains, how he might betray him unto them" (Luke 22:3-4). Given their persistent efforts to kill Jesus, it comes as no surprise that "they were glad, and covenanted to give him money" (Luke 22:5). Matthew reveals the amount as thirty pieces of silver (see Matthew 26:15). From that time, Judas "sought opportunity to betray him unto them in the absence of the multitude" (Luke 22:6).

Nothing better illustrates the shallow, devious character of this man than this despicable transaction. Not only did it pave the way for the Savior's physical death, but it stands as a final, glaring insult, revealing the paltry value he placed on the Master's life. Undoubtedly Jesus saw the fatal character flaw in Judas from the time of his call to the Twelve. We see a hint of this in the Savior's parting words to Judas following the Last Supper. While it is easy and justified to condemn Judas for his perfidy, we cannot help feel genuine regret and pathos for one who was lifted so high and who fell so low.

Arrangements for the Passover Meal

On the day of unleavened bread, the Savior "sent Peter and John, saying, Go and prepare us the passover, that we may eat" (Luke 22:8). When they asked where He wished to partake of the meal, He told them that when they entered the city, they would encounter a man carrying a pitcher of water. They were told to:

> follow him into the house where he entereth in.
> And ye shall say unto the goodman of the house, The Master saith unto thee, Where is the guestchamber, where I shall eat the passover with my disciples?
> And he shall shew you a large upper room furnished: there make ready. (Luke 22:10-12)

The two apostles did as they were directed, found the room, and made ready the Passover.

Matthew's account of the incident, while essentially the same, does not identify the disciples who were sent, nor does it indicate the man they would meet would be carrying a pitcher, referring to him only as "such a man" (see Matthew 26:17-19). Mark's version of the incident does not name the disciples sent and describes the banquet room as "a large upper room, furnished *and* prepared" (see Mark 14:13-15).

This incident illustrates the precise foreknowledge Jesus had of the final events. It also illustrates again the differences in the narration of the same event, explained by differences in the data available to the narrator.

The Passover Meal

As Jesus and the apostles filed into the banquet room, they found a large table in the center of the room with thirteen place settings. At the outset, "there was also a strife among them, which of them should be accounted the greatest" (Luke 22:24). Jesus quieted this display of self-seeking, noting this was an unbecoming characteristic of the gentiles, "But ye *shall* not *be* so:

but he that is the greatest among you, let him be as the younger; and he that is chief, as he that doth serve" (Luke 22:26).

Apparently Peter and John, who had arranged for the room, arrived first and had taken seats facing each other at one end of the long table. As it fell out following the discord over precedence, Jesus was seated to the left of John, the beloved apostle, who was the Savior's first cousin; and to the left of Jesus was Judas Iscariot (see Edersheim, Book 5, Chapter 10, p. 815, for a diagram of the seating arrangement). That Judas ended up at the side of the Savior created a situation of tension and conflict. Judas, who was regarded by some as "more a Pharisee than a Christian," had already made the despicable arrangement with the Jewish leaders to betray the Master. He was a bold and arrogant man and seemed to feel no embarrassment at having maneuvered his way to a seat next to Jesus, who knew with clarity what Judas had done.

Judas was the only Judean among the twelve apostles, the others being fishermen or men connected with the fishing industry near the Sea of Galilee, whose pickled fish were a delicacy known throughout the Roman Empire. It seems clear that Judas always considered himself to be superior to the other apostles, upon whom he looked with condescension. He obviously regarded himself as an urban elite and looked upon the other apostles as being deficient in education and sophistication. Because of his knowledge of finance and commerce, Judas had gravitated to the management of the finances of the Twelve and thus was known as the one who had the bag. The love of money and the influence money created was a principal focus of this man's life, and obviously it outweighed any sense of love or loyalty he had for the Savior.

Jesus Washes the Feet of the Apostles

Jesus arose from the supper table "and laid aside his garments; and took a towel, and girded himself" (John 13:4). He then poured water into a basin and began to wash the feet of the apostles, drying them with the towel. When the Savior approached Peter, the chief apostle asked with dismay, "Lord, dost thou wash my feet?" Answering, Jesus explained that while Peter did not understand the purpose now, he would understand later, to which Peter responded with some vehemence, "Thou shalt never wash my feet," whereupon Jesus said, "if I wash thee not, thou hast no part with me." This evoked a typically exuberant response from this loyal disciple: "Lord, not my feet only, but also *my* hands and *my* head" (John 13:6-9).

Finishing, Jesus said, "Ye are clean, but not all," an obvious reference to Judas Iscariot, "For he knew who should betray him; therefore said he, Ye are not all clean" (John 13:10-11). When the Savior had finished, He removed the towel, replaced the garment He had removed, and resumed His place at the table. He then inquired, "Know ye what I have done to you?" (John 13:12) Answering His own question, Jesus said: "If I then, *your* Lord and Master, have washed your feet; ye also ought to wash one another's feet. For I have given you an example, that ye should do as I have done to you" (John 13:14-15). The premier lesson taught by this incident is that of genuine humility. If the teacher lacks this quality, he teaches in vain.

The Passover Meal: The Sacrament

After all was ready following the washing of feet, Jesus said: "With desire I have desired to eat this Passover with you before I suffer: For I say unto you, I will not any more eat thereof, until it be fulfilled in the kingdom of God" (Luke 22:15-16). He then took the cup and gave thanks and instructed the apostles to divide it among themselves, following which He said, "I will not drink of the fruit of the vine, until the kingdom of God shall come" (Luke 22:18).

He then took bread and brake it and, having given thanks, gave it to the apostles, saying: "This is my body which is given for you: this do in remembrance of me." Likewise the cup after supper, saying, "This cup *is* the new testament of my blood, which is shed for you." (Luke 22:19-20)

Thus was instituted the holy sacrament of the Lord's Last Supper, which has been celebrated in Christian congregations over the centuries. It is a simple yet impressive means of regularly reminding the followers of Jesus of the central theme of His earthly ministry, that He gave His body and His blood as a willing sacrifice for all mankind, thereby atoning for their sins on condition of their repentance and their obedience to all the laws and ordinances of the gospel.

On April 6, 1830, the day on which The Church of Jesus Christ of Latter-day Saints was organized, the Prophet Joseph Smith received a revelation that included the exact wording to be used by Latter-day Saints in partaking of the emblems of the sacrament (see D&C 20:77,79). The participants in a Latter-day Saint sacrament service partake of the emblems in remembrance of the atoning flesh and blood of the Lord Jesus Christ, at the same time covenanting they will take upon them the name of the Son, will always remember him, and will always keep His commandments, to the end that they might always have His spirit to be with them.

Some believers in Christ have twisted the purpose and intent of the sacrament to mean the emblems are, in some miraculous way, converted into the actual flesh and blood of the

Savior. This concept, transubstantiation, has been condemned as an egregious heresy.

The Savior's allusion to His suffering portended the agonizing events that would soon take place.

Jesus Indicates His Betrayer

At one point in the meal, Jesus was troubled in spirit and said: "Verily, verily I say unto you, that one of you shall betray me" (John 13:21). Startled by this unexpected comment, the apostles looked around at those seated at the table, wondering who the guilty one could be. Simon Peter beckoned to John across the table to suggest he ask the Savior "of whom he spake" (John 13:24). John, who was lying on Jesus' breast, asked, "Lord, who is it?" Jesus answered saying: "He it is, to whom I shall give a sop, when I have dipped *it*." When Jesus had dipped the sop, "he gave *it* to Judas Iscariot" (John 13:25-36). Assuming John relayed this information to Peter, both of the apostles knew the identity of the betrayer. After Jesus dipped the sop and gave it to Judas, Satan entered into him. Then Jesus said unto Judas, "That thou doest, do quickly" (John 13:27). No one at the table knew what the Savior had said to Judas. Some speculated He had given instructions about disbursements from the bag. All they knew for sure was that Judas Iscariot had gone alone into the night.

When Judas departed, only Peter and John knew for certain he was the betrayer. Others may have suspected it because of Judas's character and conduct. But all would know it for certain before the night ended.

Because of the rapidity with which the final events of the evening passed, Peter and John likely were unable to reflect upon the enormity of what Judas had done. Imagine betraying the Savior of the world, and for the insignificant sum of thirty pieces of silver! As for Judas, who was inordinately proud of his skill in money matters, did he ever stop to calculate the difference between his betrayal fee and the riches he might have received as a worthy heir of the kingdom? Moreover, did he ever pause to consider that his relatively insignificant betrayal fee added insult to his perfidy by implying the meager value he placed on the Savior's life? Could it be that these realities weighed heavily in his decision to commit suicide?

Jesus Foretells His Death: A New Commandment

After Judas had departed into the night, Jesus told the remaining apostles, "Now is the Son of man glorified, and God is glorified in him" (John 13:31). Then focusing on His imminent departure, He said: "Little children, yet a little while I am with you. Ye shall seek me: and as I said unto the Jews, Whither I go, ye cannot come" (John 13:33). He then uttered a mandate that, if obeyed, would eliminate the self-seeking He had observed among the apostles and would provide a unity among them, which would insure the success and the perpetuation of the Kingdom of God on earth. Said He:

> A new commandment I give unto you, That ye love one another; as I have loved you, that ye also love one another.
> By this shall all *men* know ye are my disciples, if ye have love one to another. (John 13:34-35)

Peter Declares His Loyalty

After the sacrament was instituted among the Twelve, Jesus suddenly turned to Peter and said: "Simon, Simon, behold, Satan hath desired *to have* you, that he may sift *you* as wheat: But I have prayed for thee, that thy faith fail not: and when thou art converted, strengthen thy brethren" (Luke 22:31-32). This startling comment shocked Peter, evoking from him the statement: "Lord, I am ready to go with thee, both into prison, and to death." Instead of receiving commendation for this show of support, Peter received this warning from the Savior: "I tell thee, Peter, the cock shall not crow this day, before that thou shalt thrice deny that thou knowest me" (Luke 22:33-34).

Still looking into the future, Jesus told the apostles that whereas in the past they had gone forth without purse and scrip, in the future they should take both. He also told them to take a sword with them, obviously for defensive, not offensive, purposes. When it was reported they had two swords, He said, "It is enough" (Luke 22:38).

In reflecting upon these instructions and comments later, the apostles doubtless realized the Master was endeavoring to prepare them for the time when He would no longer be with them to give them personal direction. It also foreshadowed a time when they would have to be more self-reliant than they had been in the past. Moreover, it suggested that when Jesus had completed His earthly mission and had gone on, the brunt of priestly ire and conspiracy that had fallen upon Him would then be directed toward them. It was a sobering and stressful thing to contemplate.

As to Peter, he doubtless pondered long and frequently about the Savior's implication that he was not yet converted. What would his conversion entail? And by what means would he strengthen his brethren? Also, what would be the effect upon him of the knowledge that he was to be a principal focus of Satan in his efforts to thwart or destroy the kingdom of God on earth? Peter and his brethren of the Twelve would have to grapple with these and other grave issues in the not too distant future.

Could it be that the key to Peter's conversion lay in the power of the Savior's prayer that his faith would not fail? Peter had witnessed the consequence of a failure of his faith when he commenced to walk on the water toward the Savior and then began to sink after his faith failed. The success of his ministry as the chief apostle upon the Master's departure would depend on the power and the consistency of his faith. That the Savior had prayed explicitly that his faith would not fail doubtless was a great consolation and encouragement to him.

A Discourse About the Comforter

Immediately following the Savior's challenge to Peter, He sat in counsel with the Twelve. He began with the admonition, "Let not your heart be troubled: ye believe in God, believe also in me" (John 14:1). The Savior explained that in His Father's house there were many mansions and that He would go in advance to prepare a place for them. In answer to the question of Thomas as to how the apostles would know the way in which to follow him, He answered: "I am the way, the truth, and the life: no man cometh unto the Father, but by me" (John 14:6). In response to Phillip's request that they be shown the Father, Jesus answered, "he that hath seen me has seen the Father" (John 14:9), thereby signifying the remarkable likeness of the Father and the Son in their appearance and demeanor.

After explaining to the apostles that their love for Him would be measured by their obedience to His teachings, the Savior taught them the means by which they could teach the doctrine of Christ with complete accuracy and confidence, notwithstanding His absence from them. Said He: "But the Comforter, *which is* the Holy Ghost, whom the Father will send in my name, he shall teach you all things, and bring all things to your remembrance, whatsoever I have said unto you" (John 14:26).

Jesus Teaches on the Mount of Olives

The events of the Last Supper were concluded with the singing of a hymn, whereupon, they all walked to the Mount of Olives (Matthew 26:30). When all were comfortably seated, the Master began to teach them.

Allegory of the True Vine

Said He: "I am the true vine, and my Father is the husbandman" (John 15:1). Every branch of the vine which is barren is removed, while "every *branch* that beareth fruit, he purgeth it, that it may bring forth more fruit" (John 15:2). As a branch cannot bear fruit of itself, neither can a person bear fruit of himself "except ye abide in me," and "He that abideth in me, and I in him, the same bringeth forth much fruit: for without me ye can do nothing" (John 15:4-5). There comes to the person who abides in the Savior and in His words this supernal blessing: "ye shall ask what ye will, and it shall be done unto you" (John 15:7). In this the Father is glorified, "that ye bear much fruit; so shall ye be my disciples" (John 15:8).

Jesus Speaks Again of Love

As Jesus completed His discussion of the true vine, He turned to a subject that often claimed His attention. Said He, "As the Father hath loved me, so have I loved you: continue ye in my love" (John 15:9). The Savior defined those who reside within the orbit of His love and the way in which He remains within the orbit of the Father's love: "If ye keep my commandments, ye shall abide in my love; even as I have kept my Father's commandments, and abide in his love" (John 15:10). He said He had taught them this that their joy might be full and that He would be able to realize a fullness of joy in them. He added emphasis to this teaching in these words: "This is my commandment, That ye love one another, as I have loved you" (John 15:12). The Master provided this insight into the magnitude of the love He had for His disciples: "Greater love hath no man than this, that a man lay down his life for his friends" (John 15:13). Jesus also explained how one qualified to be regarded as His friend: "Ye are my friends, if ye do whatsoever I command you" (John 15:14).

The Savior proceeded to differentiate between a friend and a servant. Said He: "Henceforth I call you not servants; for the servant knoweth not what the Lord doeth: but I have called you friends; for all things that I have heard of my Father I have made known unto you" (John 15:15). The Savior reminded the brethren, "Ye have not chosen me, but I have chosen you, and ordained you, that you should go and bring forth fruit, and *that* your fruit should remain: that whatsoever ye shall ask of the Father in my name, he may give it you" (John 15:16).

After admonishing the brethren again to love one another, He said the world hated Him and the Father and would also hate them. The Master clearly explained the reason for this hatred in these words: "If I had not come and spoken unto them, they had not had sin: but now they have no cloak for their sins" (John 15:22). This occurred, the Savior said, "that the word might be fulfilled that is written in their law, They hated me without a cause" (John 15:25). The Savior concluded, saying the Comforter, whom the Father would send to them, would testify of Him and that "ye also shall bear witness, because ye have been with me from the beginning" (John 15:27).

Jesus Again Explains His Death

Speaking of His death and the circumstances which would exist following it, Jesus told His disciples: "They shall put you out of the synagogues: yea, the time cometh, that whosoever killeth you will think that he doeth God service" (John 16:2). This travesty does not sound unfamiliar today, as there is a small group of Satan-inspired zealots among us who indiscriminately kill innocents and babies as the presumed agents of God. Their twisted mentality has convinced them that these horrific acts will be rewarded hereafter with multiple wives. Jesus told the disciples that He had not spoken of these ghoulish things before, "because I was with you" (John 16:4). He told them it was expedient that He now go away, otherwise the Comforter would not come to them.

As to the sorrow His disciples would experience at His departure, He said: "Verily, verily, I say unto you, That ye shall weep and lament, but the world shall rejoice: and ye shall be sorrowful, but your sorrow shall be turned into joy" (John 16:20). He explained this sudden change in emotion by analogy to the mother in travail during childbirth, which suddenly turned to joy when the baby had been born.

The Savior concluded, saying the apostles would soon be scattered, and He would be left alone, although He would not really be alone, "because the Father is with me" (John 16:32).

The Great Prayer

The great prayer was uttered by the Savior on the Mount of Olives following the Last Supper. As He prayed, He "lifted up his eyes to heaven, and said, Father, the hour is come; glorify thy Son, that thy Son also may glorify thee" (John 17:1). The glory of the Savior, "denotes the fulness of the majesty of God, revealed in the world and made known to men" (Bible Dictionary, p. 611). That the glory of the Son would result in the glorification of the Father illustrates the truth that the "work and the glory" of God is to bring to pass the immortality and the eternal life of man. Since Jesus had been given "power over all flesh," He was empowered to "give eternal life to as many as thou hast given him" (John 17:2). Then followed, in the words quoted below, a definition of eternal life, and a confirmation of Christ's glorification on earth:

> And this is life eternal, that they might know thee, the only true God, and Jesus Christ, whom thou has sent.
> I have glorified thee on the earth: I have finished the work which thou gavest me to do.
> And now, O Father, glorify thou me with thine own self with the glory which I had with thee before the world was. (John 17:3-5)

Here we see confirmation of the exalted status that Jesus occupied in the preexistence.

The prayer then focused on the apostles, "which thou gavest me out of the world: thine they were, and thou gavest them me; and they have kept thy word" (John 17:6). These men understood that Jesus "came out from thee, and they have believed that thou didst send me" (John 17:8). The Savior prayed for the apostles: "I pray not for the world, but for them which thou hast given me." The Savior described how He, the Father, and the apostles work in unity of purpose and objective, "for they are thine. And all mine are thine, and thine are mine; and I am glorified in them" (John 17:9-10). The Savior uttered a fervent plea for unity among the apostles: "Holy Father, keep through thine own name those whom thou hast given me, that they may be one, as we *are*" (John 17:11).

Speaking again of the apostles, Jesus said, "none of them is lost but the son of perdition; that the scripture might be fulfilled" (John 17:12). The reference to the lost apostle, or the son of perdition, is, of course, to Judas Iscariot. We can only surmise the feelings of pathos and regret Jesus must have had for this brother who had been among His inner circle and who had shared the challenges and the privations of the work for many months. Such feelings of regret would have been magnified by His knowledge of the dire consequences that inure to those who inherit this condemnation:

> they shall go away into everlasting punishment, which is endless punishment, which is eternal punishment, to reign with the devil and his angels in eternity, where their worm dieth not, and the fire is not quenched, which is their torment—
>
> And the end thereof, neither the place thereof, nor their torment, no man knows;
>
> Neither was it revealed, neither is, neither will be unto man, except to them who are made partakers thereof;
>
> Nevertheless, I, the Lord, show it by vision unto many, but straightway shut it up again;
>
> Wherefore, the end, the width, the height, the depth and the misery thereof, they understand not, neither any man except those who are ordained unto this condemnation. (D&C 76:44-48)

Jesus turned to the status of the apostles in the world and the attitude of the world toward them. Said He: "I have given them thy word; and the world hath hated them, because they are not of the world, even as I am not of the world" (John 17:14). Yet this hatred would not be a deterrent to their remaining in the world but would place them in a special status, that of being in the world but not of the world. Said the Savior, "They are not of the world, even as I am not of the world" (John 17:16).

The Savior then spoke of sanctification. Said He, "I sanctify myself, that they also might be sanctified through the truth" (John 17:19). In referring to sanctification, the Savior speaks of the "process of becoming a saint, holy and spiritually clean and pure, by purging all sin from the soul" (Encyclopedia of Mormonism,

Vol. 3, p. 1259). The Savior made it clear that sanctification was not to be restricted to himself and the apostles. He said:

> Neither pray I for these alone, but for them also which shall believe on me through their word;
> That they all may be one; as thou, Father, *art* in me, and I in thee, that they also may be one in us: that the world might believe thou hast sent me.
> And the glory which thou gavest me I have given them; that they may be one, even as we are one:
> . . . that they may be made perfect in one. (John 17:20-23)

It is easy to see why this is called the great prayer, speaking as it does of both heaven and hell, of love and hatred, and of the unity between God, the Savior, the apostles, and those who hearken to the word of the apostles. Finally, it speaks of glorification, sanctification, perfection, and eternal life, and of the pathway that leads to them. It is a veritable cornucopia of eternal truth embraced in a few concise and inspired sentences.

Jesus Prays in Gethsemane

As Jesus entered the Garden of Gethsemane with the apostles, He said to them: "Sit ye here, while I go and pray yonder" (Matthew 26:36). He then took with Him, "Peter and the two sons of Zebedee, and began to be sorrowful and very heavy" (Matthew 26:37). He then told the three apostles, "My soul is exceedingly sorrowful, even unto death: tarry ye here, and watch with me" (Matthew 26:38). He then went a little further and fell on His face, and prayed, saying, "O my Father, if it be possible, let this cup pass from me: nevertheless, not as I will, but as thou *wilt*" (Matthew 26:39). Returning to the three apostles, He found them asleep, and, speaking to Peter, He said: "What, could ye not watch with me one hour? Watch and pray, that ye enter not into temptation: the spirit indeed *is* willing but the flesh *is* weak" (Matthew 26:40). He then went away the second time and prayed, saying, "O my Father, if this cup may not pass away from me, except I drink it, thy will be done" (Matthew 26:42). Returning to the three apostles, He found them asleep again. He then went away to pray again for the third time, using the same words as before. Returning to the three apostles, He found them still asleep and said to them: "Sleep on now, and take *your* rest: behold, the hour is at hand, and the Son of man is betrayed into the hands of sinners. Rise, let us be going: behold, he is at hand that doth betray me" (Matthew 26:45-46).

The account of the Savior's prayer in Gethsemane found in Mark 14:32-42 is essentially the same as the account in Matthew, related above. John did not record the incident. As appears from the following, Luke's account of the incident is significantly different from the others:

According to Luke, as the Savior gathered with the apostles in the Garden of Gethsemane, "he was withdrawn from them about a stone's cast, and kneeled down, and prayed, Saying, Father, if thou be willing, remove this cup from me. Nevertheless not my will, but thine, be done" (Luke 22:41-42). Then there appeared to Him an angel from heaven, strengthening Him, following which, "being in an agony he prayed more earnestly: and his sweat was as it were great drops of blood falling to the ground" (Luke 22:44). When Jesus arose from His prayer, He came to His disciples and found them sleeping from sorrow, and said unto them, "Why sleep ye? rise and pray, lest ye enter into temptation" (Luke 22:46).

In all the accounts of Jesus praying in Gethsemane, it is clear He would have welcomed a release from performing the sacrifice had it been in accord with the will of the Father. But He did not shrink from it, if to perform it represented the Father's will. In this perceived hesitancy is there evidence of His mother's impact on His physical being? Perhaps. The will to live among humankind, generally speaking, is powerful and persistent. Thus the idea of voluntarily giving up life among Mary and her family members would have been unnatural. So the tendency of Jesus to resist death could have been a natural endowment from His mother.

The events in Gethsemane completed the first vital phase of the Savior's supernal atonement for the sins of all mankind. The second and final phase of this cosmic achievement would take place on the cross at Golgotha.

The human mind cannot grasp fully how the amazing transference occurs, how the sins of the truly repentant and obedient are transferred from the sinner to the Savior. Still, mankind easily perceives and understands the peace and the serenity that accompany a true repentance from personal sin.

Peter Declares His Loyalty

As Jesus spoke to the apostles, He said to them, "All ye shall be offended because of me this night: for it is written, I will smite the shepherd, and the sheep of the flock shall be scattered abroad" (Matthew 26:31). He added that after He had "risen again," He would go before the brethren into Galilee. Peter responded to this, saying, "Though all *men* shall be offended because of thee, *yet* will I never be offended (Matthew 26:33). Jesus then told him that before the cock crowed that night, Peter would deny him three times. Peter answered saying: "Though I should die with thee, yet will I not deny thee. Likewise also said all the disciples" (Matthew 26:35).

Mark's account of this incident (see Mark 14:27-31) is essentially the same, except he said Peter's denial would come before the cock had crowed twice. Also, Mark reported that in responding to Jesus the second time, Peter "spake the more vehemently," again portraying the whole-souled exuberance which seemed to characterize all that this faithful servant did.

This incident illustrates again the precise foreknowledge the Master had of the fateful events that lay ahead. Also, Matthew's wording, "for it is written," reminds us of the apparent scripted nature of the Savior's life.

The Betrayal and Arrest

The Savior had barely completed the solemn prayer in Gethsemane when there came a great multitude, some bearing swords and staves. Said Jesus, "behold, the hour is at hand, and the Son of man is betrayed into the hands of sinners" (Matthew 26:45). Among the raucous throng was Judas, who had concluded his dastardly arrangement with the Jewish leaders. Judas had given his coconspirators a sign that, "Whomsoever I shall kiss, that same is he: hold him fast" (Matthew 26:48). Then in his customary, cavalier way, Judas approached Jesus, saying "Hail, master; and kissed him. And Jesus said unto him, Friend, wherefore art thou come? (Matthew 26:49-50) According to the account of Luke, Jesus also said, "Judas, betrayest thou the Son of man with a kiss?" (Luke 22:48)

Following this dialogue, Jesus was taken into custody, whereupon one of His followers grasped a sword and severed the ear of one of the servants of the high priest.

After He "touched his ear, and healed him" (Luke 22:51), the Savior remonstrated with the one wielding the sword, telling him that he who lived by the sword would die by the sword. He then reminded the people that legions would come to His defense if it were necessary for His safety.

Jesus deplored the theatrical aspect of His arrest, the clamorous, unruly crowd, and the presence of armed personnel. Said He: "Are ye come out as against a thief with swords and staves for to take me? I sat daily with you teaching in the temple, and ye laid no hold on me." Then Matthew interposed "But all this was done, that the scriptures of the prophets might be fulfilled. Then all the disciples forsook him, and fled" (Matthew 26:55-56).

Thus was the Savior left alone to face His accusers, to bear the indignity of the personal assaults made upon him, and to witness the denial of Him by His most intimate friends who but recently had declared their fervent love and loyalty for Him. And at the end of it all was the dreaded cross and the horrific events which would be played out there. All this would test the faith and the endurance of Jesus Christ to the maximum degree.

Jesus Is Taken to Annas

Once Jesus had been taken into custody near the Garden of Gethsemane, He was in the grasp of the Jewish legal system. He was first taken to the home of Annas, a former presiding high priest and the "father in law to Caiaphas, which was the high priest that same year" (John 18:13). No reason is given for taking the Savior to Annas, since he no longer had an official status within the system. However, he was still recognized as a man of distinction by the hierarchy due to his former role as the presiding high priest. That he was the father-in-law of the incumbent presiding high priest added significant heft to his present status. But none of these distinctions could obscure the fact that the Savior's appearance before Annas was a violation of Jewish legal procedure and that he lacked the authority to bind Him as he did.

Before Caiaphas

Leaving the house of Annas, those who had arrested Jesus "led *him* away to Caiaphas the high priest, where the scribes and the elders were assembled" (Matthew 26:57). This was an unusual night session of the Jewish leaders, and the fact that the scribes and the elders were already present, awaiting the arrival of Jesus, suggests the events of the evening had been carefully choreographed. Peter, who with the other apostles had fled when the Savior was arrested, followed the procession "afar off unto the high priest's palace, and went in, and sat with the servants, to see the end" (Matthew 26:58). Luke advises us that the servants "had kindled a fire in the midst of the hall, and were set down together, [and] Peter sat down among them" (Luke 22:55).

The Night Examination

Once the Savior had been brought into the council room, "the chief priests, and elders, and all the council, sought false witness against Jesus, to put him to death" (Matthew 26:59). Through a long process of interrogation, the prosecutors had found nothing until, at the end, two false witnesses came forward saying: "This *fellow* said, I am able to destroy the temple of God, and to build it in three days" (Matthew 26:61). When the high priest requested a response to this charge, Jesus remained silent, whereupon, the high priest said: "I adjure thee by the living God, that thou tell us whether thou be the Christ, the Son of God" (Matthew 26:63). Jesus answered, saying, "Thou hast said: nevertheless I say unto you, Hereafter shall ye see the Son of man sitting on the right hand of power, and coming in the clouds of heaven" (Matthew 26:64). At this, the high priest rent his clothes, saying Jesus had spoken blasphemy and asked of the assembly, "What think ye?" They answered, saying, "He is guilty of death.

Then did they spit in his face, and buffeted him; and others smote *him* with the palm of their hands, Saying, Prophesy unto us, thou Christ, Who is he that smote thee?" (Matthew 26:66-68) This ended the travesty of a trial, held at night, and otherwise in violation of the basic rules of Jewish jurisprudence.

The crude and callous conduct of Christ's enemies cried out for justice. But there was to be no victory or vindication for Him as yet. This would await the commission of other despicable acts against Jesus, this sinless and selfless man, until, at the end, He would writhe in agony, alone on the cross. Then would come His victory and vindication, the victory over Satan, death, and hell, thereby providing a pathway toward forgiveness and redemption for gross sinners like those who now thirsted for His blood.

Peter Denies the Christ

All four gospels contain this story (see Matthew 26:69-75; Mark 14:66-72; Luke 22:55-62; and John 18:15-18, 25-17). All four versions are essentially the same, except John says there was another disciple with Peter (John 18:15) and, according to John, one of those who identified Peter as a disciple of Jesus was the servant of the high priest, whose ear was severed in Gethsemane (John 18:26). This verse of scripture also identifies Peter as the one who smote off the ear of the servant of the high priest.

The scene of Peter's denial was set in the hall of the high priest's palace, where several servants had built a fire for warmth and Peter had joined them. It was there "a damsel came unto him [Peter] saying, "thou also wast with Jesus of Galilee" (Matthew 26:69). Answering, Peter "denied before *them* all, saying, I know not what thou sayest" (Matthew 26:70). Then when Peter left the hall and walked out on to the porch, "another *maid* saw him, and said unto them that were there, This *fellow* was also with Jesus of

Nazareth" (Matthew 26:71). Then Peter denied with an oath, "I do not know the man" (Matthew 26:72). Then others who stood nearby came to Peter, saying, "Surely thou also art *one* of them; for thy speech bewrayeth thee," suggesting the dialect of the Galilean fishermen marked them and set them apart. Annoyed by this accusation, Peter spoke out with vehemence, "Then began he to curse, and to swear, *saying*, I know not the man. And immediately the cock crew" (Matthew 26:74). Then Peter remembered the words Jesus had spoken to him, "Before the cock crow, thou shalt deny me thrice. And he went out, and wept bitterly" (Matthew 26:75). This story demonstrated again the Savior's remarkable foreknowledge of events, while providing an important lesson for Peter, who all too soon would become the Lord's mouthpiece on earth. That process was attended by incidents of dire consequence, typified by the bitter tears he shed on remembering the Savior's prediction about his denial. This story also illustrates the importance of repentance and forgiveness. The bitter tears shed by Peter was the beginning of his repentance for the weakness shown by his denials, a process which led to healing and redemption. The significance of the Savior's forgiveness of Peter was demonstrated by the way He later showed confidence in His wavering disciple.

The Formal Trial and Condemnation

On the day following the irregular night examination, "the elders of the people and the chief priests and the scribes came together, and led him into their council" (Luke 22:66). This was a convocation of the highest ecclesiastical court known to the Jews. Because this tribunal was subordinate to Roman rule, the members were well aware that they lacked the authority to impose a sentence of death upon Jesus, the thing they earnestly sought. Yet they knew if they had any hope of persuading the

Roman rulers to levy a judgment of death, it would be necessary to demonstrate that the Jews sought this result. Thus the tribunal and Jesus were both well aware of what was at stake and the significance of the procedure.

Once the assembly was called to order and Jesus was placed in the dock, the Jewish leaders lost no time coming to the point, asking, "Art thou the Christ? tell us." The Savior's answer was forthright, but inconclusive: "If I tell you, ye will not believe: And if I ask *you*, ye will not answer me, nor let *me* go. Hereafter shall the Son of man sit on the right hand of the power of God" (Luke 22:67-69). Since the answer hardly met their expectations, they followed with this question, "Art thou then the Son of God? And he said unto them, Ye say that I am" (Luke 22:70). Apparently frustrated at their inability to obtain a clear statement from the Savior about His true identity, they said, "What need we any further witness? For we ourselves have heard of his own mouth" (Luke 22:71). What His accusers did not hear from His mouth was that He was the Son of God. This is what they wanted to hear in order to charge Him with blasphemy. Lacking that, they concluded, by inference and supposition, He had said what He did not say. From this it is apparent that the ecclesiastical trial against Jesus was a farce, wholly devoid of legitimacy.

The Savior's calm and self-confident demeanor in this stressful situation is a source of amazement. Here He stood alone in the midst of the most powerful set of men in the nation, men who openly sought His death. Yet He was calm, confident, and well spoken as He faced down His accusers, while frustrating them in their efforts to manipulate His responses. At the end they were left to claim a hollow victory where none existed. Even at Golgotha, where He expired in agony on the cross, there was no victory for them, since His voluntary death was soon swallowed up in the glory of His resurrection.

Judas Iscariot Commits Suicide

Once the Jewish leaders had concluded the ecclesiastical trial of Jesus, they bound Him and "led *him* away, and delivered him to Pontius Pilate the governor" (Matthew 27:2). When Judas Iscariot, who had witnessed the trial, saw Jesus bound and under guard, he was suddenly overwhelmed with oppressive feelings of guilt and remorse. When the enormity of what he had done was brought home to him, he "repented himself, and brought again the thirty pieces of silver to the chief priests and elders" (Matthew 27:3). Telling the Jewish leaders he had sinned grievously in that he had "betrayed the innocent blood," they scoffed at him, saying, "What is *that* to us? see thou *to that*" (Matthew 27:4). This was a terrible and terrifying moment for Judas when he realized he stood alone, condemned, with no one to turn to for support. His co-conspirators had spurned him. The brethren of the Twelve despised and detested him for the dastardly thing he had done. And he could hardly look to God for solace, seeing he had committed the unpardonable sin. It was in this extremity that Judas "cast down the pieces of silver in the temple, and departed, and went and hanged himself" (Matthew 27:5).

Jewish law prohibited the high priest from placing the thirty silver coins in the treasury because they were toxic, "the price of blood" (Matthew 27:6). So they took counsel and decided to use the money to purchase a plot of ugly, forbidding ground, once occupied by a pottery, which became a cemetery in which heathen and other strangers were buried. "Wherefore that field was called, The field of blood, unto this day" (Matthew 27:8). This place was also known as the potter's field, the final resting place for the unwashed and unwanted. Fittingly, Judas Iscariot was buried here.

Jesus Appears Before Pilate

After the proceedings before the high priest, Caiaphas, "the whole multitude of them arose, and led him unto Pilate" (Luke 23:1). Pontius Pilate was the Roman ruler who had jurisdiction over the area around Jerusalem. The hearing before Pilate was held in the Roman Judgment Hall in Jerusalem. According to John's account of this hearing (see John 18:28-38), the Jewish leaders refused to enter the Judgment Hall out of concern that they would thereby become defiled. So in John's account, Pilate is shown as going back and forth between the judgment hall and the Jewish leaders outside.

According to Luke, the proceedings began when the Jews accused Jesus, saying, "We found this *fellow* perverting the nation, and forbidding to give tribute to Caesar, saying that he himself is Christ a king" (Luke 23:2). Turning to Jesus, Pilate asked, "Art thou the King of the Jews? And he answered him and said, Thou sayest *it*" (Luke 23:3). Then Pilate said to the chief priests and to the people, "I find no fault in this man" (Luke 23:4).

Then, becoming "more fierce" in their accusations, the Jewish leaders said, "He stirreth up the people, teaching throughout all Jewry, beginning from Galilee to this place" (Luke 23:5). Hearing the word Galilee and confirming that Jesus was a Galilean, Pilate saw a way out of deciding this difficult matter and ordered that the case be transferred to Herod, who had Roman jurisdiction over Galilee.

Jesus Appears Before Herod

On the order of Pilate, Jesus was taken before Herod, who was in Jerusalem at the time, apparently for the Passover feast. The record is silent as to the place in Jerusalem where the interview took place. At first, Herod was pleased at this opportunity to meet with the Savior, "for he was desirous to see him of a long *season*, because he had heard many things of him; and he hoped to have seen some miracle done by him" (Luke 23:8). In his excitement to at last see this man of such widespread fame, Herod questioned him "in many words." It obviously was a serious disappointment when Jesus "answered him nothing" (Luke 23:9). It was then the chief priests and scribes who were present "stood and vehemently accused him." Then, in apparent retaliation for the silent treatment Jesus had given him, "Herod with his men of war set him at nought, and mocked *him*, and arrayed him in a gorgeous robe, and sent him again to Pilate" (Luke 23:10-11).

An interesting consequence of this episode is that "the same day Pilate and Herod were made friends together: for before they were at enmity between themselves" (Luke 23:12).

The utter contempt Jesus had for this shallow, verbose man is obvious. The idea Jesus would perform a miracle to satisfy the curiosity of this evil man was an affront to the Master's majesty and dignity. And in His treatment of Herod, perhaps Jesus also had in mind Herod's frivolous and deadly action in ordering the beheading of John the Baptist in the Machaerus prison.

Jesus Is Again Brought Before Pilate

Following His appearance before Herod, Jesus was again brought before Pilate in the Roman Judgment Hall. The first issue to be resolved involved the tradition that during the feast a felon be released from custody. At the time there was a notable criminal named Barabbas who was guilty of sedition and murder. "Therefore when they were gathered together, Pilate said unto them, Whom will ye that I release unto you? Barabbas, or Jesus which is called Christ?" (Matthew 27:17) Before asking for comment, Pilate, as he sat on the judgment seat, was approached by his wife, who said, "Have thou nothing to do with that just man [speaking of Jesus]: for I have suffered many things this day in a dream because of him" (Matthew 27:19). Meanwhile the chief priests and elders had "persuaded the multitude that they should ask Barabbas, and destroy Jesus" (Matthew 27:20). Pilate then put the question to them which of the two he should release to them, and they answered Barabbas. When he asked what should be done with Jesus, they all said, "Let him be crucified" (Matthew 27:22). When Pilate asked what Jesus had done to deserve this, "they cried out the more, saying, Let him be crucified" (Matthew 27:23). When Pilate saw nothing could sway the multitude, he took water and washed his hands before them, saying, "I am innocent of the blood of this just person: see you *to it*. Then answered all the people, and said, His blood *be* on us, and on our children" (Matthew 27:24-25).

Barabbas Is Freed: Crucifixion Is Ordered for Jesus

Seeing that the multitude was determined that Jesus be crucified, and recognizing his inability to stop it, Pilate relinquished Barabbas to them, "scourged Jesus," and "delivered *him* to be crucified" (Matthew 27:26).

The scourging was a bloody and brutal affair. Several of Pilate's powerful soldiers, whips in hand, delivered a severe beating to the defenseless Savior, raising great red welts on His body and drawing blood, which created a most pitiful and gory sight. When the whippers had completed their bloody work, they "took Jesus into the common hall, and gathered unto him the whole band of *soldiers*" (Matthew 27:27).

Jesus Is Mocked and Humiliated

Amidst the soldiers, Jesus was subjected to a litany of insults and gross ribaldry. They first "stripped him, and put on him a scarlet robe" (Matthew 27:28). Then when they had plaited a crown of thorns,

> they put *it* upon his head, and a reed in his right hand: and they bowed the knee before him, and mocked him, saying, Hail, King of the Jews!
>
> And they spit upon him, and took the reed, and smote him on the head.
>
> And after that they had mocked him, they took the robe off from him, and put his own raiment on him, and led him away to crucify *him*. (Matthew 27:28-32)

The Procession to Golgotha

Following the despicable actions of the soldiers in the common hall, then began the mournful march to Golgotha, the place of a skull, where the crucifixion was to take place. "And as they came out, they found a man of Cyrene, Simon by name: him they compelled to bear his cross" (Matthew 27:32). Along the route of the procession to Golgotha were seen hordes of jostling, clamoring people who were caught up in the morbid excitement of a crucifixion. Fantasy has invested this march with an imaginary structure of stops along the way with the Savior occasionally shown as struggling under the weight of the cross.

Arriving at the site of the crucifixion, Jesus was lifted up on His cross between the crosses of two men who were crucified at the same time. When His cross was in place, "They gave him vinegar to drink mingled with gall: and when he had tasted *thereof*, he would not drink" (Matthew 27:34). The soldiers then divided His garments by lot, which, according to Matthew, was done, "that it might be fulfilled which was spoken by the prophet, They parted my garments among them, and upon my vesture did they cast lots" (Matthew 27:35). Above the Savior's head on the cross was written the words, THIS IS JESUS THE KING OF THE JEWS" (Matthew 27:37).

Jesus Is Disrespected on the Cross

As Jesus hung on the cross between two thieves, "they that passed by reviled him, wagging their heads, And saying, Thou that destroyest the temple, and buildest *it* in three days, save thyself. If thou be the Son of God, come down from the cross" (Matthew 27:39). Then followed mocking comments from the chief priests, the scribes, and the elders:

> He saved others; himself he cannot save. If he be the King of Israel, let him now come down from the cross, and we will believe him.
> He trusted in God; let him deliver him now, if he will have him: for he said, I am the Son of God. (Matthew 27:42-43)

Then the two thieves joined in the condemnation and "cast the same in his teeth" (Matthew 27:44).

From the sixth hour to the ninth hour, there was darkness over all the land, "And about the ninth hour Jesus cried with a loud voice, saying, Eli, Eli, lama sabachthani? that is to say, My God, my God, why hast thou forsaken me?" (Matthew 27:46) Some standing near the cross said Jesus had called for Elias. At the same time another "ran, and took a sponge, and filled *it* with vinegar, and put *it* on a reed, and gave him to drink. The rest said, Let be, let us see whether Elias will come to save him" (Matthew 27:48-49).

The Final Culminating Events

The final culminating events occurred soon after, when Jesus "cried again with a loud voice, [and] yielded up the ghost" (Matthew 27:50). Thus was accomplished the essential act which completed Christ's great atonement for the sins of all mankind. Jesus knew the terrible moment would come when the Almighty would withdraw His presence from Him, leaving Him entirely alone. While He knew what would happen, when it did happen He was anxious and terrified, asking why the Father had forsaken Him. By that final act, He had achieved total victory over death, hell, and Satan, and had fully qualified as the Savior and redeemer of all mankind.

Following these supernal acts, "the veil of the temple was rent in twain from the top to the bottom; and the earth did quake, and the rocks rent" (Matthew 27:51). Then after His resurrection, "the graves were opened; and many bodies of the saints which slept arose, And came out of the graves after his resurrection, and went into the holy city, and appeared unto many" (Matthew 27:52). Observing these astonishing events, the centurion said, "Truly this was the Son of God" (Matthew 27:54). [NOTE: The timing of these events is unclear, since Jesus was the first to be resurrected.]

That evening a wealthy man, Joseph of Arimathaea, a disciple of the Savior, received permission from Pilate to take charge of the body and prepare it for burial. "He wrapped it in a clean linen cloth, And laid it in his own new tomb, which he had hewn out in the rock: and he rolled a great stone to the door of the sepulchre, and departed" (Matthew 27:57-60).

The day following the day of preparation, the chief priests and Pharisees went to Pilate requesting that a watch be set on the tomb of the Savior. They remembered Him saying that after three days He would rise again, and they wished to prevent His disciples from fabricating that He had risen. Pilate told them, "Ye have a watch . . . make *it* as sure as ye can. So they went, and made the sepulchre sure, sealing the stone, and setting a watch" (Matthew 27:65-66).

CHAPTER TWENTY-EIGHT

Events Following the Resurrection

An Angel Opens the Tomb

Near dawn of the first day of the week "came Mary Magdalene and the other Mary to see the sepulchre" (Matthew 28:1). They were hardly prepared for the dramatic events that ensued. "And, behold, there was a great earthquake: for the angel of the Lord descended from heaven, and came and rolled back the stone from the door and sat upon it" (Matthew 28:2). Then followed a description of the heavenly being: "His countenance was like lightning, and his raiment white as snow" (Matthew 28:3). The guards who had been set to watch the tomb were so shocked by this sudden, brilliant display they were "as dead *men*." Meanwhile, the women arrived and were terrified. Addressing them, the angel said:

> Fear not ye: for I know that ye seek Jesus, which was crucified.
> He is not here: for he is risen, as he said. Come, see the place where the Lord lay.
> And go quickly, and tell his disciples that he is risen from the dead; and, behold, he goeth before you into Galilee; there shall ye see him: lo, I have told you."
> (Matthew 28:5-7)

Then the women departed quickly from the sepulchre "with fear and great joy; and did run to bring his disciples word" (Matthew 28:8).

Mary Tells Peter and John

In great excitement and haste, Mary Magdalene ran to the disciples to report what she had seen and heard at the sepulchre. To Peter, who was with John, she said: "They have taken away the Lord out of the sepulchre, and we know not where they have laid him" (John 20:2). Alarmed by this distressing information, the two apostles began to run at full speed toward the sepulchre. John outran Peter and, arriving first and "stooping down, *and looking in*, saw the linen clothes lying; yet went he not in" (John 20:5). On the other hand, when Peter arrived later, he, in his customary forthright way, "went into the sepulchre, and seeth the linen clothes lie, And the napkin, that was about his head, not lying with the linen clothes, but wrapped together in a place by itself" (John 20:6-7). The detail with which John described the scene lends credence to its reality.

Having inspected the burial site, the two apostles returned home. It is obvious from the following statement of John that the reality of the Savior's resurrection had not yet been understood by the two apostles: "For as yet they knew not the scripture, that he must rise again from the dead" (John 20:9). Not only were the apostles unaware of this scripture, but they had overlooked, or had forgotten, the several instances when the Savior had told them explicitly about His death and resurrection.

Jesus Appears to Mary Magdalene

After Peter and John left the sepulchre, Mary Magdalene was standing alone outside the tomb weeping, "and as she wept, she stooped down, *and looked* into the sepulchre, And seeth two angels in white sitting, the one at the head, and the other at the feet, where the body of Jesus had lain" (John 20:11-12). When the angels asked Mary why she wept, she answered, "Because they have taken away my Lord, and I know not where they have laid him" (John 20:13). Turning back, she saw Jesus but did not know who it was. Whereupon, He spoke to her saying, "Woman, why weepest thou? whom seekest thou? She, supposing him to be the gardener, said unto him, Sir, if thou have borne him hence, tell me where thou hast laid him, and I will take him away"(John 20:15). Jesus then spoke to her, saying, "Mary," whereupon,

> She turned herself, and saith unto him, Rabboni; which is to say, Master.
> Jesus saith unto her, Touch me not; for I am not yet ascended to my Father: but go to my brethren, and say unto them, I ascend unto my Father, and your Father; and *to* my God, and your God. (John 20:16-17)

Mary Magdalene Reports to the Apostles

Obedient to the instructions of the Savior given to her at the sepulchre, Mary Magdalene went immediately to the apostles, explaining the circumstances of the Savior's appearance to her and that He was to ascend to the Father (see John 20:18).

Other Women Come to the Tomb

Luke has provided a different account of the visit of Mary Magdalene and other women to the tomb. He identifies these other women as "Joanna, and Mary *the mother* of James, and other *women that were* with her" (Luke 24:10). [NOTE: There seems to be a discrepancy here, since the mother of James and John elsewhere is known as Salome.] According to Luke, these women came to the tomb very early in the morning of the first day of the week, "bringing the spices which they had prepared, and certain *others* with them" (Luke 24:1). Finding the stone rolled away from the entrance, they entered the sepulchre,

> and found not the body of the Lord Jesus . . . [But] behold, two men stood by them in shining garments:
>
> And as they were afraid, and bowed down *their* faces to the earth, they said unto them, Why seek ye the living among the dead?
>
> He is not here, but is risen: remember when He spake unto you when He was yet in Galilee,
>
> Saying, The Son of man must be delivered into the hands of sinful men, and crucified, and the third day rise again.
>
> And they remembered his words,
>
> And returned from the sepulchre, and told all these things unto the eleven, and to all the rest. (Luke 24:3-8)

The following statement suggests the level of credence the apostles gave to the words of these women: "And their words seemed to them as idle tales, and they believed them not" (Luke 24:11).

The Women See and Worship Jesus

As Mary Magdalene and other women went to tell the disciples that Jesus had risen from the dead,

> behold, Jesus met them, saying, All hail. And they came and held him by the feet, and worshipped him.
>
> Then said Jesus unto them, Be not afraid: go tell my brethren that they go into Galilee and there shall they see me. (Matthew 28:9-10)

Thus these women bore two important messages for Christ's disciples: first, that He was risen from the dead, and second, that they had seen Him personally and had worshipped at His feet.

One thing that stands out among these heavenly visitations was the usual admonition that those visited not be afraid. The heavens had been closed for so many hundreds of years that it was a great oddity for heavenly beings to appear to men and women on the earth. The novelty of the experiences enjoyed by Zacharias and Mary when Gabriel appeared to them had not worn thin, so that an appearance from the unseen world was something new and exciting, even fearsome, thus prompting the frequently repeated admonition not to be afraid.

The High Priests Told of the Resurrection

Some of the soldiers who were assigned to guard the tomb went into the city following the events at the tomb. The high priests were alarmed at the news, for it corresponded with the pronouncements of the Savior that His body would be resurrected after three days in the tomb. After hearing the report of the soldiers and counseling together, the high priests "gave large money unto the soldiers, Saying, Say ye, His disciples came by night, and stole him *away* while we slept" (Matthew 28:12-13). Presumably the soldiers balked at this scenario because death was the Roman penalty for sleeping while on watch. For the high priests, the solution to this problem was simple: "And if this come to the governor's ears, we will persuade him, and secure you" (Matthew 28:14). So the soldiers "took the money, and did as they were taught: and this saying is commonly reported among the Jews until this day" (Matthew 28:15).

On the Road to Emmaus

On the first day of the week, two disciples were walking together toward Emmaus, talking about reports of the Savior's resurrection. As they walked, "Jesus himself drew near, and went with them. But their eyes were holden that they should not know him" (Luke 24:15-16).

When Jesus asked about their sad appearance and earnest conversation, one of them named Cleopas, after expressing surprise that the man was unaware of the amazing story, briefed Him about the background of the Savior and His death and the story of certain women who had "seen a vision of angels, which said that He was alive. And certain of them which were with us went to the sepulchre, and found *it* so as the women had said: but him they saw not" (Luke 24:23-24). After censuring unbelievers, Jesus, "beginning at Moses and all the prophets, . . . expounded unto them in all the scriptures the things concerning himself" (Luke 24:27). At journey's end, as Jesus sat at meat with them, He broke and blessed bread and gave it to them, and as He did so, "their eyes were opened, and they knew him; and He vanished out of their sight" (Luke 24:31).

After exclaiming to each other about the miraculous thing which had occurred to them, the pair returned to Jerusalem and, finding the eleven and others assembled together, declared to them "what things *were done* in the way, and how he was known to them in breaking of bread" (Luke 24:35).

The Risen Lord Appears Unto Peter

It is clear from the scriptural record that the Savior appeared to Simon Peter following His resurrection.

However, the documentation supporting this event is sparse. It consists of this: When the pair returned from Emmaus and met with the eleven and others, they were told, "The Lord is risen indeed, and hath appeared to Simon" (Luke 24:34). Then in his first epistle to the Corinthian saints, in enumerating the different instances when the Lord appeared to different men and women upon the earth, Paul wrote this: "And that he was seen of Cephas, then of the twelve" (1 Corinthians 15:5). It was appropriate and needful that the Master appear personally to Peter, given the fact that very soon he would have the principal responsibility to guide the fledgling church in its earthly ministrations.

Jesus Appears to the Apostles

When the pair returned from Emmaus and reported to the apostles:

> Jesus himself stood in the midst of them, and saith unto them, Peace *be* unto you.
> But they were terrified and affrighted, and supposed that they had seen a spirit.
> And he said unto them, Why are ye troubled? and why do thoughts arise in your hearts?
> Behold my hands and my feet, that it is I myself: handle me, and see; for a spirit hath not flesh and bones, as ye see me have. (Luke 24:36-39)

Then, as if to demonstrate the reality of His resurrected body, He asked, "Have ye here any meat?" (Luke 24:41) And they provided Him with a piece of boned fish and a honeycomb, which He ate before them.

This incident presents significant information about a resurrected body, while posing deep questions about its composition and functioning. Apparently, the Savior's resurrected body had substance, for the disciples handled him. Yet, the walls of the enclosed room where the disciples were assembled were not an impediment to His passing through them. And the Savior's act of eating the kind of food mortals eat to sustain life causes wonderment about the nutritional requirements of a resurrected body.

John provided other important details about this remarkable appearance, reporting that the Savior "shewed unto them *his* hands and his side" and told them, as His Father had sent Him, "even so send I you" (John 20:20-21) When He had done and said these things, the Savior "breathed on *them*, and saith unto them, Receive ye the Holy Ghost: Whose soever sins ye remit, they are remitted unto them; *and* whose soever *sins* ye retain, they are retained" (John 20:22-23).

Thomas of the Twelve was not present when Jesus appeared to the apostles. When informed about it, Thomas responded: "Except I shall see in his hands the print of the nails, and put my finger into the print of the nails, and thrust my hand into his side, I will not believe" (John 20:25). Eight days later, as the apostles gathered, Thomas being among them, and the doors being shut, then came Jesus,

> and stood in the midst, and said, Peace *be* unto you.
> Then saith he to Thomas, Reach hither thy finger, and behold my hands; and reach hither thy hand, and thrust it into my side: and be not faithless, but believing. (John 20:26-27)

After Thomas had exclaimed "My Lord and my God," the Savior continued speaking, saying, "Thomas, because thou hast seen me, thou hast believed: blessed *are* they that have not seen, and *yet* have believed" (John 20:28-29).

Jesus Appears at the Sea of Tiberias

Following the events in Jerusalem pertaining to the resurrection of the Savior, the following disciples were gathered at the Sea of Tiberias: Simon Peter, Thomas, Nathaniel, the sons of Zebedee, James and John, and "two other of his disciples" (John 21:2). As these visited at the Sea of Tiberias, and despite the supernal events which had occurred in Jerusalem, including the direction the Savior had given to the disciples to meet Him in Galilee, "Simon Peter saith unto them, I go a fishing. They say unto him, we also go with thee" (John 21:3). They immediately boarded a ship and fished all night, but caught nothing.

The following morning, Jesus, whose identity was unknown to the disciples, appeared on the beach, calling to them, "Children, have ye any meat?" When they answered, no, He said, "Cast the net on the right side of the ship, and ye shall find" (John 21:5-6). After they had complied, the "multitude of fishes" they caught was so great they could not draw in the net.

At this juncture, John recognized Jesus and said to Peter "it is the Lord," whereupon, Peter put on his fisher's coat, for he was naked, "and did cast himself into the sea" (John 21:7). Then "Simon Pater went up, and drew the net to land full of great fishes, an hundred and fifty and three" (John 21:11). Given the quantity and great size of these fishes, John marveled that the net was not broken.

A fire having been laid on the beach, "Jesus then cometh, and taketh bread, and giveth them, and fish likewise" (John 21:13). The disciples knew instinctively it was Jesus who served them, but none of them "durst ask him, Who art thou?" (John 21:12)

Of this gathering, John observed: "This is now the third time that Jesus shewed himself to his disciples, after that he was risen from the dead" (John 21:14). John apparently had in mind this appearance and the two appearances in Jerusalem following the return of the pair from Emmaus. Actually, counting the appearances to Mary Magdalene and Peter and the women and the pair on the road to Emmaus, this was the seventh appearance of Jesus following His resurrection.

The meal having been finished, Jesus turned to Peter asking, "Simon, *son* of Jonas, lovest thou me more than these? He saith unto him, Yea, Lord; thou knowest that I love thee. He saith unto him, Feed my lambs" (John 21:15). This dialogue was repeated two other times with the words "feed my sheep" being substituted for the words "feed my lambs." When this question was put to him the third time, Peter is reported to have been "grieved" by the repetition. This incident could be regarded as a mild reproof of Peter for his focus on fishing at a time when his role as a fisher of men should have been predominate in his thoughts.

Still speaking to Peter, the Savior sketched a brief narrative of his life, signifying that in his youth he would care for his own needs and would walk where he wished, but in his old age others would "gird thee, and carry *thee* whither thou wouldest not." He explained He had related this, "signifying by what death he should glorify God. And when he had spoken this, he saith unto him: Follow me" (John 21:18-19).

It is generally believed that Peter outlived the Savior by about thirty-five years, so that at his death he would have been considered to be an old man, according to the calculations of that day. It is also believed that Peter was a martyr, like the Savior, thus fulfilling the Master's prophetic utterance with exactness.

Seeing John among the group, Peter said, "Lord, what shall this man do?" Jesus answered him, saying, "If I will that he tarry till I come, what *is that* to thee? follow thou me" (John 21:22). This is the origin of the general understanding that John the Beloved, like the three Nephites, would not taste of death according to the customary pattern, but would remain on earth to minister as God's servant until the end.

The Savior's somewhat abrupt answer to Peter's inquiry about the status of John is a good reminder to all, as it was to Peter, that the primary concern of the individual should be about his own mission and status, not that of others.

John concluded his narrative of the Savior's life, saying that if everything Jesus said or did in life were recorded, "I suppose that even the world itself could not contain the books that should be written" (John 21:25).

Jesus Is Seen by More Than Five Hundred

The largest group to see the risen Lord was reported by the Apostle Paul in these words: "After that, he was seen of above five hundred brethren at once; of whom the greater part remain unto this present, but some are fallen asleep" (1 Corinthians 15:6). The precise location of this appearance is not specified. Some scholars have speculated that this occurred at the designated mountain in Galilee where the Savior met with His apostles.

Jesus Appears to Saul of Tarsus

Saul of Tarsus, later called Paul, was a highly intelligent and educated man, who was a student of Gamaliel, a distinguished Jewish scholar. Saul was in the forefront of those who persecuted Jesus and His followers. And Saul "went unto the high priest, And desired of him letters to Damascus to the synagogues, that if he found any of this way, whether they were men or women, he might bring them bound unto Jerusalem" (Acts 9:1-2). As Saul came near to Damascus, "suddenly there shined round about him a light from heaven: And he fell to the earth, and heard a voice saying unto him, Saul, Saul, why persecutest thou me?" (Acts 9:3-4) Astonished, Saul asked, "Who art thou, Lord? And the Lord said, I am Jesus whom thou persecutest: *it is* hard for thee to kick against the pricks" (Acts 9:5). Trembling and astonished, Saul said, "Lord what will thou have me to do?"(Acts 9:6)

He was told to go into the city, where he would be told what to do. When Saul arose from the earth, he could not see and was led by the hand into Damascus. There he remained for three days, blind and without food. Then the Lord appeared in a dream to a disciple named Ananias, telling him to go to the house of Judas, on the street called Straight, and to inquire about a man named Saul of Tarsus, who had seen a vision in which a man named Ananias would come to give him sight (see Acts 9:11-12). Ananias counseled the Lord about the evil things Saul was reported to have done, whereupon the Lord said Saul was a chosen vessel to bear His name among the gentiles, among kings, and among the house of Israel. Ananias then blessed Saul, who received his sight and bore testimony of the divinity of Christ in the synagogues at Damascus.

James Sees the Savior

This appearance is attested to only by this scripture: "After that, he was seen of James" (1 Corinthians 15:7). James and John were brothers, the sons of Zebedee. It will be remembered that their mother asked Jesus that her two sons be permitted to stand at his side in the kingdom to come. He declined, saying only God could decide that. Of the two brothers, John, by far, was the most prolific writer of the pair, being the author of a narrative of the Savior, of the book of Revelation, and of three letters in the New Testament, while James wrote only one general letter, which also is found in the New Testament. In appraising the impact of the writings of these brothers, as contrasted with the volume of their writings, it is well to bear in mind the impact of James 1:5-7, which impelled Joseph Smith to pray in the Sacred Grove, and of which he was heard to say that no other scripture had come to the heart of man with greater power than this one did to him (see HC 1:4).

So this scripture, uttered by James, stands at the very threshold of the restoration of the gospel of Jesus Christ in the latter days.

Jesus Appears to the Eleven Apostles in Galilee

Jesus appeared before the eleven apostles in Galilee on a "mountain where Jesus had appointed them." And when they saw him, they worshipped him: but some doubted" (Matthew 28:16-17). The Savior then spoke to them saying:

> All power is given unto me in heaven and in earth.
> Go ye therefore, and teach all nations, baptizing them in the name of the Father, and of the Son, and of the Holy Ghost:
> Teaching them to observe all things whatsoever I have commanded you: and, lo, I am with you alway, *even* unto the end of the world. Amen. (Matthew 28:18-20)

This mandate broadened the scope of the apostles' responsibility to include teaching "all nations." The subject of their teaching was to be all that Jesus had commanded them. They were consoled with the knowledge the Savior would be with them until the end of the world, an undoubted reference to the influence of the Holy Ghost. They had already been promised that the Holy Ghost would bring to their remembrance all things He had taught them. These supernal promises and assurances undoubtedly imbued the apostles with enormous self-confidence as they faced the future.

It is surprising that there yet remained doubt among some of the apostles at this late stage of the Savior's earthly ministry. Because of the way the doubts Thomas had about the actuality of the resurrection had been resolved, with no later questions being raised about that issue, it is unlikely there was any remaining doubt among them about it. That being said, and recognizing the loyalty and obedience these remaining apostles had always shown toward the Savior, the doubt mentioned here presumably did not rise to the level of disbelief or rejection, but was more akin to questions and uncertainties about the future, which seem to afflict most of mankind.

It is significant that the Savior told the apostles He had been given all power both on earth and in heaven, which would have given the apostles more confidence in the permanence and the eternal significance of their message.

The Ascension

Following the significant events in Galilee, the apostles returned to Jerusalem, where they were found mingling with and being taught by the Savior. He reminded them that, "repentance and remission of sins should be preached in his name among all nations, beginning at Jerusalem" (Luke 24:47). Then one day He led them out of Jerusalem as far as Bethany, where occurred the final, amazing incident of His storied, earthly life. There, as He blessed them, "he lifted up his hands" and as He did so, "he was parted from them, and carried up into heaven" (Luke 24:51). At this the disciples worshiped Him and returned to Jerusalem with great joy.

This incident tends to remind the Latter-day Saints of the incident when the Angel Moroni appeared to the Prophet Joseph Smith in his bedroom near Palmyra, New York. There Moroni appeared to him, standing suspended in the air near his bed while he delivered his message. That being accomplished, he ascended through the air in much the same way that Jesus was seen ascending into heaven as He departed from His disciples. This was an amazing thing to them, causing wonderment about the Savior's new mobility and about the apparent lack of gravitational pull on a resurrected body. These, and many other things connected with the resurrection the disciples would learn about and experience as they pursued and fulfilled their life's mission. In the meantime, they faced important and challenging events connected with their apostolic callings.

One of the most significant of these was the day of Pentecost, which lay immediately ahead, when the apostles would observe and experience the mighty power and influence of the Holy Ghost, who would become their constant guide and companion.

CHAPTER TWENTY-NINE

Jesus Appears and Ministers in America

The Book of Mormon, which was translated by the Prophet Joseph Smith from a set of metallic plates given to him by the Angel Moroni, contains the account of three groups of people who migrated from the Eastern Hemisphere to the Western Hemisphere. There they multiplied and thrived, but then disintegrated through disobedience to divine law. The Apostle John, while relating the story of the good shepherd, had this to say about some of those involved in these migrations, and their descendants: "And other sheep I have, which are not of this fold: them also I must bring, and they shall hear my voice; and there shall be one fold, *and* one shepherd" (John 10:16).

This prophecy foretold the appearance of Jesus Christ in the Western Hemisphere and the promulgation of His gospel there. An inspired narrator among the descendants of the people who migrated to the Western Hemisphere, wrote this: "soon after the ascension of Christ into heaven he did truly manifest himself unto them [people in the Western Hemisphere]—Showing his body unto them, and ministering unto them; and an account of his ministry shall be given hereafter" (3 Nephi 10:18-19).

The Book of Mormon is another witness of the divinity of Jesus Christ and of His atoning sacrifice in behalf of men and women everywhere. As the above quotation from Third Nephi indicates, the Book of Mormon also contains an account of His ministry in the Western Hemisphere, as the following narrative attests.

Signs in the Western Hemisphere at Christ's Birth

Several years before the birth of Jesus Christ, a prophet named Samuel the Lamanite appeared to people in the Western Hemisphere, predicting that the Savior, Jesus Christ, would be born soon, and that His birth would be attended by marvelous signs and wonders. He predicted that on the night before the birth, there would be no darkening of the light of the sun, so that a day and a night and a day would appear as a single day. At the same time, he predicted that a new star would appear in the heavens.

At the time of these predictions, there was a division among the people at Zarahemla in the Western Hemisphere. There were some who believed what Samuel had said, while others disbelieved: "there was a day set apart by the unbelievers, that all those who believed in those traditions should be put to death except the sign should come to pass, which had been given by Samuel the prophet" (3 Nephi 1:9).

Concerned about this crisis, Nephi, the leader of the believers,

> cried mightily unto the Lord all that day; and behold, the voice of the Lord came unto him, saying:
> Lift up your head and be of good cheer; for behold, the time is at hand, and on this night shall the sign be given, and on the morrow come I into the world, to show unto the world that I will fulfill all that which I have caused to be spoken by the mouth of my holy prophets.
> . . . And behold, the time is at hand, and on this night shall the sign be given. (3 Nephi 1:13-14)

There followed the night when there was no darkness and the day as Samuel had predicted. At the same time "a new star did appear, according to the word" (3 Nephi 1:21).

There was great jubilation among the believers, however, "from this time forth there began to be lyings sent forth among the people, by Satan, to harden their hearts . . . but notwithstanding these lyings and deceivings the more part of the people did believe, and were converted unto the Lord" (3 Nephi 1:22).

Dire Events Following the Crucifixion

More than three decades following the appearance of the signs which attended the birth of Jesus Christ, the Nephites looked forward with great fear to the signs given by Samuel the Lamanite, "for the time that there should be darkness for the space of three days over the face of the land" (3 Nephi 8:3). This prophecy began to be fulfilled in the thirty-fourth year following the birth of Christ, when "there was also a great and terrible tempest; and there was terrible thunder, insomuch that it did shake the whole earth as if it was about to divide asunder" (3 Nephi 8:6). This was accompanied by sharp lightnings, such as had never been seen before. Immediately afterward, the city of Zarahemla took fire, and the city of Moroni sank into the sea. At the same time, the earth was carried up upon the city of Moronihah, which became a mountain. And "the whole face of the land was changed, because of the tempest and the whirlwinds, and the thunderings and the lightnings, and the exceedingly great quaking of the whole earth" (3 Nephi 8:15). Meanwhile, the roads were broken up, the rocks were rent, and many other cities were destroyed or seriously damaged. The human toll was equally devastating, with untold numbers being killed or maimed. Adding to the misery and devastation, a thick darkness covered the whole earth so thick and stifling that there was no light at all.

In the midst of the cries and groanings were heard voices crying and expressing regret they had failed to heed the warnings of the prophets.

A Voice Is Heard

As the people lamented over their failure to heed the words of the prophets, "there was a voice heard among all the inhabitants of the earth, upon all the face of this land" (3 Nephi 9:1). The voice explained that those who died in the chaos did so, "because of their iniquity and abominations" (3 Nephi 9:2). Then followed a recital of various cities which had been destroyed because of their iniquities, and of those who had lost their lives, "and many great destructions have I caused to come upon this land, and upon this people, because of their wickedness and their abominations" (3 Nephi 9:12). Those who survived were told they were spared because they "were more righteous than they" and that they might obtain eternal life if they would now "return unto me" (3 Nephi 9:13). Then followed these supernal words:

> Behold, I am Jesus Christ the Son of God. I created the heavens and the earth, and all things that in them are. I was with the Father from the beginning. I am in the Father, and the Father in me; and in me hath the Father glorified his name. (3 Nephi 9:15)

Finally, the voice said, "in me is the law of Moses fulfilled. I am the light and the life of the world. I am Alpha and Omega, the beginning and the end" (3 Nephi 9:17-18).

In the place of the sacrifices required by the Law of Moses,

> ye shall offer as a sacrifice unto me a broken heart and a contrite spirit. And whoso cometh unto me with a broken

heart and a contrite spirit, him will I baptize with fire and with the Holy Ghost . . .

Therefore, whoso repenteth and cometh unto me as a little child, him will I receive, for of such is the kingdom of God. Behold, for such I have laid down my life, and have taken it up again; therefore repent, and come unto me ye ends of the earth, and be saved. (3 Nephi 9:20,22)

By this miraculous means, through a voice heard by all, the gospel of Jesus Christ was introduced, in its fullness, to the inhabitants of the Western Hemisphere.

Beginning with humility and repentance, those who heard the voice were taught the process which leads to eternal life, baptism, the ministrations of the Holy Ghost, contrition, and Godly conduct. In the process they were taught that the Law of Moses had been fulfilled in Christ and that the Father was glorified in Christ. Also, the essence of Christ's teachings—a broken heart and a contrite spirit—was illustrated and emphasized. This laid the groundwork for the emergence of the disciples of Christ as a force among the people in the Western Hemisphere.

There Is Silence in the Land

There came a time in the midst of the sorrow and anguish of the survivors over the loss of their possessions and loved ones, that the marvel of the voice and its message began to dominate their thinking, and they fell silent.

For so great was the astonishment of the people that they did cease lamenting and howling for the loss of their kindred which had been slain; therefore there was silence in all the land for the space of many hours. (3 Nephi 10:2)

The sudden change from lamenting and howling to complete silence by the survivors, followed by long hours when nothing was heard from them, is a source of amazement. Any answer or comment explaining it lies completely within the realm of speculation. Can it be that the survivors, suddenly shocked into the realization that Jesus Christ is a real person, a divine being, who had outlined a process by which they might attain eternal life, caused them, perhaps for the first time, to appraise their status in the eyes of God? Such an appraisal, like, perhaps, the introspective process through which the repentant sinner passes, could have been time consuming, accounting for their hours of silence.

The Voice Is Heard Again

Following the period of silence, the voice was heard again by all the survivors "and did witness of it." The voice was first directed to the survivors of the great cities that had fallen, "who are descendants of Jacob, yea, who are of the house of Israel." Of these the voice then commented, "how oft have I gathered you as a hen gathereth her chickens under her wings, and have nourished you." The voice then repeated these words, directing them to "ye people of the house of Israel, ye that dwell in Jerusalem." (3 Nephi 10:3-5)

The voice, then being directed again to the survivors, who had been spared, said,

> how oft will I gather you as a hen gathereth her chickens under her wings, if ye will repent and return unto me with full purpose of heart,
> But if not, O house of Israel, the places of your dwellings shall become desolate until the time of the fulfilling of the covenants to your fathers. (3 Nephi 10:6-7)

When the survivors had heard these words, "they began to weep and howl again because of the loss of their kindred and friends" (3 Nephi 10:8).

In these scriptures from the Book of Mormon are found the fulfillment of the prediction of the Apostle John, uttered in the Eastern Hemisphere, that Christ had other sheep than those in the Eastern Hemisphere; that these other sheep were of the house of Israel; that Christ would visit and teach these other sheep, bringing them into a single fold, led and nourished by a single shepherd, even the Lord Jesus Christ.

Significantly, it was made clear to the followers of Christ in the Western Hemisphere that their status in the fold of Christ was dependent upon their obedience to the laws and commandments of the Savior.

The Darkness Disappears: The Earth Is Restored

Following the three days of darkness, "the earth did cease to tremble, and the rocks did cease to rend, and the dreadful groanings did cease, and all the tumultuous noises did pass away" (3 Nephi 10:9). At the same time, the mourning and the weeping of the people "was turned into joy, and their lamentations into the praise and thanksgiving unto the Lord Jesus Christ, their Redeemer" (3 Nephi 10:10).

These portentous events were described in and fulfilled the scriptures "which had been spoken by the prophets" (3 Nephi 10:11). They pertained to the more righteous part of the people who were not guilty of any disrespect of or of any violence toward the prophets. "And it was they who had not shed the blood of the saints, who were spared" (3 Nephi 10:12). All these devastations fulfilled "the prophecies of many of the holy prophets" (3 Nephi 10:14). Among these prophets were Zenos and Zenock, who "spake concerning these things, because they testified, particularly concerning us, who are the remnant of their seed" (3 Nephi 10:16). The narrator then observed,

> Behold, our father Jacob also testified concerning a remnant of the seed of Joseph. And behold, are not we a remnant of the seed of Joseph? And these things which testify of us, are they not written upon the plates of brass which our father Lehi brought out of Jerusalem?" (3 Nephi 10:17)

Prediction of Christ's Appearance in the Western Hemisphere

> And it came to pass, that in the ending of the thirty and fourth year, . . . soon after the ascension of Christ into heaven he did truly manifest himself unto them—
> Showing his body unto them, and ministering unto them. (3 Nephi 10:18-19)

In anticipation of this supernal event, the people were gathered at the temple in the land Bountiful:

> and they were marveling and wondering one with another, and were showing one to another the great and marvelous change which had taken place.
> And they were also conversing about this Jesus Christ, of whom the sign had been given concerning his death. (3 Nephi 11:1-2)

As they were conversing together,

> they heard a voice as if it came out of heaven; and they cast their eyes round about, for they understood not the voice which they heard; and it was not a harsh voice, neither was it a loud voice; nevertheless, and notwithstanding it

being a small voice it did pierce them that did hear to the center, insomuch that there was no part of their frame that it did not cause to quake; yea, it did pierce them to the very soul, and did cause their hearts to burn. (3 Nephi 11:3)

When the voice sounded the second time, they still did not understand it, but when it sounded the third time, "they did understand the voice" and it said unto them: "Behold my Beloved Son, in whom I am well pleased, in whom I have glorified my name—hear ye him" (3 Nephi 11:6-7). At this, they did cast their eyes upward toward heaven, and

> they saw a Man descending out of heaven; and he was clothed in a white robe; and he came down and stood in the midst of them; and the eyes of the whole multitude were turned upon him, and they durst not open their mouths, even one to another, and wist not what it meant, for they thought it was an angel that had appeared unto them. (3 Nephi 11:8)

Soon this heavenly being stretched forth His hand toward them and said,

> Behold, I am Jesus Christ, whom the prophets testified shall come into the world. And behold, I am the light and the life of the world; and I have drunk out of that bitter cup which the Father hath given me, and have glorified the Father in taking upon me the sins of the world, in the which I have suffered the will of the Father in all things from the beginning. (3 Nephi 11:11)

After Jesus had uttered these words, the multitude fell to the earth, remembering it had been prophesied that Christ would show himself unto them after His ascension. The Lord then said to them:

> Arise and come forth unto me, that ye may thrust your hands into my side, and also that ye may feel the prints of the nails in my hands and my feet, that ye may know that I am the God of Israel, and the God of the whole earth, and have been slain for the sins of the world. (3 Nephi 11:14)

When the multitude had done what Jesus had bidden and realized that this was, indeed, the promised Messiah, they did cry out with one accord saying: "Hosanna! Blessed be the name of the Most High God! And they did fall down at the feet of Jesus, and did worship him" (3 Nephi 11:17).

Nephi and Others Commanded to Baptize

Following these supernal events, Jesus called forth Nephi, a leader who was present. Responding, Nephi bowed himself before Jesus and kissed His feet. Being commanded to do so, Nephi stood before Jesus, who said to him,

> I give unto you power that ye shall baptize this people when I am again ascended into heaven.
> And again the Lord called others, and said unto them likewise; and he gave unto them power to baptize. And he said unto them, On this wise shall ye baptize; and there shall be no disputations among you. (3 Nephi 11:21-22)

Jesus said that whosoever repented of their sins through their words, should be baptized. The officiator was directed to use these words: "Having authority given me of Jesus Christ, I baptize you in the name of the Father, and of the Son, and of the Holy

Ghost. Amen" (3 Nephi 11:25). Having said this, the officiator was to immerse the candidate in the water. Jesus said there was to be no dispute about this procedure and warned that "the spirit of contention is not of me, but is of the devil, who is the father of contention, and he stirreth up the hearts of men to contend with anger, one with another" (3 Nephi 11:29).

The Savior then affirmed the unity of the Godhead in these words, "I say unto you, that the Father, and the Son, and the Holy Ghost are one; and I am in the Father, and the Father in me, and the Father and I are one" (3 Nephi 11:27).

The Doctrine of Christ Is Announced

Finally, Jesus said:

I will declare unto you my doctrine.

And this is my doctrine, and it is the doctrine which the Father hath given unto me; and I bear record of the Father, and the Father beareth record of me, and the Holy Ghost beareth record of the Father and me; and I bear record that the Father commandeth all men, everywhere, to repent and believe in me.

And whoso believeth in me, and is baptized, the same shall be saved; and they are they who shall inherit the kingdom of God.

And whoso believeth not in me, and is not baptized, shall be damned. (3 Nephi 11:31-34)

The Savior then affirmed that this was His doctrine, and that "whoso buildeth upon this buildeth upon my rock, and the gates of hell shall not prevail against them" (3 Nephi 11:39). He also warned that anyone who taught anything different from this was moved by an evil intent.

Calling of the Twelve

Following this discourse, several were called to promulgate these teachings: "now the number of them who had been called, and received power and authority to baptize, was twelve" (3 Nephi 12:1). The Savior stretched forth His hand to the multitude saying,

> Blessed are ye if ye shall give heed unto the words of these twelve whom I have chosen from among you to minister unto you, and to be your servants; and unto them I have given power that they may baptize you with water; and after that ye are baptized with water, behold, I will baptize you with fire and with the Holy Ghost; therefore blessed are ye if ye shall believe in me and be baptized, after that ye have seen me and know that I am. (3 Nephi 12:1)

Christ's Teachings in the Western Hemisphere

Having called the Twelve, Jesus proceeded to instruct them in the subjects they were to teach the masses. He assured them that:

> more blessed are they who shall believe in your words because that ye shall testify that ye have seen me, and that ye know that I am. Yea, blessed are those who shall believe in your words, and come down into the depths of humility and be baptized, for they shall be visited with fire and with the Holy Ghost, and shall receive a remission of their sins. (3 Nephi 12:2)

Things Taught in the Eastern Hemisphere, Which Also Apply in the Western Hemisphere

The Savior then repeated many of the things He had taught to those in the Eastern Hemisphere, which also apply to His followers in the Western Hemisphere. These are recorded in Matthew 5. They began with the most needy and vulnerable of all, invoking blessings upon the poor, upon those who mourn, upon the meek, those who hunger and thirst after righteousness, the sorrowful and pure in heart and the peacemakers, indeed, all those who may be called "the salt of the earth" whose reward in heaven shall be great. (3 Nephi 12:4-13)

However, implying that these blessings would not come automatically, they were told, "if the salt shall lose its savor wherewith shall the earth be salted? The salt shall be thenceforth good for nothing, but to be cast out and to be trodden under the foot of men" (3 Nephi 12:13).

Ye are the Light of this People

Christ's teachers were told, "I give unto you to be the light of this people," and as such it was not intended they be hidden from view, but should be as a candle to be seen by all in the house. "Therefore let your light so shine before this people, that they may see your good works and glorify your Father who is in heaven." (3 Nephi 12:14-16)

Jesus to Fulfill the Law

The people were assured that Jesus had not come to destroy the law or the prophets, but rather to fulfill the law. "I say unto you, one jot nor one tittle hath not passed away from the law, but in me it hath all been fulfilled" (3 Nephi 12:18).

Believe, Repent, and Keep the Commandments

The Savior declared He had given the people the law and the commandments of the Father,

> that ye shall believe in me, and that ye shall repent of your sins, and come unto me with a broken heart and a contrite spirit. Behold, ye have the commandments before you, and the law is fulfilled.
>
> Therefore come unto me and be ye saved; for verily I say unto you, that except ye shall keep my commandments, which I have commanded you at this time, ye shall in no case enter into the kingdom of heaven. (3 Nephi 12:19-20)

Thou Shalt not Kill

Jesus recalled that under the law whoever killed was in danger of the judgment of God. However under the mandate of Christ,

> whosoever is angry with his brother shall be in danger of his judgment. And whosoever shall say to his brother, Raca, shall be in danger of the council; and whosoever shall say, Thou fool, shall be in danger of hell fire. (3 Nephi 12:22)

Along with these radical changes in the law governing personal relationships, the Nephites were told that if in approaching God they recalled a conflict with another, they were first to "be reconciled to thy brother, and then come unto me with full purpose of heart, and I will receive you" (3 Nephi 12:24). Moreover, they were to "agree with thine adversary quickly (3 Nephi 12:25) as a means of avoiding needless and complicated personal conflicts. The practice of reconciliation as opposed to retaliation was a significant change in Nephite culture and would have served them well in practice, as it would serve their cousins well who are in the Middle East today.

The Law Against Adultery Radically Changed

The Savior observed, "Behold, it is written by them of old time, that thou shalt not commit adultery" (3 Nephi 12:27). But Jesus decreed, "whosoever looketh on a woman, to lust after her, hath committed adultery already in his heart" (3 Nephi 12:28). Herein lies the most radical change in personal conduct brought about by the teachings of the Savior. The carnal commandments specified under the Law of Moses placed restraints on physical conduct as a means of controlling or eliminating practices deemed detrimental to the common good. The higher law, however, proscribed even the thought of engaging in physical conduct that was forbidden under the law. Thus taught King Benjamin in the Book of Mormon, "watch yourselves, and your thoughts, and your words, and your deeds" (Mosiah 4:30).

After the announcement of the change in the law of adultery, there followed a litany of principles Christ's disciples were expected to teach and to follow, to the end that they "should be perfect even as I, or your Father who is in heaven is perfect" (3 Nephi 12:48).

Other Principles the Disciples Were to Teach

The disciples were told it is better to deny themselves of evil practices "than that ye should be cast into hell." It was written anciently that whosoever put his wife away should give her a writing of divorcement. Now, however, whosoever shall put his wife away, except for fornication, causes her to commit adultery, "and whoso shall marry her who is divorced committeth adultery." (3 Nephi 12:30-32)

While in the past the individual was taught not to forswear himself, now he is taught to perform his oaths unto the Lord. Indeed, the individual was to swear not at all, neither by heaven, or by earth, or by thy head. "But let your communication be Yea, yea; Nay, nay; for whatsoever cometh of more than these is evil." (3 Nephi 12:33-37)

In the past it was written "an eye for an eye, and a tooth for a tooth." But now,

> whosoever shall smite thee on the right cheek, turn to him the other also.
>
> And if any man sue ye at the law and take away thy coat, let him have thy cloak also;
>
> And whosoever shall compel thee to go a mile, go with him twain.
>
> Give to him that asketh thee, and from him that would borrow of thee, turn thou not away. (3 Nephi 12:38-42)

While in the past the people were taught to love their neighbors and hate their enemies, now they were taught to "love your enemies, bless them that curse you, do good to them that hate you, and pray for them who despitefully use you and persecute you" (3 Nephi 12:43-44).

All these changes were effected:

> That ye may be the children of your Father who is in heaven; . . .
>
> Therefore, those things which were of old time, which were under the law, in me are all fulfilled.
>
> Old things are done away, and all things have become new. (3 Nephi 12:45-47)

Giving Alms

The disciples were warned to give heed and not to give alms before men in the synagogues or in the streets, sounding a trump before them as the hypocrites do. "But when thou doest alms let not thy left hand know what thy right hand doeth; That thine alms may be in secret; and thy Father who seeth in secret, himself shall reward thee openly" (3 Nephi 13:3-4).

The Manner of Prayer

Turning to the manner of prayer, Jesus told them:

> And when thou prayest thou shall not do as the hypocrites, for they love to pray, standing in the synagogues and in the corner of the streets, that they may be seen of men. Verily I say unto you, they have their reward.
>
> But thou, when thou prayest, enter into thy closet, and when thou hast shut the door, pray to thy Father who is in secret; and thy Father, who seeth in secret, shall reward thee openly. (3 Nephi 13:5-6)

They were warned not to use vain repetitions in their prayers and then were presented with the example of an acceptable prayer:

> Our Father who art in heaven, hallowed be thy name.
> Thy will be done on earth as it is in heaven.
> And forgive us our debts, as we forgive our debtors.
> And lead us not into temptation [JST 6:14 translates this as "suffer us not to be led into temptation"], but deliver us from evil.
> For thine is the kingdom, and the power, and the glory, forever. Amen. (3 Nephi 13:9-13)

The disciples were reminded, with emphasis, that forgiveness for their debts was conditioned upon their forgiveness of the debts of others.

The Procedure in Fasting

The Savior warned His disciples in fasting not to be like the hypocrites. These, He noted, accompanied their fasting with disfigured faces and actions designed to demonstrate their discomfort and to evoke sympathy. These, He told the disciples, have their reward.

> But thou, when thou fastest, anoint thy head, and wash thy face;
> That thou appear not unto men to fast, but unto thy Father, who is in secret; and thy Father who seeth in secret, shall reward thee openly. (3 Nephi 13:17-18)

Lay up Heavenly Treasures

The disciples were told not to lay up treasures on earth, where moth and rust doth corrupt and thieves steal. Rather they should, "lay up for yourselves treasures in heaven, where neither moth nor rust doth corrupt, and where thieves do not break through nor steal" (3 Nephi 13:19-20). Significantly the Savior remarked that their hearts and their focus in life should be where their treasure was found.

The Light of the Body

Jesus said the light of the body is the eye. "If, therefore, thine eye be single, thy whole body shall be full of light." But if the eye is evil, the whole body shall be full of darkness, "and how great is that darkness." (3 Nephi 13:22-23)

No Man Can Serve Two Masters

The Savior concluded His great discourse to the Nephites with these words: "No man can serve two masters; for either he will hate the one and love the other, or else he will hold to the one and despise the other. Ye cannot serve God and Mammon" (3 Nephi 13:24).

With this, Jesus had repeated, in both form and substance, the message He had delivered to His followers in the Eastern Hemisphere in the Sermon on the Mount and the sermon on the plain. In these are the substance and the essence of Christ's moral teachings, which were and are intended to direct and bless His followers and disciples, whether in the Eastern Hemisphere or the Western Hemisphere or elsewhere.

A Message to the Twelve

Having completed His discourse, Jesus then turned to the Twelve and said:

> Remember the words which I have spoken. For behold, ye are they whom I have chosen to minister unto this people. Therefore I say unto you, take no thought for your life, what ye shall eat, or what ye shall drink; nor yet for your body, what ye shall put on. Is not the life more than meat, and the body than raiment?
>
> Behold the fowls of the air, for they sow not, neither do they reap nor gather into barns; yet your heavenly Father feedeth them. Are ye not much better than they?
>
> Which of you by taking thought can add one cubit unto his stature?
>
> And why take ye thought for raiment? Consider the lilies of the field how they grow; they toil not, neither do they spin;

And yet I say unto you, that even Solomon, in all his glory, was not arrayed like one of these.

Wherefore, if God so clothe the grass of the field, which today is, and tomorrow is cast into the oven, even so will he clothe you, if ye are not of little faith.

Therefore take no thought, saying, What shall we eat? or, What shall we drink? Or, Wherewithal shall we be clothed?

For your heavenly Father knoweth that ye have need of all these things.

But seek ye first the kingdom of God and his righteousness, and all these things shall be added unto you.

Take therefore no thought for the morrow, for the morrow shall take thought for the things of itself. Sufficient is the day unto the evil thereof. (3 Nephi 13:25-34)

Instructions to the Multitude

When Jesus had finished delivering His message to the Twelve, "he turned again to the multitude, and did open his mouth unto them again" (3 Nephi 14:1). His first instruction to the multitude was about judgment.

Judge Not That Ye Be Not Judged

The multitude was first warned that, "with what judgment ye judge, ye shall be judged; and with what measure ye mete, it shall be measured to you again" (3 Nephi 14:2). Here is a perfect example of the rule of reciprocity. So you will be judged by the same standard you apply in judging your brother. The wise should beware and guard the tongue. The hypocrisy of one sinner presuming to judge another sinner is made clear. "Thou hypocrite, first cast the beam out of thine own eye; and then shalt thou see clearly to cast the mote out of thy brother's eye" (3 Nephi 14:5).

Share Not Sacred Things With the Unrighteous

The admonition not to share sacred things with the unrighteous was expressed in these blunt words: "Give not that which is holy unto the dogs, neither cast ye your pearls before swine, lest they trample them under their feet, and turn again and rend you" (3 Nephi 14:6). It is foolish and fruitless to cause the ignorant and boorish to understand and appreciate sensitive, spiritual things. Therefore, the wise will refrain from the attempt.

Ask, Seek, and Knock

The multitude was admonished to ask, to seek, and to knock for the things that are needful. "For every one that asketh, receiveth; and he that seeketh, findeth; and to him that knocketh, it shall be opened" (3 Nephi 14:8). To illustrate this law of plentitude, the Savior then asked whether a man, having a son, would give him a stone when he asked for bread or a serpent when he asked for a fish. Answering His own question, the Master said, "If ye then, being evil, knoweth how to give good gifts unto your children, how much more shall your Father who is in heaven give good things to them that ask him?" (3 Nephi 14:11) The Savior then reaffirmed the law of reciprocity in these words: "Therefore, all things whatsoever ye would that men should do to you, do ye even so to them, for this is the law and the prophets" (3 Nephi 14:12).

Inherent in the principle announced here, that in order to receive the blessings of the Lord, we must take the initiative to ask, to seek, or to knock, is the reality that God remains neutral in the affairs of men until His children implore Him to act.

Otherwise, all would be God's doing and the purpose of earth life, namely to prove ourselves, would be frustrated.

Enter at the Strait Gate

The disciples were warned to avoid entering the kingdom by means of the broad gate, for "broad is the way, which leadeth to destruction, and many there be who go in thereat" (3 Nephi 14:13). Instead the disciples were told to enter through the strait gate, "Because strait is the gate, and narrow is the way, which leadeth unto life, and few there be that find it" (3 Nephi 14:14).

Beware of False Prophets

The disciples were also told to beware of false prophets "who come to you in sheep's clothing, but inwardly they are ravening wolves." They were told they would recognize them by their fruits. "Do men gather grapes of thorns, or figs of thistles? Even so every good tree bringeth forth good fruit; but a corrupt tree bringeth forth evil fruit." Finally they were told that every tree which did not bring forth good fruit would be cut down and cast into the fire. (3 Nephi 14:15-18)

Only the House Built Upon Rock Shall Stand

Jesus warned His followers that not everyone who declares, "Lord, Lord, shall enter into the kingdom of heaven, but he that doeth the will of my Father who is in heaven" (3 Nephi 14:21). To those who protested because they had "done many wonderful works" in His name, the Savior declared unto them, "I never knew you; depart from me, ye that work iniquity" (3 Nephi 14:22-23). By way of elaboration, the Savior then uttered these telling words:

Therefore, whoso heareth these sayings of mine and doeth them, I will liken him unto a wise man, who built his house upon a rock—

And the rains descended, and the floods came, and the winds blew, and beat upon that house; and it fell not, for it was founded upon a rock.

And every one that heareth these sayings of mine and doeth them not shall be likened unto a foolish man who built his house upon the sand—

And the rains descended, and the floods came, and the winds blew, and beat upon that house; and it fell, and great was the fall of it. (3 Nephi 14:24-27)

Jesus' Relationship to the Law of Moses Explained

When Jesus had finished teaching the Nephite multitude the things He had taught to His disciples in the Eastern Hemisphere before His ascension, He declared there were some who "understood not the saying that old things had passed away, and that all things had become new" (3 Nephi 15:2). He began by noting that He gave the law and He had fulfilled the law; "therefore it hath an end" (3 Nephi 15:5). However He went on to say, "I do not destroy the prophets, for as many as have not been fulfilled in me, verily I say unto you, shall all be fulfilled" (3 Nephi 15:6).

He also made it clear that His statement that old things had passed away did not refer to "things which are to come" (3 Nephi 15:7). By way of warning, Jesus said, "The covenant which I have made with my people is not all fulfilled; but the law which was given unto Moses hath an end in me" (3 Nephi 15:8). Jesus concluded saying,

> Behold, I am the law, and the light. Look unto me, and endure to the end, and ye shall live; for unto him that endureth to the end will I give eternal life.
>
> Behold, I have given unto you the commandments; therefore keep my commandments.
>
> And this is the law and the prophets, for they truly testify of me. (3 Nephi 15:9-10)

Instructions to the Twelve About the Other Sheep

Following His instructions to the multitude about the Law of Moses, Jesus turned to the Twelve. He told them that they were His disciples, "a light unto this people, who are a remnant of the house of Joseph," that this was the land of their inheritance and that the Father had given it to them (3 Nephi 15:11-13). Because of the stiffneckedness of their ancestors in Jerusalem, they were not told about those whom the Lord had led away, except for those about whom He had said, "other sheep I have which are not of this fold; them also I must bring, and they shall hear my voice; and there shall be one fold, and one shepherd" (3 Nephi 15:17, John 10:16).

Following this revelation, the Savior discoursed further about the matter and about the Gentiles in these words:

> And they understood me not, for they supposed it had been the Gentiles; for they understood not that the Gentiles should be converted through their preaching.
>
> And they understood me not that I said they shall hear my voice; and they understood me not that the Gentiles should not at any time hear my voice—that I should not manifest myself unto them save it were by the Holy Ghost.

But behold, ye have both heard my voice, and seen me; and ye are my sheep, and ye are numbered among those whom the Father hath given me. (3 Nephi 15:22-24)

Christ Tells of Other Scattered Sheep

Jesus then told the Nephites, "I have other sheep, which are not of this land, neither of the land of Jerusalem, neither in any part of that land round about whither I have been to minister" (3 Nephi 16:1). As to these scattered people Jesus said, "I shall go unto them, and . . . they shall hear my voice, and shall be numbered among my sheep, that there may be one fold and one shepherd; therefore I go to show myself unto them." (3 Nephi 16:3)

Knowledge about some of these other sheep arose out of the first area general conference held in Manchester, England, in August 1971. At a testimony meeting held in the Picadilly Hotel in Manchester, President Spencer W. Kimball, Acting President of the Twelve, alluded to the diary of his grandfather, Heber C. Kimball, covering his mission to England in 1837. An entry in this diary, said President Spencer W. Kimball, told of the experience of Heber C. Kimball who, while walking between two English villages, was so overwhelmed with emotion he twice had to go to a nearby stream to bathe his face. Later, in America, he related this experience to Joseph Smith. The prophet told him his emotion resulted from the fact he was then in an area where the Savior had been during his earthly ministry. This writer was present at the meeting in the Piccadilly Hotel in Manchester and heard President Spencer W. Kimball relate this experience.

When the Savior had finished instructing the Nephites about His other sheep, He commanded them to make a record of the things He had told them, to the end the Gentiles "may be brought to a knowledge of me, their Redeemer" (3 Nephi 16:4).

Then followed this comment about the gathering of the house of Israel: "And then will I gather them in from the four quarters of the earth; and then will I fulfill the covenant which the Father hath made unto all the people of the House of Israel" (3 Nephi 16:5).

The Gentiles are Blessed and Warned

Following comments about covenants made with the House of Israel, the Savior said: "And blessed are the Gentiles, because of their belief in me, in and of the Holy Ghost, which witnesses unto them of me and of the Father" (3 Nephi 16:6). Then the Father, speaking of the latter days, said:

> Behold, because of their belief in me, saith the Father, and because of the unbelief of you, O house of Israel, in the latter day shall the truth come unto the Gentiles, that the fulness of these things shall be made known unto them." (3 Nephi 16:7)

However, at the very zenith of the power and influence of the Gentiles came this heavenly warning: "But wo, saith the Father, unto the unbelieving of the Gentiles" (3 Nephi 16:8). After describing the total dominance the Gentiles had attained over the Nephites through bullying, intimidation, and murders, whereby the Nephites had become "a hiss and a by-word" among them, the Father decreed that "when the Gentiles shall sin against my gospel, and shall reject the fullness of my gospel, and shall be lifted up in the pride of their hearts . . . I will bring the fulness of my gospel from among them" (3 Nephi 16:9-10). The Father then decreed He would remember the covenant He had made with the House of Israel with the result, "the Gentiles shall not have power over you . . . and ye shall come unto the knowledge of the fulness of my gospel" (3 Nephi 16:12).

Yet with all that, the Father also decreed: "But if the Gentiles will repent and return unto me, . . . behold they shall be numbered among my people, O house of Israel" (3 Nephi 16:13).

Finally, the Savior said to the multitude,

> Verily, verily, I say unto you, thus hath the Father commanded me—that I should give unto this people this land for their inheritance.
>
> And then the words of the prophet Isaiah shall be fulfilled, which say:
>
> Thy watchmen shall lift up the voice; with the voice together shall they sing, for they shall see eye to eye when the Lord shall bring again Zion.
>
> Break forth into joy, sing together, ye waste places of Jerusalem; for the Lord has comforted his people, he hath redeemed Jerusalem.
>
> The Lord has made bare his holy arm in the eyes of all the nations; and all the ends of the earth shall see the salvation of God. (3 Nephi 16:16-20, see Isaiah 52:8-10)

He Tells Them to Ponder His Words

When Jesus had finished His discourse, He observed that the multitude seemed weak and unable to understand all His words. Therefore, He urged them to go to their homes to ponder what He had said, "and ask of the Father, in my name, that ye may understand, and prepare your minds for the morrow, and I come unto you again" (3 Nephi 17:3). Meanwhile, Jesus said He intended to "go unto the Father, and also to show myself unto the lost tribes of Israel" (3 Nephi 17:4). He added they were not lost to Him, as He knew very well where He had led them.

The Savior detected there was a strong sentiment among the multitude that the interview with Him not be terminated. This prompted Him to say that His bowels were filled with compassion toward them, which caused Him to say, "Have ye any that are sick among you? Bring them hither" (3 Nephi 17:7). As He had done in Jerusalem, the Savior then proceeded to bless all those who came to Him who were afflicted with all manner of diseases and physical disabilities. Significantly, in doing this, He said, "I see that your faith is sufficient that I should heal you." He then healed them, "every one" (3 Nephi 17:8-9).

Jesus Blesses the Little Children

Such was the gratitude of the multitude on this supernal occasion, that as many of them as could do so "did kiss his feet, insomuch that they did bathe his feet with their tears" (3 Nephi 17:10).

It was then that Jesus commanded that the little children be brought forward. Hundreds of them came from among the multitude, estimated to number twenty-five hundred souls. When all were gathered around Jesus, He commanded that they kneel upon the ground. Jesus then "groaned within himself, and said: Father, I am troubled because of the wickedness of the people of the house of Israel" (3 Nephi 17:14). The Savior then kneeled upon the ground and prayed, and the things which He prayed "cannot be written and the multitude did bare record who heard him" (3 Nephi 17:15). The people did bare record in this manner, saying, "The eye hath never seen, neither hath the ear heard, before, so great and marvelous things as we saw and heard Jesus speak unto the Father" (3 Nephi 17:16). Jesus then commanded the multitude to arise, saying,

> And now behold, my joy is full.
> And when he had said these words, he wept, and the multitude bare record of it, and he took their little

children, one by one, and blessed them, and prayed unto the Father for them.

And when he had done this, he wept again. (3 Nephi 17:20-22)

Then addressing the multitude, Jesus told them, "Behold your little ones," whereupon they all cast their eyes toward heaven, "and they saw angels descending out of heaven as it were in the midst of fire; and they came down and encircled those little ones about, and they were encircled about with fire; and the angels did minister unto them." (3 Nephi 17:23-24) The multitude saw, heard, and bore record of these miraculous things.

The Multitude Is Fed: The Sacrament

Jesus commanded the disciples to bring bread and wine to Him. While they were gone, He directed the multitude to be seated upon the ground. When the disciples had returned with the bread and wine, "he took of the bread and brake and blessed it; and he gave unto the disciples and commanded that they should eat" (3 Nephi 18:3). When they had done this, Jesus commanded they should serve the multitude. They were instructed to follow this procedure always, "even as I have done, even as I have broken bread and blessed it and given it unto you" (3 Nephi 18:6). They were told:

> And this shall ye do in remembrance of my body, which I have shown unto you. And it shall be a testimony unto the Father that ye do always remember me. And if ye do always remember me ye shall have my Spirit to be with you. (3 Nephi 18:7)

The disciples then partook of the wine and gave to the multitude to partake in remembrance of His blood. They were commanded always to do these things and were told that in doing them, "ye are built upon my rock" (3 Nephi 18:12).

In order to handle the preparation and distribution of the sacred emblems in an orderly manner, they were directed to appoint one to perform this duty (see 3 Nephi 18:5). Later the Saints were authorized to use water instead of wine in partaking of the sacrament (see D&C 27:2).

Jesus Teaches Prayer

When the Savior had finished speaking to the disciples, He turned again to the multitude, saying, "ye must watch and pray always lest you enter into temptation; for Satan desireth to have you, that he may sift you as wheat" (3 Nephi 18:18). Their prayers were to be offered to the Father, always in the name of Jesus. "And whatsoever ye shall ask the Father in my name, which is right, believing that ye shall receive, behold it shall be given unto you" (3 Nephi 18:20). Herein lie the criteria for any effective prayer: It must be offered to the Father in the name of Jesus; it must be for an appropriate purpose; and the petitioner must believe, or have faith, he will receive the blessing sought. The multitude was admonished to meet together often and not to forbid others from joining them. Finally, they were told to hold up their light, "that it might shine unto the world. Behold I am the light which ye shall hold up" (3 Nephi 18:24). The multitude also was admonished to do the things the Savior had done.

Other Instructions Given About the Sacrament

After giving these instructions to the multitude, the Savior turned again to the disciples whom He had chosen, saying, "I give unto you another commandment, and then I must go unto my

Father that I may fulfill other commandments which he hath given me" (3 Nephi 18:27).

Then the Savior gave His disciples this commandment: "ye shall not suffer any one knowingly to partake of my flesh and blood unworthily, when ye shall minister it" (3 Nephi 18:28). Jesus warned that anyone who partook of the sacred emblems unworthily would eat and drink "damnation" to his own soul (3 Nephi 18:29). Nevertheless, such as these were not to be cast out, but should be retained in brotherhood, looking toward their repentance and redemption.

As Jesus departed, He touched and spoke privately to each of the disciples. No one among the multitude heard what Jesus said to them, but they later bore record that "he gave them power to give the Holy Ghost" (3 Nephi 18:37). Following this, a cloud overshadowed them. After the cloud lifted, the multitude discovered Jesus had departed.

The Multitude Gather and Pray

When the multitude had returned to their homes to ponder, and Jesus had departed, the word spread before nightfall that Jesus had appeared and ministered unto the people, and that He would return on the morrow. Then all that night,

> it was noised abroad concerning Jesus; and insomuch did they send forth unto the people that there were many, yea, an exceedingly great number, did labor exceedingly all that night, that they might be on the morrow in the place where Jesus should show himself unto the multitude. (3 Nephi 19:3)

On the morrow as the multitude gathered, the twelve disciples whom Jesus had called, namely Nephi and his brother Timothy whom Nephi had raised from the dead, and Jonas the son of Timothy; and Mathoni; and Mathonihah his brother; and Kumen; and Kumenonhi; and Jeremiah; and Shemnon; and Jonas; and Zedekiah; and Isaiah were among them. The numbers of the multitude were so great that they were divided into twelve groups. The multitude was then directed to pray unto the Father in the name of Jesus. (3 Nephi 19:4-6)

Then the disciples "did pray unto the Father also in the name of Jesus," after which "they arose and ministered unto the people" repeating the same words Jesus had spoken, "nothing varying" (3 Nephi 19:7-8).

The Twelve Are Baptized and Receive the Holy Ghost

The disciples then prayed for that which they desired most, "and they desired that the Holy Ghost should be given unto them" (3 Nephi 19:9). When they had thus prayed, the multitude followed them down to the water's edge. Then Nephi was baptized, following which he baptized all those who had been chosen by Jesus. This being accomplished, "the Holy Ghost did fall upon them, and they were filled with the Holy Ghost and with fire" (3 Nephi 19:13). It was then that angels descended from heaven and ministered unto them. In the midst of this panoply of heavenly splendor, "Jesus came and stood in the midst and ministered unto them" (3 Nephi 19:15).

Then addressing the multitude, Jesus "commanded them that they should kneel down again upon the earth, and also that His disciples should kneel down upon the earth" (3 Nephi 19:16). Then after commanding the disciples to pray, "they did pray unto Jesus, calling him their Lord and their God" (3 Nephi 19:18). Jesus then withdrew a short distance from the multitude and, bowing to the earth, thanked the Father for giving the Holy Ghost to His disciples, adding this significant statement: "Father, I pray thee that thou will give the Holy Ghost unto all them that shall believe in their words" (3 Nephi 19:21).

Jesus explained why His followers deviated from the norm in praying directly to him, saying, "they pray unto me because I am with them" (3 Nephi 19:22). Jesus then offered a special prayer for His disciples and "for all those who shall believe on their words, that they may believe in me, that I may be in them as thou, Father, art in me, that we may be one" (3 Nephi 19:23).

The Disciples Are Purified

As the disciples continued to pray unto Jesus with fervor and persistence, this extraordinary incident occurred:

> the light of his countenance did shine upon them, and behold they were as white as the countenance and also the garments of Jesus; and behold the whiteness thereof did exceed all the whiteness, yea, even there could be nothing upon the earth so white as the whiteness thereof. (3 Nephi 19:25)

Following this supernal event, the Savior turned aside again, saying,

> Father, I thank thee that thou hast purified those whom I have chosen, because of their faith, and I pray for them, and for them who shall believe on their words, that they may be purified in me, through faith on their words, even as they are purified in me. (3 Nephi 19:28)

The Magnitude of Christ's Power and Blessings

Here Jesus turned aside again and prayed to the Father, "And tongue cannot speak the words which he prayed, neither can be written by man the words which he prayed" (3 Nephi 19:32). After He had finished praying and had returned to the multitude, Jesus said:

> So great faith have I never seen among all the Jews; wherefore I could not show unto them so great miracles because of their unbelief.
>
> Verily I say unto you, there are none of them that have seen so great things as ye have seen, neither have they heard so great things as ye have heard. (3 Nephi 19:35-36)

Jesus Again Administers the Sacrament

After Jesus had commanded His disciples and the multitude to cease praying, He also commanded them that "they should not cease to pray in their hearts" (3 Nephi 20:1). Then according to His command, the disciples and the multitude arose and stood upon their feet, whereupon "he brake bread again and blessed it, and gave to the disciples to eat" (3 Nephi 20:3). He then commanded the disciples to break bread and give it to the multitude to eat. He then gave the Twelve wine to drink "and commanded them that they should give unto the multitude" (3 Nephi 20:5). Neither the Twelve nor the multitude had brought either bread or wine with them, "But he truly gave unto them bread to eat, and also wine to drink" (3 Nephi 20:7).

When the process of blessing and distributing the holy emblems had been completed and all had been filled, Jesus said unto them: "He that eateth this bread eateth of my body to his soul; and he that drinketh of this wine drinketh of my blood to his soul; and his soul shall never hunger nor thirst, but shall be filled" (3 Nephi 20:8).

Now when they all had eaten and drunk, "behold, they were filled with the Spirit; and they did cry out with one voice, and gave glory to Jesus, whom they both saw and heard" (3 Nephi 20:9). Then Jesus concluded, saying, "Behold now I finish the commandment which the Father hath commanded me concerning this people, who are a remnant of the house of Israel" (3 Nephi 20:10).

Jesus Quotes Isaiah

Jesus said that when the words of Isaiah had been fulfilled, "then is the fulfilling of the covenant which the Father hath made unto his people, O house of Israel" (3 Nephi 20:12). In speaking of the last days, the prophet Isaiah said:

> And it shall come to pass in the last days, *that* the mountain of the LORD's house shall be established in the top of the mountains, and shall be exalted above the hills; and all nations shall flow unto it. (Isaiah 2:2)

This process, which foreshadowed the gathering of Israel, was an integral part of the grand plan that led to the fulfilling of the covenant that the Father made with His people.

The Savior then confirmed the actuality of the gathering, saying, "And then shall the remnants, which shall be scattered abroad upon the face of the earth, be gathered in" (3 Nephi 20:13). As an important element of the gathering, the Savior declared, "the Father hath commanded me that I should give unto you this land, for your inheritance" (3 Nephi 20:14).

The Savior predicted dire consequences for the Gentiles should they fail to repent, saying: "the sword of my justice shall hang over them at that day; and except they repent it shall fall upon them, saith the Father, yea, even upon all the nations of the Gentiles" (3 Nephi 20:20). On the other hand, the Savior foresaw this favorable consequence for the children of Jacob:

> And behold, this people will I establish in this land, unto the fulfilling of the covenant which I made with your father Jacob; and it shall be a New Jerusalem. And the powers of heaven shall be in the midst of this people; yea, even I will be in the midst of you." (3 Nephi 20:22)

Jesus Proclaims His Identity

After discoursing on the prophecies of Isaiah, Jesus identified himself saying, "I am he of whom Moses spake, saying: A prophet shall the Lord your God raise up unto you of your brethren, like unto me" (3 Nephi 20:23). The people were to hear and obey this prophet in all things, but the disobedient were to be cut off. All the prophets from Samuel onward testified of this most distinguished prophet. The Nephites were said to be children of the prophets and of the house of Israel and of "the covenant which the Father made with your fathers, saying unto Abraham: And in thy seed shall all the kindred of the earth be blessed" (3 Nephi 20:25). The glory of all the kindred of the earth was to be accomplished by "the pouring out of the Holy Ghost through me upon the Gentiles, which blessing upon the Gentiles shall make them mighty above all, unto the scattering my people, O house of Israel" (3 Nephi 20:27).

While the Gentiles were to be a scourge unto the people of the land, "Nevertheless, when they shall have received the fulness of my gospel, then if they shall harden their hearts against me I will return their iniquities upon their own heads, saith the Father" (3 Nephi 20:28).

Discourse on the Glory of Israel

As to the promised gathering of scattered Israel, Jesus declared,

> I have covenanted with them that I would gather them together in mine own due time, that I would give unto them again the land of their fathers for their inheritance, which is the land of Jerusalem, which is the promised land unto them forever, saith the Father. (3 Nephi 20:29)

Then the fullness of the gospel will be preached to them again. Then shall they believe that Jesus Christ is "the Son of God, and shall pray unto the Father in my name" (3 Nephi 20:31). Then shall the Father "gather them together again, and give unto them Jerusalem for the land of their inheritance" (3 Nephi 20:33). Then will the people break forth in joy and sing for the Lord has redeemed Jerusalem and comforted His people. In this the Father has "made bare his holy arm in the eyes of all the nations; and all the ends of the earth shall see the salvation of the Father; and the Father and I are one" (3 Nephi 20:35). In that day,

> my people shall know my name; yea, in that day they shall know that I am he that doth speak.
> And then shall they say: How beautiful upon the mountains are the feet of him that bringeth good tidings unto them, that publisheth peace; that bringeth good tidings unto them of good, that publisheth salvation; that saith unto Zion: Thy God reigneth! (3 Nephi 20:39-40)

Finally, the Savior declared,

> all these things shall surely come, even as the Father hath commanded me. Then shall this covenant which the Father hath covenanted with his people be fulfilled; and then

shall Jerusalem be inhabited again with my people, and it shall be the land of their inheritance. (3 Nephi 20:46)

The Sign of the Gathering

The remnant of the house of Israel, which Jesus found among the Nephites when He appeared in the Western Hemisphere, was weak and dissolute because of their iniquity. They were a minority group among a society dominated by the Gentiles. This iniquitous remnant had been scattered throughout the land by the Gentiles. The Father had covenanted with the house of Israel that, having been scattered, they would be gathered to the land of their inheritance. The Savior gave the Nephites a sign whereby they would know that the process of gathering had begun. It was known that it was the will of the Father that the Nephite remnant should learn of their identity through the Gentiles. This was made known to "the Gentiles that they may know concerning this people who are a remnant of the house of Jacob, and concerning this my people who shall be scattered by them" (3 Nephi 21:2). The Savior explained why the Father wished this knowledge would come to the remnant through the Gentiles:

> that he may show forth his power unto the Gentiles, for this cause that the Gentiles, if they will not harden their hearts, that they may repent and come unto me and be baptized in my name and know of the true points of my doctrine, that they may be numbered among my people, O house of Israel. (3 Nephi 21:6)

Jesus said when the remnant shall come to know these things, it shall be a sign unto them, that they may know that the work of the Father hath already commenced unto the fulfilling of the covenant which he hath made unto the people who are of the house of Israel. (3 Nephi 21:7)

As a consequence of these things,

my people who are a remnant of Jacob shall be among the Gentiles, yea, in the midst of them as a lion among the beasts of the forest, as a young lion among the flocks of sheep, who, if he goeth through, both treadeth down and teareth in pieces, and none can deliver.
Their hand shall be lifted up upon their adversaries and all their enemies shall be cut off. (3 Nephi 21:12-13)

The Woes of the Gentiles

Despite the benign and significant role the Gentiles played in the initiation of the gathering, the Father had serious words of warning for them:

Yea, wo be unto the Gentiles except they repent; for it shall come to pass in that day, saith the Father, that I will cut off thy horses out of the midst of thee, and I will destroy thy chariots. (3 Nephi 21:14)

All their cities were to be cut off and their strongholds thrown down. They were to abandon witchcrafts, soothsayers, and graven images; and all lyings, deceiving, strifes, and whoredoms were to be eliminated.

For it shall come to pass, saith the Father, that at that day whosoever will not repent and come unto my Beloved Son, them will I cut off from among my people, O house of Israel,

And I will execute vengeance and fury upon them, even as upon the heathen, such as they have not heard. (3 Nephi 21:20-21)

The amplitude of the beliefs and practices of the Gentiles that required their repentance suggests the level of degradation to which the Nephite nation had fallen. This had a significant and lasting impact upon the remnant of the house of Israel, found intermixed with the dominant Gentiles.

How the Gentiles Share in the Glories

Despite the dire, condemning words about the Gentiles, the Savior promised that if they would repent and not harden their hearts,

> I will establish my church among them, and they shall come in unto the covenant and be numbered among this the remnant of Jacob, unto whom I have given this land for their inheritance.
> And they shall assist my people, the remnant of Jacob, and also as many of the house of Israel as shall come, that they may build a city which shall be called the New Jerusalem.
> And they shall assist my people that they may be gathered in, who are scattered upon the face of the land, in unto the New Jerusalem.
> And then shall the power of heaven come down among them; and I also will be in the midst.
> And then shall the work of the Father commence at that day even when the gospel shall be preached among the remnant of the people. Verily I say unto you at that day the work of the Father shall commence among all the dispersed of my people, yea, even the tribes which have been lost which the Father hath led away out of Jerusalem.

Yea, the work shall commence among all the dispersed of my people, with the Father to prepare the way whereby they may come unto me, that they may call on the Father in my name. (3 Nephi 21:22-27)

That the Gentiles were involved in the organization of the Church, in the gathering of the lost remnants, and in the building of the New Jerusalem implies they had become sufficiently repentant and submissive that they were adopted into the House of Israel. In this status, they were in a position to share in the richest blessings God has provided for His faithful and obedient children, even the blessing of a fullness.

The Father Will Initiate the Gathering

After dwelling upon the work and the status of the Gentiles in the latter days, the Savior declared, "Yea, and then shall the work commence, with the Father among all nations in preparing the way whereby his people may be gathered home to the land of their inheritance" (3 Nephi 21:28). Then was initiated the global process of the gathering and the somewhat leisurely pace with which it was achieved. "And they shall go out from all nations; and they shall not go out in haste, nor go by flight, for I will go before them, saith the Father, and I will be their rearward" (3 Nephi 21:29).

A significant example of this gathering process occurred when, shortly after the first missionary effort in England in 1837, Mormon converts began to immigrate to the United States of America. This process continued in regular increments until August 1971, when at the area general conference held in Manchester, England, the English and other British saints were urged to remain in their native countries and build up the Church there instead of immigrating to America.

Jesus Again Quotes Isaiah

Word of the gathering was met with joy unbounded.

> And then shall that which is written come to pass: Sing, O barren, thou that didst not bear; break forth into singing, and cry aloud, thou that didst not travail with child; for more are the children of the desolate than the children of the married wife, saith the Lord. (3 Nephi 22:1; Isaiah 54:1)

The prophet then laments over the scattered children and then rejoiced over their recovery:

> For a small moment have I forsaken thee, but with mercies will I gather thee.
> In a little wrath I hid my face from thee for a moment, but with everlasting kindness will I have mercy on thee, saith the Lord thy Redeemer. (3 Nephi 22:7-8)

The Lord promised that as He had affirmed that the waters of Noah would not return, "so have I sworn that I would not be wroth with thee" (3 Nephi 22:9).

As a consequence of these things, and quoting from Isaiah, the Lord made this promise to His servants:

> No weapon that is formed against thee shall prosper; and every tongue that shall revile against thee in judgment thou shall condemn. This is the heritage of the servants of the Lord, and their righteousness is of me, saith the Lord. (3 Nephi 22:17; see Isaiah 54:17)

President Ezra Taft Benson carried a copy of this scripture in his wallet for many years (see *Ezra Taft Benson, Statesman, Patriot, Prophet of God* by Francis Marion Gibbons).

The People to Search the Scriptures

In reference to the writings of Isaiah, Jesus told the people, "Ye ought to search these things. Yea, a commandment I give unto you that ye search these things diligently; for great are the words of Isaiah" (3 Nephi 23:1). Jesus observed that Isaiah spoke of all things concerning His people, the house of Israel, "therefore, it must needs be that he speak also to the Gentiles" (3 Nephi 23:2).

The people were also admonished to give heed to the words of Jesus: "write the things which I have told you; and according to the time and the will of the Father they shall go forth unto the Gentiles" (3 Nephi 23:4). The Savior then promised, "whosoever will hearken unto my words and repenteth and is baptized, the same shall be saved." Then followed this admonition: "Search the prophets, for many there be that testify of these things" (3 Nephi 23:5). Following these exhortations, the Savior uttered these final, enigmatic words: "Behold, other scriptures I would that ye should write, that ye have not" (3 Nephi 23:6).

The Records Are Questioned

At this juncture, Jesus told Nephi, "Bring forth the record which ye have kept." After the record had been brought forth and Jesus had scanned it, He reminded the disciples He had commanded Samuel the Lamanite to testify that many Saints had risen at the time "the Father should glorify his name in me." When Jesus asked why this historic event had been omitted from the record, "Nephi remembered that this thing had not been written," whereupon "Jesus commanded that it should be written; therefore it was written according as he commanded." After Jesus had expounded all the scriptures, "he commanded them that they should teach the things which he had expounded unto them." (3

Nephi 23:7-14) Herein are taught the importance of the scriptures and the duty to record and to perpetuate them.

The Nephites Write Scriptures From Malachi

The Savior instructed the Nephites to write certain scriptures from Malachi, which He then expounded to them.

> And these are the words which he did tell unto them, saying: Then said the Father unto Malachi—Behold, I will send my messenger, and he shall prepare the way before me, and the Lord whom ye seek shall suddenly come to his temple, even the messenger of the covenant, whom ye delight in; behold, he shall come, saith the Lord of Hosts. (3 Nephi 24:1)

The messenger here alluded to is John the Baptist (see D&C 45:9 and Matthew 3:1).

Then, anticipating the day of Christ's second coming, the question was posed: "But who may abide the day of his coming, and who shall stand when he appeareth?" (3 Nephi 24:2) Then was described the rigid testing which the children would undergo:

> For he is like a refiner's fire, and like fuller's soap.
> And he shall sit as a refiner and purifier of silver; and he shall purify the sons of Levi, and purge them as gold and silver, that they may offer unto the Lord an offering in righteousness.
> Then shall the offering of Judah and Jerusalem be pleasant unto the Lord, as in the days of old, and as in former years. (3 Nephi 24:2-4)

In the day of judgment, the Lord will be:

a swift witness against the sinner and the sorcerers, and against the adulterers, and against false swearers, and against those that oppress the hireling in his wages, the widow and the fatherless, and that turn aside the stranger, and fear not me, saith the Lord of Hosts. (3 Nephi 24:5)

After declaring himself to be the Lord, Jesus chided the sons of Jacob for having abandoned the Lord and His holy ordinances, but then declared, "Return unto me and I will return unto you, saith the Lord of Hosts. But ye say: Wherein shall we return?" (3 Nephi 24:7) Answering, Jesus inquired, "Will a man rob God?" explaining that they had robbed God in their failure to pay their tithes and offerings. After admonishing them to resume paying their tithes and offerings, He promised, "prove me now herewith, saith the Lord of Hosts, if I will not open you the windows of heaven, and pour you out a blessing that there shall not be room enough to receive it" (3 Nephi 24:10). They were also promised that their fields would produce bounteously so that "all nations shall call you blessed, for ye shall be a delightsome land, saith the Lord of Hosts" (3 Nephi 24:12).

The Lord also accused the people of speaking against Him. When they asked how they had done so, the Lord answered, "Ye have said: It is vain to serve God, and what doth it profit that we have kept his ordinances and that we have walked mournfully before the Lord of Hosts?" (3 Nephi 24:14) Then, among those who feared the Lord,

> a book of remembrance was written before him for them that feared the Lord, and that thought upon his name.
> And they shall be mine, saith the Lord of Hosts, in that day when I make up my jewels; and I will spare them as a man spareth his own son that serveth him.

> Then shall ye return and discern between the righteous and the wicked, between him that serveth God and him that serveth him not. (3 Nephi 24:16-18)

Then alluding to the circumstances that shall exist at the time of the Second Coming, the Lord said,

> For behold, the day cometh that shall burn as an oven; and all the proud, yea, and all that do wickedly, shall be stubble; and the day that cometh shall burn them up, saith the Lord of Hosts, that it shall leave them neither root nor branch.
>
> But unto you that fear my name, shall the Son of Righteousness arise with healing in his wings; and ye shall go forth and grow up as calves in the stall.
>
> And ye shall tread down the wicked; for they shall be ashes under the soles of your feet in the day I shall do this, saith the Lord of Hosts.
>
> Remember ye the law of Moses, my servant, which I commanded unto him in Horeb for all Israel, with the statutes and judgments.
>
> Behold, I will send you Elijah the prophet before the coming of the great and dreadful day of the Lord;
>
> And he shall turn the heart of the fathers to the children, and the heart of the children to their fathers, lest I come and smite the earth with a curse. (3 Nephi 25:3-6)

Thus the Nephites were instructed in the significant role Elijah was to play in the windup of the great plan of happiness the Lord has in store for His children, a role which is more significant and dramatic today with the multiplication of holy temples throughout the earth where are performed the sacred ordinances, linking individuals and families together in an eternal union.

The Scriptures Are Expounded

It came to pass after Jesus had told the disciples about the prophecies of Malachi, "he expounded them unto the multitude." More than that, "he did expound all things unto them, both great and small" (3 Nephi 26:1). Jesus explained that, "These scriptures which ye had not with you, the Father commanded that I should give unto you; for it is wisdom in him they should be given unto future generations" (3 Nephi 26:2). The Savior therein undertook to describe the broad scope, the height, and the depth of the things to be recorded:

> And he did expound all things, even from the beginning unto the time that he should come in his glory—yea, even all things which should come upon the face of the earth, even until the elements should melt with fervent heat, and the earth should be wrapped together as a scroll, and the heavens and the earth should pass away;
>
> And even unto the great and last day, when all people, and all kindreds, and all nations and tongues shall stand before God to be judged of their works, whether they be good or whether they be evil—
>
> If they be good, to the resurrection of everlasting life; and if they be evil, to the resurrection of damnation; . . . according to the mercy, and the justice, and the holiness which is in Christ, who was before the world began. (3 Nephi 26:3-5)

This epic historic-prophetic narrative is not found among the Nephite scriptures. Did it suffer the fate of Samuel the Lamanite's omitted story, lacking a recorder?

Or was it merely part of the enormous mass of omitted materials, the quantity of which is suggested by this: "And now there cannot be written in this book even a hundredth part of the things which Jesus did truly teach unto the people" (3 Nephi 26:6).

Mormon Comments on the Record

Following the statement that the book could not contain even a hundredth part of what Jesus taught the people, Mormon continued to comment on the Nephite record. First he noted that "the plates of Nephi do contain the more part of the things which he [Jesus] taught the people" (3 Nephi 26:7). He also noted that the things he had written were "a lesser part of the things which he had taught the people" and that he had written them "to the intent that they may be brought again unto this people, from the Gentiles, according to the words which Jesus had spoken" (3 Nephi 26:8).

If at that time the people will not believe these things, "then shall the greater things be withheld from them, unto their condemnation" (3 Nephi 26:10). Mormon noted that he was about to quote these things which were engraved on the plates of Nephi, "but the Lord forbade it, saying: I will try the faith of my people" (3 Nephi 26:11).

In conclusion, Mormon declared, "Therefore I, Mormon, do write the things which have been commanded me of the Lord. And now I, Mormon, make an end of my sayings, and proceed to write the things which have been commanded me" (3 Nephi 26:12).

The Duration and Content of Christ's Teachings

Mormon recorded "that the Lord truly did teach the people, for the space of three days; and after that he did show himself unto them oft, and did brake bread oft, and bless it, and give it unto them" (3 Nephi 26:13). The Savior also taught and ministered unto the children, "and he did loose their tongues, and they did speak unto their fathers great and marvelous things, even greater than he had revealed unto the people" (3 Nephi 26:14). The Savior then:

> healed all their sick, and their lame, and opened the eyes of their blind, and unstopped the ears of the deaf, and even had done all manner of cures among them, and raised a man from the dead, and had shown forth his power unto them, and had ascended unto the Father—" (3 Nephi 26:15)

It was then the disciples whom Jesus had chosen began their ministry. "And they who were baptized in the name of Jesus were called the church of Christ" (3 Nephi 26:21).

Another Warning

After the disciples had commenced their ministry and were teaching and baptizing in the name of Jesus, they were gathered together, engaged in mighty prayer, when the Savior appeared and stood in their midst and said, "What will ye that I shall give unto you?" (3 Nephi 27:2) In answer, they asked the name by which the church would be known, for there were disputations among them.

In responding, Jesus asked whether they had

> read the scriptures, which say ye must take upon you the name of Christ, which is my name? For by this name shall ye be called at the last day;
> And whoso taketh upon him my name, and endureth to the end, the same shall be saved at the last day.
> Therefore, whatsoever ye shall do, ye shall do it in my name; therefore ye shall call the church in my name; and

ye shall call upon the Father in my name that he will bless the church for my sake. (3 Nephi 27:5-7)

Moreover "if ye call upon the Father, for the church, if it be in my name, the Father will hear you" (3 Nephi 27:9).

In this discourse it was taught that Christ's church must be built upon His gospel. In giving emphasis to this truth, Jesus said in conclusion:

> But if it be built not upon my gospel, and is built upon the works of men, or upon the works of the devil, verily I say unto you they have joy in their work for a season, and by and by the end cometh, and they are hewn down and cast into the fire, from whence there is no return.
>
> For their works do follow them, for it is because of their works that they are hewn down; therefore remember the things that I have told you. (3 Nephi 27:11-12)

Jesus Again Declares Himself

Jesus declared He had given His gospel to the people, and that His gospel consisted of this: "that I came into the world to do the will of my Father, because my Father sent me" (3 Nephi 27:13). He then explained why the Father had sent him:

> that I might be lifted up upon the cross; and after that I had been lifted up upon the cross, that I might draw all men unto me, that as I have been lifted up by men even so should men be lifted up by the Father, to stand before me, to be judged of their works, whether they be good or whether they be evil— (3 Nephi 27:14)

The Savior concluded, saying, "And for this cause have I been lifted up; therefore, according to the power of the Father I will draw all men unto me, that they may be judged according to their works" (3 Nephi 27:15).

Baptism Explained

Jesus declared that whosoever repents and is baptized shall be filled, "and if he endureth to the end, behold, him will I hold guiltless before my Father at that day when I shall stand to judge the world" (3 Nephi 27:16). He who does not endure to the end is to be "hewn down and cast into the fire, from whence they can no more return, because of the justice of the Father" (3 Nephi 27:17).

The Savior declared further that no unclean thing can enter the kingdom of God, because only those whose garments have been washed clean and pure through the atoning blood of the Savior can enter the kingdom of God.

> "Now this is the commandment: Repent all ye ends of the earth, and come unto me and be baptized in my name, that ye may be sanctified by the reception of the Holy Ghost, that ye may stand spotless before me at the last day. (3 Nephi 27:20)

Jesus then declared that this was His gospel, and that His followers must do what they had seen Him do. "Therefore, if you do these things blessed are ye, for ye shall be lifted up at the last day" (3 Nephi 27:22).

Nephites Urged to Keep Records

Jesus taught the Nephites,

> Write the things which ye have seen and heard, save it be those which are forbidden.

> Write the works of the people, which shall be, even as hath been written, of that which hath been. (3 Nephi 27:23-24)

Then was given the reason for this command: "For behold, out of the books which have been written, and which shall be written, shall this people be judged, for by them shall their works be known unto men" (3 Nephi 27:25). Then was added this: "And behold, all things are written by the Father; therefore of the books which shall be written shall the world be judged" (3 Nephi 27:26). Then is explained the connection between the judgment of God and the judgment of men, together with the standard of conduct to which men should aspire:

> And know ye that ye shall be judges of this people, according to the judgment which I shall give unto you, which shall be just. Therefore, what manner of men ought ye to be? Verily I say unto you, even as I am. (3 Nephi 27:27)

Ask for Desired Blessings

As Jesus prepared to return to the Father, He said to the Nephites,

> And now I go unto the Father. And verily I say unto you, whatsoever things you shall ask the Father in my name shall be given unto you.
> Therefore, ask, and ye shall receive; knock, and it shall be opened unto you; for he that asketh, receiveth; and unto him that knocketh, it shall be opened. (3 Nephi 27:28-29)

Herein lies a great truth governing God's relationship with His children on earth. That is that the Father acts affirmatively in blessing His children only in response to pleadings of the children. Otherwise, it would be God's actions, not those of His children, so to that extent the purpose of earth life would be frustrated, that purpose being to prove one's worthiness to return to the presence of God. So it was that the perceptive artist drew the door to the garden with a knob on only one side. So in his dealings with the Almighty, the individual must take the initiative in asking or knocking.

None of This Generation Is Lost

Following the Savior's instructions about taking the initiative to seek and to knock, He told the people:

> And now, behold, my joy is great, even unto fulness, because of you, and also this generation; yea, and even the Father rejoiceth, and also all the holy angels, because of you and this generation; for none of them are lost. (3 Nephi 27:30)

Then to make His meaning crystal clear, the Savior added this: "Behold, I would that ye should understand; for I mean them who are now alive of this generation; and none of them are lost; and in them I have fulness of joy." (3 Nephi 27:31)

The Fourth Generation To Be Held Captive

In the midst of rejoicing over the current generation, the Savior grieved over another.

> But behold, it sorroweth me because of the fourth generation from this generation, for they are led away captive by him even as was the son of perdition; for they will sell me for silver and for gold, and for that which moth doth corrupt and thieves can break through and

steal. And in that day will I visit them, even in turning their work upon their own heads. (3 Nephi 27:32)

Here is illustrated how joy and success become sorrow and failure when the principles of righteousness and integrity are trampled upon and the dire consequences thereof are turned upon the heads of evildoers.

Further Instructions

When Jesus had ended these sayings, He admonished His disciples in these words:

> Enter ye in at the strait gate; for strait is the gate, and narrow is the way that leads to life, and few there be that find it; but wide is the gate, and broad the way which leads to death, and many there be that travel therein, until the night cometh, wherein no man can work. (3 Nephi 27:33)

These precise words left no doubt that the way of the successful disciple would be characterized by continued and undeviating obedience to the words and the works of the Savior and the Father. There was to be no leeway whatsoever whereby one could tweak or manipulate the words of the Almighty into some meaning or implication He did not intend. The pathway to life and safety was clearly marked, and the choice given to the disciple was defined with precision.

The Savior's Gifts to the Nine Disciples

When Jesus had finished His discourse about the chosen few, "he spake unto the disciples, one by one, saying unto them: What is it that ye desire of me, after that I am gone to the Father?"

(3 Nephi 28:1) All except three of the disciples answered, saying: "We desire that after we have lived unto the age of man, that our ministry, wherein thou hast called us, may have an end, that we may speedily come unto thee in thy kingdom" (3 Nephi 28:2). Jesus responded, saying, "Blessed are ye because ye desire this thing of me; therefore, after that ye are seventy and two years old ye shall come unto me in my kingdom; and with me ye shall find rest" (3 Nephi 28:3).

That the target age of 72 as representing the age of man may be shifting is suggested by the fact that the patriarch, Eldred G. Smith died at age 106; Joseph Anderson, long-time secretary to the First Presidency died at age 102 and this writer is near age 93 and in good health.

When Jesus had finished blessing the nine disciples, He turned to the other three, saying, "What will ye that I should do unto you, when I am gone unto the Father?" (3 Nephi 28:4) The three disciples were sorrowful in their hearts and reluctant to tell the Savior what they desired of Him. Perceiving their thoughts, Jesus said to them, "Behold, I know your thoughts, and ye have desired the thing which John, my beloved, who was with me in my ministry, before that I was lifted up by the Jews, desired of me" (3 Nephi 28:6). The Savior then undertook to describe various aspects of their future life. He said to them:

> Therefore, more blessed are ye, for ye shall never taste of death; but ye shall live to behold all the doings of the Father unto the children of men, even until all things shall be fulfilled according to the will of the Father, when I shall come in my glory with the powers of heaven. (3 Nephi 28:7)

The three Nephites were promised they would never suffer the pains of death, and that when Jesus appeared in His glory they would be changed in the twinkling of an eye to immortality and would then take their place in the kingdom of heaven. "And again ye shall not have pain while ye shall dwell in the flesh, neither sorrow save it be for the sins of the world" (3 Nephi 28:9).

For their faithful service, the three Nephites were promised:

> ye shall have fullness of joy; and ye shall sit down in the kingdom of my Father; yea, your joy shall be full, even as the Father hath given me fullness of joy; and ye shall be even as I am, and I am even as the Father; and the Father and I are one;
>
> And the Holy Ghost beareth record of the Father and me; and the Father giveth the Holy Ghost unto the children of men, because of me. (3 Nephi 28:10-11)

Jesus Departs; the Three Caught Up Into Heaven

Before He departed, Jesus "touched every one of them with his finger save it were the three who were to tarry, and then he departed" (3 Nephi 28:12). The three were then "caught up into heaven, and saw and heard unspeakable things. And it was forbidden them that they should utter; neither was it given unto them power that they could utter the things which they saw and heard" (3 Nephi 28:13-14). They could not tell whether they were in or out of their bodies, "for it did seem unto them like a transfiguration of them, that they were changed from this body of flesh into an immortal state, that they could behold the things of God" (3 Nephi 28:15).

Therefore, the three disciples continued to minister on earth, "nevertheless, they did not minister of the things which they had heard and seen, because of the commandment which was given them in heaven" (3 Nephi 28:16).

Ministry of the Three

The narrator did not know whether the three Nephites were mortal or immortal from the time of their transfiguration,

> But this much I know, according to the record which hath been given—they did go forth upon the face of the land, and did minister unto all the people, uniting as many to the church as would believe in their preaching; baptizing them, and as many as were baptized did receive the Holy Ghost. (3 Nephi 28:18)

Then were recorded various incidents regarding the early ministry of the three Nephites: They were cast into prison and the prison could not hold them; they were cast into the earth, but were delivered; they were cast into a furnace but were not touched by the flame; they were cast into a den of beasts but were not harmed. And in this manner they did go forth among the people of Nephi,

> and did preach the gospel of Christ unto all people upon the face of the land; and they were converted unto the Lord, and were united unto the Church of Christ, and thus the people of that generation were blessed, according to the word of Jesus. (3 Nephi 28:23)

Other Comments About the Three Nephites

At this juncture, Mormon interjected to comment on the three Nephites, beginning with these words:

> And now I, Mormon, make an end of speaking concerning these things for a time.
>
> Behold, I was about to write the names of the three who were never to taste of death, but the Lord forbade; therefore, I write them not, for they are hid from the world. (3 Nephi 28:24-25)

Mormon said he had seen them, and that they had ministered unto him. He said they would minister to the Gentiles and the Jews, and they would know them not, and that:

> when the Lord seeth fit in his wisdom that they will minister unto all the scattered tribes of Israel, and unto all nations, kindred, tongues and people, and shall bring out of them unto Jesus many souls, that their desire may be fulfilled, and also because of the convincing power of God which is in them. (3 Nephi 28:29)

Mormon also said they were as the angels of God and could show themselves to whomever they wished by praying to God in the name of Jesus. "Therefore, great and marvelous works shall be wrought by them, before the great and coming day when all people must surely stand before the judgment seat of Christ" (3 Nephi 28:31). Mormon said that at the last day Jesus would not receive those who had failed to receive His word or the word of His servants and for such as these it would have been better they had not been born (see 3 Nephi 28:34-35).

Mormon then commented as follows about the change that was effected in the bodies of the three Nephites:

> But behold, since I wrote, I have inquired of the Lord, and he hath made it manifest unto me that there must be a change wrought upon their bodies, or else it must needs be they must taste of death. (3 Nephi 28:37)

The change wrought in their bodies was from mortality to immortality so that:

> Satan could have no power over them, that he could not tempt them; and they were sanctified in the flesh, that they were holy, and that the powers of the earth could not hold them.
>
> And in this state they were to remain until the judgment day of Christ; and at that day they were to receive a greater change, and to be received into the kingdom of the Father to go no more out, but to dwell with God eternally in the heavens. (3 Nephi 28:39-40)

The Gathering: Final Words to the Gentiles

The appearance of the Book of Mormon in the hands of the Gentiles signified that the gathering of the tribes of Israel to the lands of their inheritance had begun. The great drama of the gathering was global in scope and complex in its operation. For the Latter-day Saints, the gathering of converts from Europe and Great Britain to the United States over a period of almost two hundred years was of special importance and interest. The process was attended by hymns of the gathering, whose lyrics contained urgent calls to the scattered ones—*Israel, Israel, God is Calling*, or, *Come to Zion, Come to Zion*. This flow of converts to America significantly ended in August 1971 with the holding of the first area general conference in Manchester, England. There the conferees were urged to remain in their home countries and to build up the Church there. Similar area general conferences were held in other parts of the world with the same message being given—remain in your home countries.

The role and the status of the Gentiles were given special attention in the windup of the account contained in Third Nephi.

There the Gentiles were denounced for their evil ways and misconduct and were called to repentance.

Christ invites all to:

> Come unto me, and be baptized in my name, that ye may receive a remission of your sins, and be filled with the Holy Ghost, that ye may be numbered with my people who are of the house of Israel. (3 Nephi 30:2)

INDEX

Aaronic Priesthood, 142
Adam, 8
Alma the Younger, 6
Amos, 1
Andrew, 56, 143
   follows John the Baptist, 15
   proclaims Jesus as the
      Messiah, 32
Angel
   opens Christ's tomb, 331
Angels, 6
Anna, 18
Annas, 317
Apostles
   Jesus appears to, 337
Archangel, 8
Arrest, 316
Ascension, 344
Augustus Caesar, 27
Authority of Jesus, 270
Baptism
   explained by the Lord, 397
Barabbas, 325
Bartholomew, 56, 131
Bartimaeus, 261
Bathsaida, 53
Benedictus, the, 13
Bethabara, 31
Bethany, 28, 204, 266, 297

Bethlehem, 15
Bethphage, 268
Bethsaida, 143, 155, 162, 192
   home of Peter, Andrew
      and Philip, 39
Betrayal, 297, 316
Bloody Way, 204
Book of Mormon, 347
Caesarea Philippi, 155, 165,
   168, 175, 179
Caiaphas, 318, 323
Cana, 37, 49
Capernaum, 39, 49, 52, 77,
   123, 137, 143, 149, 155, 183,
   192
Children, 253
   blessed by the Lord, 374
Chorazin, 192
Christ
   the doctrine of Christ is
      taught, 357
Cleopas, 336
Comforter, 307
Corban
   a sacrifice or offering, 150
Cornelius, 77
Covetousness, 239
Cowdery, Oliver, 142, 174
Dalmanutha, 161

David's son, 280
Decapolis, 115, 155, 165
Divorce, 250
Elias, 173, 189
Elijah, 6, 173
Elisabeth, 4, 13
   salutes Mary, 9
Ephraim (city), 245
Feast of Dedication, 195, 221
Feast of Lights, 195
Feast Of Tabernacles, 195, 200
Final Judgment, 294
Fishing, 71, 103, 180
   Peter goes fishing after resurrection, 339
Gabriel, 6, 173
Gadarene Demoniac, 111
Galilee, 33, 136, 179
Garden of Gethsemane, 204, 313
Gathering, 387, 405
Gennesaret, 71
Gentiles, 405
   blessed and warned, 372
   woes of the, 385
Gerasa, 111
Gergasa, 155
Gethsemane, 175
Golgotha, 175, 326
Great Intercessory Prayer, the, 310

Guardian Angels, 6
Herod
   Jesus appears before, 323
Herod Antipas, 46, 79, 226
   beheads John the Baptist, 139
Herodians, 76
Herodias, 46
Hosanna, 270
Isaiah, 388
Jairus, 117
James, 6, 56, 71, 171, 260, 339
   brother of the Lord, 27
   sees resurrected Lord, 342
James the *son* of Alpheus, 56
James, the brother of the Lord, 128
James, the son of Alpheus, 131
Jensen, Ella
   raised from dead by Lorenzo Snow, 121
Jericho, 28, 261
Jerusalem, 24, 28, 39, 204, 259
   Christ sets his face toward, 189
   Christ's final journey to, 245
   Jesus enters on a colt, 267
   Jesus laments over, 283
   winding up scenes at, 179

Jesus Christ
  alludes to his burial, 86
  anointed by a sinful woman, 81
  anointed in Bethany, 297
  appears before Herod, 323
  appears before Pontius Pilate, 323
  appears on the road to Emmaus, 336
  appears to Apostles, 337
  appears to Apostles on Sea of Tiberias, 339
  appears to eleven Apostles in Galilee, 343
  appears to Mary Magdalene, 333
  appears to Peter, 336
  attributes of, 41
  baptism of, 30
  before Caiaphas, 318
  betrayal and arrest, 316
  birth of, 15
  blesses the little children, 252, 374
  brought again before Pilate, 324
  cleanses the temple, 269
  clears the Temple, 39
  curses the barren fig tree, 268
  David's son, 280
  declares himself the Christ, 48
  denounces scribes and Pharisees, 281
  disrespected on the cross, 327
  divine nature of, 23
  doctrine of, 45, 47, 74, 87, 149, 161, 199, 202, 210, 221, 226, 239, 248, 259, 278
  a new commandment, 305
  discourse about the Comforter, 307
  discourse on forgiveness, 186
  marriage and divorce, 250
  persistence in prayer, 207
  prayer, 206
  qualifications of a disciple, 230
  repentance and forgiveness, 241
  sermon on meekness, 183
  taught in Western Hemisphere, 358
  the Light of the World, 200

early life, 24
enters Jerusalem on a colt, 267
events following resurrection, 331
expounding in Temple, 25
final events before death, 328
final journey to Jerusalem, 245
foretells his death, 305
formal trial and condemnation, 320
Galilean ministry, 49, 71
indicates his betrayer, 304
laments over Jerusalem, 283
miracles of
    a demoniac is healed, 177
    a dumb devil cast out, 208
    blind made to see, 123
    blind, dumb man healed, 83
    centurion's servant healed, 77
    crippled woman healed on Sabbath, 223
    daughter of Greek woman healed, 153
    deaf man healed, 156
    dumb made to speak, 125
    feeding of five thousand, 143
    feeding of four thousand, 158
    healing at Bethsaida, 53
    healing on the sabbath, 75
    healing ten lepers, 246
    healing the blind near Jericho, 261
    heals a blind man, 162
    heals a man blind from birth, 216
    Lazarus is raised, 241
    leper healed, 72
    miracle at Cana, 37
    miracle of the tribute money, 180
    one with palsy healed, 73
    raises son of widow, 78
    raising daughter of Jairus, 117
    the Gadarene demoniac, 111
    the storm is stilled, 107
    walks on the sea, 146
mocked and humiliated, 326
moral mandates of, 61

nighttime examination, 318
Olivet discourse, 287
on the Mount of
    Transfiguration, 171
parables of, 89
    man with dropsy healed
        on Sabbath, 228
    the foolish rich man, 212
    the good Samaritan, 202
    the good shepherd, 219
    the gospel net, 103
    the guests at the great
        feast, 229
    the hidden treasure, 101
    the importunate
        neighbor, 208
    the importunate widow,
        248
    the King's son, 274
    the laborers in the
        vineyard, 256
    the leaven, 101, 225
    the lost sheep, 233
    the mustard seed, 99,
        224
    the pearl of great price,
        102
    the Pharisee and the
        publican, 249
    the prodigal son, 235
    the rich man and
        Lazarus the beggar,
        239
    the seed growing
        secretly, 96
    the sower of the seed, 92
    the talents, 292
    the ten pieces of silver,
        234
    the ten pounds, 264
    the ten virgins, 291
    the two sons, 271
    the unforgiving servant,
        187
    the unjust steward, 238
    the wedding feast, 229
    the wheat and the tares,
        97
    the wicked
        husbandmen, 272
prays in Gethsemane, 313
presented in Temple, 17
rejected at Nazareth, 127
returns to Bethany, 266
seen by five hundred after
    resurrection, 341
sentenced to be crucified,
    325
Sermon on the Mount, 56
Sermon on the Plain, 68
sojourn in Egypt, 21
taken to Annas, 317

teaches of his death and
resurrection, 168
Teachings on Mount of
Olives, 308
Allegory of the Ture
Vine, 308
Jesus explains His death,
309
Jesus speaks of love, 308
temptation of, 33
the great intercessory
prayer, 310
the procession to Golgatha,
326
washes the feet of the
Apostles, 302
with the rich young ruler,
254
Jewish weights and
measures, 101
John, 6, 56, 71, 171, 219, 260,
304, 339
follows John the Baptist, 15
learns of resurrection, 332
John the Baptist, 6, 29
appears on banks of
Susquehanna River, 142
beheaded, 139
birth, 13
disciples of, 74
imprisoned, 79

imprisonment and
beheading, 45
ministry begins, 27
Jordan River, 27, 155
Christ's baptism in, 30
Joseph, 8
instructed in a dream, 11
Joseph of Arimathaea, 45
Josephus, 23, 195
Joses, 128
Juda, 128
Judas
betrays the Savior, 316
Judas Iscariot, 56, 131
arranges the betrayal, 299
commits suicide, 322
identified as betrayer by
Jesus, 304
Judas *the brother* of James, 56
Judea, 136
Kimball, Heber C., 371
Kimball, Spencer W., 371
King Herod, 19, 20
Kirtland Temple, 174
Last Supper, 308
Law of Moses, 200
Lawyers, 202, 229
denounced by Savior, 211
Lazarus, 204, 266
raised from the dead, 241
Lebbaeus, 131
Lepros, 72

Lord's Prayer, 206
Lucifer, 112
Magdala, 161
Magi, 18
Magnificat, the, 10
Malachi, 1
Mariamne, 19
Mark, 73, 96
Marriage, 250, 277
Martha, 204, 241
Mary, 4, 15, 37, 128
  conception, 8
  imprint on the Savior, 147
Mary Magdalene, 82, 161, 332
  reports to the Apostles, 333
  sees and worships the resurrected Lord, 334
  tells Peter and John of resurrection, 332
Mary, sister of Lazarus, 204, 241
Matthew, 56, 123
  emphasis, 12
  source material, 21
Mediterranean, 136
Melchizedek Priesthood, 142
Michael, 8
Mormon, 394
Moroni, 6, 174, 344
Mosaic Law, 58
Moses, 6, 173
Mount Hermon, 155, 171

Mount of Olives, 28, 268, 308
Mount of Transfiguration, 171
Nain, 78
Nathaniel, 32, 339
Nazareth, 26, 50, 197
Nephi
  commanded to baptize, 356
New Commandment, 305
Nicodemus, 43
Olivet Discourse, 287
Palmyra, New York, 344
Paneas,, 165
Parables
  defined, 90
  Rabbinic, 91
Passover, 24, 39, 195, 266
  arrangements for Passover meal, 299
Passover Meal, 302
Paul, 337
  sees risen Lord, 341
Pentecost, 195, 345
Perea, 136, 223, 252
Peter, 6, 32, 53, 56, 71, 143, 150, 171, 179, 304, 307, 313, 315, 339
  declares his loyalty, 305
  denies the Christ, 319
  irrepressible nature, 147
  learns of resurrection, 332

risen Lord appears to, 336
  testifies of Christ, 165
Pharisees, 28, 76, 89, 149, 161, 200, 210, 212, 229, 240, 281
  warn Jesus, 226
Philip, 32, 56
Phillip, 131
Phoenicia, 153, 155
Pontius Pilate, 322, 324
  Jesus appears before, 323
Prayer, 62
  persistence in, 207
Purim, 195
Reactive Commandments, 69
Red Path, 204
Resurrection, 277
  events following, 331
Road to Emmaus, 336
Roman Army, 77
Roman Empire, 71
Roman Legion, 77
Sabbath, 75, 195
Sacrament, 302, 375
Sacred Grove, 343
Sadducees, 28, 161
Salome, 141, 260
Samaria, 46, 189
Samaria, Woman of, 46
Samuel the Lamanite, 348
Sanhedrin, 43
Satan
  tempts Christ, 33

Scribes, 281
Sea of Galilee, 107, 147, 155, 161, 165
Sea of Tiberias, 339
Sermon on the Mount, 55
  the beatitudes, 56
Seventy
  called and sent forth, 190
  return and report, 192
Shewbread, 75
Sidon, 68, 153, 192
Signs, 85, 161
Simeon, 17
Simon, 128
Simon called Zelotes, 56
Simon the Canaanite, 131
Simon the Leper, 299
Sisters of the Lord, 128
Smith, Joseph Jr.
  on the parable of the wheat and the tares, 98
Smith, Joseph, Jr., 6, 142, 174
Snow, Lorenzo
  raises girl from the dead, 121
Suicide, 322
Susquehanna River, 142
Sychar, 47
Temple of Herod, 1
Ten Commandments, 173
  the King James translation, 207

Thomas, 56, 131, 307, 339
Three Nephites, 403
Tiberius Caesar, 27
Timaeus, 261
Tribute, 276
Twelve, 307, 365
   and discipleship, 57
   calling of, 55
   return and report, 136
   sent forth, 131
Tyre, 68, 153, 192
Western Hemisphere
   appearance of Christ in, 354
Widow of Nain, 78
Widow's Mite, 284
Woman Taken In Adultery, 199
Women
   come to the Lord's tomb, 333
Zacchaeus the Publican, 262
Zacharias, 2, 13, 173
Zebedee, 260

www.ingramcontent.com/pod-product-compliance
Lightning Source LLC
Chambersburg PA
CBHW060107230426
43661CB00033B/1428/J